THE WIGGLY WORLD OF ORGANIZATION

The well-ordered, fully aligned view of organization and management practice, with its unfailingly positive results, bears little relationship to the world that managers and others experience every day. This straight-line, 'do this and you'll get that' idealization is far removed from the wiggly reality. Despite this, the former continues to dominate the ways in which management is spoken about and judged in formal organizational arenas and wider society. This creates unrealistic expectations of what managers (from CEO to the front line) can sensibly achieve independently of the actions of others. Crucially, too, it distorts the ways in which they and others account formally for their actions. And so, the fantasy continues.

Against this background, the book offers a radically different way of thinking about, and engaging with, the *irreducible* complexity of organization and management practice. Using straightforward language throughout, it sets out to help managers and others to become consciously aware of what they already know deep down about how organization works and what they – and everyone else – *are actually doing in practice*. It then offers a practical approach to everyday practice that *takes complexity seriously*.

Armed with these new insights, readers will be better placed to apply their innate understanding and practical judgement to the demands that they and others face day to day. Whether these arise from their roles as managers, other practitioners, policy makers, regulatory authorities, or participants more generally.

Chris Rodgers is an independent consultant, speaker and writer on leadership, change and organizational dynamics. He is a Fellow of the Chartered Management Institute and was previously a senior manager in the UK power industry. His first book, *Informal Coalitions*, was published in 2006.

THE WIGGLY WORLD OF ORGANIZATION

Muddling Through with Purpose, Courage and Skill

Chris Rodgers

Routledge
Taylor & Francis Group
LONDON AND NEW YORK

First published 2021
by Routledge
2 Park Square, Milton Park, Abingdon, Oxon OX14 4RN

and by Routledge
52 Vanderbilt Avenue, New York, NY 10017

Routledge is an imprint of the Taylor & Francis Group, an informa business

British Library Cataloguing-in-Publication Data
A catalogue record for this book is available from the British Library

Library of Congress Cataloging-in-Publication Data
A catalog record has been requested for this book

ISBN: 978-0-367-74465-6 (hbk)
ISBN: 978-0-367-74467-0 (pbk)
ISBN: 978-1-003-15804-2 (ebk)

Typeset in Joanna
by Apex CoVantage, LLC

For Benji and Sylvie

CONTENTS

FOREWORD

For the 20 years that I have known and worked with Chris Rodgers he has been a consistent and cogent critic of the prevailing orthodoxy of management and leadership practice in organisations. His work profoundly influences my practice as a business leader and an organisational consultant as well as that of my firm, Lane4. In this book he not only describes what is really going on in organisational life but provides a coherent philosophical mindset and practical ways to better navigate its many complexities. To participate rather than pontificate; to connect and contribute rather than seek to control; to be curious rather than seek false certainty. We are all muddling through, as investors, managers or consultants to management; and yet, we can do so with purpose, courage and skill. Our organisations become places of possibility, creativity and longevity with such an approach and at a time of enormous disruption and transformation – the advent of Artificial Intelligence, Big Data and ever increasing speed of change – Chris points to the uniquely human characteristics that are needed to successfully lead our organisations of the future.

Dominic Mahony OLY
Executive Chairman
Lane4 Management Group
September 2020

PREFACE

WAKING PEOPLE UP!

A couple of years ago, I visited the Museo Picasso Málaga. Written on the wall of one of the galleries is the following quotation:[1]:

> You have to wake people up. To revolutionize their way of identifying things. You've got to create images they won't accept. Make them foam at the mouth. Force them to understand that they're living in a pretty queer world. A world that's not reassuring. A world that's not what they think it is.

As Picasso says, we're living in a pretty queer world. Odd, even. A world which doesn't operate in neat straight lines. An asymmetrical world.

Overview

Taking my lead from Picasso, my aim in writing this book is similarly to "wake people up". That is, to help them become consciously aware of *what they already know deep down* about how organization works and what they – and everyone else – are *actually doing in practice*. They will then be better placed to apply their innate understanding, practical judgement, and new insights, to the challenges that they and others face. Whether these arise from their roles as managers, consultants, policy makers, regulatory authorities or participants more generally. In this way, my hope is that they will begin to "revolutionize their way of identifying things", as Picasso says, and come to recognize and embrace the "beautiful, ugly truth" of organizational life *as they actually experience it*.[2] To do this means first exposing the seductive but misleading ways in which we have come to think and talk about organization and management, in what Ralph Stacey calls "the dominant management discourse".[3] It means setting aside the well-worn clichés, and if-you-do-this-you'll-get-that logic, that we find in business biographies, conventional organizational research, and mainstream consultancy offerings. Instead, it calls on each one of us to *take our own experience seriously*. To acknowledge the messy reality of everyday organizational life – *arising from our own and everyone else's participation in it*. And, in so doing, to base our individual and collective practice on a more credible view of how organization actually works.

According to management orthodoxy, organizational success results from formal, rational analysis of the facts; step-by-step decision-making by people whose agendas are fully aligned; and the seamless translation of those decisions into programmable action on the ground. From this perspective, good management is seen as the ability to use what are supposedly scientifically derived, evidence-based, and universally applicable models and methodologies to plan, predict, and control outcomes in line with formally stated intentions. This fits well with the notion that there is a discoverable set of concepts, tools, and techniques that can be applied universally. Indeed, it depends on this being the case. However, given the complex reality of everyday organizational life (what I shall describe later as "*wiggliness*"), this fantasized view of management practice is far removed from the detail of people's everyday lived experience. Despite this, most managers (from CEOs to those in the front line) continue to be recruited, developed, measured, recognized, rewarded, promoted, and removed in line with principles and procedures that are rooted in assumptions of scientific rationality, predictability, and control. At least supposedly so. This is further reflected in the ways in which high-profile events are dealt with in the public arena. When these hit the headlines, managers are both lauded and vilified (often in equal measure) by journalists, commentators, and members of the public at large. They also often find themselves condemned for their failure to act in line with the seemingly obvious course that is offered by the benefit of hindsight, single-issue focus and unlimited time to decide the 'rights' and 'wrongs' of the matter.

The pervasiveness of the above narrative inevitably increases pressure on managers to conform to this imaginary view of organization; contaminating their day-to-day practice and further obscuring the complex reality. It should not be at all surprising, then, that what they say they are doing – and what, in formal arenas, they argue everyone else should be doing – often bears little relationship to what they actually find themselves and others doing *in practice*. In my experience, those who take time to look at what's actually going on, and to reflect on their own experience, readily acknowledge this to be the case. However, power relations are typically such, the dominant discourse so taken for granted, and the formal recruitment, recognition, and reward structures so locked-in to this way of thinking, that openly challenging it becomes particularly difficult. For others, perhaps, the formalized responses have become so habitual that to question them remains a thought unthunk! Either way, the fantasy continues. Rather than acknowledging the complex social dynamics of organization, and exploring the implications of these for their day-to-day practice, managers often feel compelled to adopt the latest fads and fashions; and to account for what they're doing in ever more managerially 'correct' and politically acceptable ways. Ironically, this failure to confront the myths that disfigure real-world management practice, makes their job harder still.

Against this background, the book offers a radically different way of thinking about, and engaging with, the irreducible complexity of organization and management practice. My aims in writing it are twofold. First, to help managers and others become consciously aware of what they already know deep down about how organization works and what they – and everyone else – are actually doing in practice. Secondly, to provide them with practical ideas on how they might lead and manage in ways that take this complexity seriously. Aided by these new insights, they will then be in a better position to draw on their lived experience and apply their practical judgement to the demands that they and others face every day.

Central to this is the recognition that managers themselves unavoidably participate in – and contribute to – the ongoing wiggliness. That is, they are always acting forwards, moment to moment, into a continuously emerging and unknowable future. A future which they and everyone else are jointly creating through their ongoing participation. Put simply, they are *muddling through*. Crucially, this is not a second-best response to the challenges that they face. It's the only thing that they – indeed, any of us – can do. As in all things, of course, some people will do this better than others. And we all do it better on some occasions than we do at other times. One of the main challenges then becomes how we might set out to do so more expertly and with greater insight. Or, as I'm describing it here, with *purpose*, *courage* and *skill*.

Organizational dynamics and the language of organization

Pivotal to this is an understanding of the underlying dynamics of organization. That is, how organization works *in practice*. By way of analogy, when I began some consultancy work in Germany a few years ago, I thought it would be interesting to learn to speak a little of the language. For this, I decided to use Michel Thomas's "natural" method. The "no writing and no revision" approach was particularly appealing! And it appeared to work – at least to my satisfaction. Contrary to the classic approach, Thomas spends very little time on vocabulary. Instead, he places most emphasis on the process of sentence formation and how this is affected, in particular, by verb usage. By adopting this approach, those learning the language are quickly able to construct relatively complicated sentences. As Thomas puts it, *once you understand the verbs, you understand the language. The rest is just vocabulary.* Although he would no doubt have agreed that this is an over-simplification, the basic point holds true. Verbs, broadly speaking, relate to process (the "doing"). And the ways in which these have come to be used tend to shape the pattern of the language and the ways in which meaning is derived from its use. Other aspects of vocabulary add in the content – the who, what, when, where, how and why etc. of the doing.

And so it is with organization. Once managers and others understand the dynamics of everyday human interaction, and how outcomes emerge from this process, they understand organization. The rest is just content. It doesn't matter whether their focus is on strategy, change, culture, business performance, innovation, leadership development, agile working, or whatever. Or whether their preferred approach is one of "command and control", empowered self-management or any other formulation. *In all cases, the underlying dynamics of interaction are the same.* The ways in which these play out, and the outcomes that emerge, will differ considerably, of course. But the *dynamics* of organization will be the same in all cases. It also follows from this that it is not possible to get to grips with organization without understanding these dynamics and their implications for management practice. However well people might have thought-through the content of what they're trying to achieve, and regardless of how committed they might be to its success, what actually happens will be wholly determined by the ways in which these dynamics play out in practice.

Outline of chapters

As I said in *Informal Coalitions*,[4] and stress again here, one of the most obvious insights that we can draw from this view of organization is that we are all walking case studies of these dynamics in action. It is not that others fall short of what's required whilst we rise above them in our pursuit of exemplary management and leadership practice. We're all contributing to the reality that we are experiencing. Readers can therefore gain the most from the book if they reflect on their own in-the-moment experiences of organizational life when interacting with the ideas contained in it.

With this in mind, Chapter 1 introduces the notion of the wiggly world of organization, drawing on the image used by philosopher Alan Watts to describe the non-linear nature of the world at large – and people's general reluctance to engage with it. This sets out the central argument for taking experience – and, with it, complexity – seriously. It provides the rationale for what follows. In particular, it contrasts what's supposed to be happening, according to management orthodoxy, with what's actually going on in organizational life *as people actually experience it*.

For those who wish to understand and explore these dynamics more fully, Chapter 2 describes the complex social process of organization in more depth. In particular, it explains why organization is best understood as an *ongoing process of conversational interaction*, rather than as a defined entity ("the organization"), which supposedly has the capacity to act in some way independently of these local interactions. It also discusses how this process occurs between *inter*dependent people, rather than as a result of individuals acting autonomously or as members of whole systems. People, that is, who are co-creating the future in the currency of their present interactions. Importantly, too, this chapter emphasizes the centrality of power and politics to everything that happens in an organizational context, positioning these as natural dynamics of human interaction rather than as signs of dysfunction that 'proper management' will cure. It also highlights the fundamentally paradoxical nature of organizational dynamics.

Against this background, Chapter 3 explores what I refer to as The Five Acts of Management. This calls into question much of the research and supposed evidence on which the plethora of n-step models, assessment questionnaires, and similar concepts, tools and techniques of organization are based. In particular, it exposes the disconnect between the reality of managers' everyday lived experience, and the way in which this is accounted for in conventional scientific and practitioner research. Also, how the latter then flows through into the policy making of government bodies, the work of regulatory agencies, and the offerings of mainstream management consultancies. These combine to present a neatly packaged, 'do this and you'll get that' view of organization, which ticks all of the expected boxes as regards diagnostic rigour and stepwise prescriptions. Unfortunately, this fails to take seriously the complex social dynamics of organization and the nature of real-world management practice, that are set out in the earlier chapters. The underpinning theme here is that organization, as a continuously emerging, socially constructed phenomenon, is not amenable to conventional scientific analysis, using the established research methodologies.

Chapter 4 goes on to explain why "muddling through" most accurately describes what managers and others *find themselves doing in practice* and why this is an inevitable consequence of the wiggliness of organization. My use of this term is deliberately provocative. It openly challenges the carefully cultivated conception of management as an elite practice, underpinned by scientifically rational decision-making and formally defined strategies, structures, systems and so on. This is the case irrespective of people's particular roles and relationships. As such, it offers some important pointers towards achieving a degree of mastery in the practice of operating within the irreducible complexity of real-word organization. Whilst, at the same time, acknowledging that this is intimately interwoven with the mystery that comes from not knowing. This chapter provides the fertile ground in which the later practical guidelines for leading, managing and consulting in the wiggly world of organization are rooted.

The first four chapters, then, set out the case for pursuing a radical shift in our understanding of the nature and dynamics of organization. And, in particular, in the way in which we view the manager's task. However, in order to realize this fully, we need to understand and escape from the suffocating grip that management orthodoxy maintains on current practice.

With this in mind, Chapter 5 exposes the wide gap that exists between the currently dominant view of organization and management practice and the complex social dynamics of organizational life as managers and others actually experience it. The established narrative implies that managers should be doing something much more sophisticated and 'manager-like' than the process in which they actually find themselves immersed every day. This fantasy is reinforced by the codification of supposed "best practice"; mechanistic performance measurement practices and reward mechanisms; one-size-fits-all competency frameworks; and so on. As such, it distorts understanding and inhibits progress towards a view that is more attuned to what's actually going on. I've illustrated this conundrum here by identifying and exploring a number of recurring themes that have come to shape people's understanding of the nature of organization; define what 'good' management is supposed to look like; and set their expectations as to what those in formal management roles are supposed to be capable of achieving. Although supposedly the touchstones of professional practice, these fail to reflect the complex reality within which managers and everyone else are perpetually immersed. Nevertheless, these generally accepted 'truths' are reinforced by everyday repetition, within and beyond the specific context of organizational practice (e.g. via the media), as well as through their official endorsement in all of its forms (such as by regulators, qualification bodies, mainstream consultancies and the like). Fuelled by this, and other dynamics that tend to maintain the established order, it can be particularly challenging for managers and others to escape from this mental and procedural straitjacket. And so, the fantasy continues.

Against this background, Chapter 6 explores in depth the "So what can I *do*?" question. In everyday discussions on these matters, this is the point at which the real-world wiggliness of organization comes face to face with the deeply ingrained expectations of order, predictability and control. If it is true that organization and management don't work in the ways that they are supposed to do, what can managers do *in practical terms* to deal more effectively with this complex reality? An essential first step is in recognizing that there are no simple tools and techniques available – at least not in the universally applicable, 'plug and play' sense that these are usually understood. On the upside, since whatever happens does so in the widespread interplay of people's everyday interactions, managers are already powerful participants in this process. They are already setting priorities, making choices and mobilizing action. But, despite being in charge of whatever is going on, within the bounds of their formal authority, neither they nor anyone else is in control of what emerges overall. They, along with everyone else, are acting forwards, moment to moment, into an unknowable future that is emerging continuously from their individual and collective participation in the process. That is to say, as set out in Chapter 4, they are muddling through. Their challenge then becomes one of how they might do so most effectively. Central to this is recognizing that muddling through is not a poor substitute for leading and managing professionally – devoid of the intentionality, insight and inspiration that textbook practice is supposed to bring to the fore. On the contrary. When enacted with purpose, courage, and skill, it is the best that managers – indeed, everyone else – can achieve in practice. Doing so skilfully, though, requires them to develop and deploy *their own* "practice theory", which might well include adaptations of concepts, tools and techniques that they find personally resonant and useful practically. This, together with other practical aspects of muddling through, is explored extensively in this chapter.

Building on the muddling-through nature of leadership and management practice, Chapter 7 considers the implications of the wiggly-world dynamics for management consultants and related practitioners (such as coaches, mentors, facilitators, developers and so on). Understandably, this reflects many of the same themes that govern management practice. In this case, though, these are viewed from the perspective of consulting and other specialist practices. In their relationships with clients, such specialists are similarly immersed in the live game of conversational interaction, through which issues, perspectives and outcomes are emerging continuously. And so, despite the formality and structure that typically circumscribes their engagement, muddling through similarly provides the most accurate description of what they find themselves doing day to day. Here again, then, striving to do this with purpose, courage and skill sits at the core of high quality practice. Within this, I've related the challenge of operating skilfully to three broad aspects of the consulting craft. These concern the ways in which consultants frame their involvement with their clients; the efforts they make to bring about beneficial changes in client capabilities, practice and performance; and, underpinning both of these, the quality of their own participation.

In light of the above, attention in Chapter 8 turns to what might happen if managers, consultants and others were to take their own experience seriously. How might they understand and talk about management and leadership practice? In this relatively short chapter, I have identified a number of shifts in the patterns of talk and action that might become evident, if the currently dominant conception of management practice were to be supplanted by one which more closely reflected the complex social reality of organizational life. This provides, in effect, my *manifesto for muddling through*.

By way of conclusion, I've included a short Postscript. This provides a very brief excursion beyond the world of organization into life more generally. It underscores the point that we are both subjected to – and, at the same time, creators of – these same, wiggly-world dynamics in our daily lives. That is to say, we are all inextricably immersed in the 'game of life'. Perpetually creating the future together – for better and for worse – through our moment-to-moment interactions.

Using the book

Overall, the structure of the book is intended to offer readers a number of options for engaging with its contents. These range from a short, practical overview to an in-depth understanding of the underlying dynamics, the practical implications, and options for further study. For those managers who want to gain a quick introduction to the wiggly world of organization, and to consider the implications of this for their own and/or others' day-to-day practice, Chapters 1, 6 and 8 should serve their purpose. In essence, these respond to the questions, "What's going on?", "What can I *do*?" and "What difference could this make to my own and others' perspectives, practices and performance?" For consultants and other specialist practitioners, adding Chapter 7 will complete a quick pass through the book. For a full exploration of the subject, all eight main chapters, together with this Preface and the Postscript, is recommended. And, as a final option, the book includes a number of endnotes that offer additional commentary and pointers to further exploration.[5]

Thanks

As I mentioned in the Preface to *Informal Coalitions*, I have had the privilege of working alongside a multitude of people whose words and actions have enriched my understanding of how organization works and what this means for management and leadership practice. All of those interactions have, in some way or other, influenced the ideas that are contained in this book. Once again, therefore, I'm grateful to friends, past colleagues, and current and past clients, for helping me to make better sense of the dynamics of organization and management practice than I might otherwise have done. There are, though, a few people whose contributions over recent years deserve particular mention.

I'd like to begin by giving special thanks to Clive Smith and Richard Shaw, who have both been long-standing supporters and keen advocates of these ideas. Clive is a friend, one-time colleague and enthusiastic client, most recently expressed during our work together in South-East Asia. Richard, who has also been a friend and client for several years, sealed his commitment to this way of thinking with the comment, "When you understand this stuff, there's no going back." I have also benefited from the long-term support and friendship of one-time GameChanger, Hans Haringa, as well as the many other friends and clients with whom I have worked and communicated over the years since the publication of *Informal Coalitions*. Most prominent amongst these have been Kevin Nix, Nina Skorupska, Hanneke Lambregts, Janke Bosma, Marinus Tabak, Guy Eccles, Sharon Varney, Gary Pass, Flemming Toft, Naomi Stanford, Ozcan Kabakcioglu, Chris Hunt, Cliff Oswick, Kevin McCullough and many friends and past colleagues within the Lane4 community. River School friends Pete Burden, Rowena Davis, Rob Warwick and Jonathan Wilson have also provided much mental stimulation, support and encouragement.

Over the past several years, during my annual attendance at the University of Herfordshire's Complexity and Management Conference, I have benefited from many stimulating conversations with members of faculty and fellow participants, many of whom I now regard as friends. These have helped to challenge, validate and reinforce the radical view of organizational dynamics on which the book is based. The many interesting conversations and reflections sparked by my running of a bimonthly network of senior organizational development (OD) practitioners since 2005 have also proved helpful. As has my regular attendance at a writers' network meeting run by another friend, Bob MacKenzie. And, of course, I want to express special thanks to Dominic Mahony. As he did in relation to my writing of *Informal Coalitions*, Dom has performed the vitally important role of "critical friend"; providing invaluable commentary on the emerging text. Finally, here, I would like to recognize the enthusiastic support and expert contribution made by Rebecca Marsh and the wider team at Routledge – most particularly, Sophie Peoples, Sj Smith and Ravinder Dhindsa – in ensuring that all aspects of the publication process were dealt with swiftly and professionally.

Coda

At the time of writing, the worldwide coronavirus pandemic has brought into sharp focus our inability to predict and control what happens as a result of the self-organizing interactions of people across the globe. It is important to recognize, though, that the emergence of COVID-19 as a pandemic is not an aberration. That is to say, the direct and indirect transmission of the virus between people is itself an expression of the complex social process of everyday human interaction – albeit involving the exchange of contaminated airborne particles, rather than conversation! As such, it is predictably unpredictable in terms of its effects; heavily context- and path-dependent; uncontrollable by any one individual or governing body, and so on. Despite this, the fundamental belief that those deemed to be in charge should be able to predict and control outcomes appears to be as deeply ingrained as ever. This perception needs to change. Not only amongst managers themselves but, equally importantly, within the ranks of those who circumscribe managers' practice with rules and regulations. Or who comment on their actions from afar. The most important learning that we can gain from this experience is recognition that all of us are continuously immersed in a world that doesn't operate in a 'do this and you'll get that' way. It is a world that is far removed from the conditions of order, predictability and control that currently dominate the official construction of what constitutes success and good practice. In short, it's a *wiggly world*. And we all have no option but to *muddle through* the multiplicity of demands that this brings. We can, though, strive to do so with *purpose*, *courage* and *skill*.

And finally . . .

As a concluding thought, before moving to the book proper, Picasso usefully identifies "foaming at the mouth" as a key performance indicator of success in waking people up. Hopefully, what follows might provoke a significant shift in readers' thinking and practice – without quite going that far!

Chris Rodgers, Cirencester UK, September 2020

Notes

1 This quotation from Picasso is recorded in André Malraux's book, *Picasso's Mask*, which was originally published in 1976 by Henry Holt & Company Inc.
2 "The beautiful, ugly truth" is how the leader writer in the *New Scientist* of 28 June 2014 headlined the argument that it is better to see things as they are, rather than as we'd like them to be.
3 Stacey, R. D. (2010) *Complexity and organizational reality.* Routledge.
4 Rodgers, C. (2007) *Informal Coalitions.* Palgrave.
5 Throughout the text, I have drawn extensively on my experience of the complex social process of organization, as gleaned from many years of working as an in-house manager and a management consultant. For the past several years, I have commented on various aspects of these dynamics in original posts on my *Informal Coalitions* blog and elsewhere. I have not, though, provided specific reference to any personally copyrighted extracts that appear in the following pages.

1

THE WIGGLY WORLD OF ORGANIZATION

TAKING EXPERIENCE SERIOUSLY

We all know how organizations work. We've read the books and journals, seen the research, and attended the courses. If we're looking for ways to change, develop, restructure, merge, demerge, turnaround, or otherwise transform the organization for the better, we are spoilt for choice. These – always "new" – ways of working are all neatly packaged, politics-free, and presented as common-sense responses to the challenges that we face. Provided that everyone follows the prescribed models, programmes, systems, and procedures, we're assured that the outcomes we're looking for will come to fruition. Sorted!

Trouble is, this well-ordered, fully aligned view of organization and management practice, with its unfailingly positive results, bears little relationship to the world that managers experience and participate in every day.

At the same time, of course, life goes on and the organizational world continues to function. Whatever our role might be, we can – *and do* – deal with the challenges that emerge. Like everyone else, we have no other option. Some people tend to do this better than others, of course. And most of us do so better on some occasions than we do on others. For most of the time, though, what we find ourselves doing bears only a passing relationship to the 'oughts' and 'shoulds' that are supposed to govern the being and doing of our formal role. It might be politically expedient, of course, to collude with the fiction that we are fully in control of what is happening around us. Or that, if we aren't, others will be. But, by doing so, we severely limit our ability to understand and enhance our own and others' practice.

In the context of organization, it is those who are formally charged with managing and leading organizational practice and performance who are most visibly exposed to the implications of not knowing and the anxieties that this can generate. In my experience, both as a practising manager and organizational consultant, most managers do their best to carry out their roles conscientiously and purposefully. However, their efforts are shaped by the felt need to satisfy the conditions of order, predictability and control that sit at the core of the established management discourse. Most damagingly, this creates unrealistic expectations about what they and others can credibly achieve in their roles. As such, it distorts their practice and limits their perspective. In this opening chapter, therefore, I want to expose some of the myths that obscure people's current understanding of the underlying nature of organization, before setting out a more reality-congruent view of how organization works *in practice*. Later, we will consider the implications of this for people's ongoing participation and seek to answer the "So what can I *do*?" question – especially for those in managerial roles of one sort or another, from CEO to the front line.

A word on managing and leading

In *Informal Coalitions* I challenged what I saw as the false dichotomy that had grown up between management and leadership, with leadership usually positioned as separate from – and superior to – management. This divide still exists today. And, if anything, the gap has widened in popular organizational discourse. Instead, I continue to argue that these are separate but complementary aspects of the same management role. With that in mind, I think that Kevin Flinn captures the spirit of this well in what he calls his "working definition":[1]

> I see leadership as making sense of the social context in which one finds oneself and then articulating an understanding/next step in which people recognise themselves and in so doing come to recognise one as leader. And I see management as coping with the context and the intended and unintended consequences of working from the new understanding and/or taking that next step into the unknown.

He goes on to echo the point that these are two sides of the same coin, which can't be separated in any meaningful sense. As he says most persuasively, it is in the process of coping with the emerging context that one makes sense of what's going on and articulates an understanding and/or potential next step around which, in my terms, people coalesce. I will later argue that leadership is an emergent property of people's everyday interactions rather than an elite practice confined to those 'at the top'. That is to say, it is a quality of relationship that might emerge and be recognized as such at any time, in any place, and involving any people – whether they are formally designated as leaders/managers or not. Of course, those who are in formal management positions, in whatever setting, are expected to perform well in both aspects of the role. That is in leading and managing, as these are described by Flinn. And much of this book is directed towards supporting them in their understanding and practice of that contribution. In this regard, and to simplify the language throughout the text, I have ordinarily used the word "management" to describe the role of managing and leading, except where more clarification is needed.

What are we dealing with?

As the following extract shows, it is not easy to escape from the well-established view that managers are fully capable of predicting and controlling people's actions and organizational outcomes:[2]

> To better manage complexity, senior leaders must recognize how employees at all levels see it, and then learn what's driving it. By doing so, companies can retain the kinds of complexity that add value, remove the kinds that don't, and channel the rest to employees, at any level, who can be trained to handle it effectively.

In this article by McKinsey consultants, the authors confidently set out their recipe for enabling managers to "put organizational complexity in its place". As such, they treat as unproblematic the idea of talking about the inherent ambiguity, uncertainty, and complexity of organizational life alongside the suggestion that, for example, appropriately trained employees can "manage whatever value-creating pockets of complexity their companies decide to maintain". They are not alone in this. Much of the recent writing on organization and management practice similarly views *so-called* complexity as a specific problem of organizational design and operational practice. A problem, that is, that managers can solve through rational analysis and intentional redesign. Various papers purport to give managers the means, for example, to "crack the complexity code"; "conquer complexity"; "lead [their] organisation out of the complexity wilderness"; eliminate or reduce "the hidden killer [of complexity]"; "tame costly complexity"; or, as here, "put organizational complexity in its place". In doing so, the authors further reinforce the view that managers can indeed ensure that events turn out as planned, provided that they follow the particular prescriptions on offer. By presenting complexity as another aspect of organizational dysfunction, that their particular remedy will cure, the authors reduce the task to one of intentional (re-)design and procedural compliance. In each of the above cases, this is essentially about designing-out *overly complicated* processes, systems, and procedures; and replacing these with new ways of working that, supposedly, hold the key to improved organizational performance and business success.

Taking time out to reflect on the continuing appropriateness or otherwise of the formal design aspects of organization is important, of course. It makes sense to eliminate or reduce any structural aspects (structures, systems, procedures, etc.) that have outlived their usefulness, and to simplify the ways in which things are supposed to be done. However, this only accounts for one part of the way in which organization is enacted in practice – and rarely the most significant part. It says nothing about the *necessarily complex* social dynamics of organization, out of which all such complications arose in the first place. And from which others will continue to emerge in the future, whether planned or otherwise. Against this background, it is very tempting for hard-pressed managers to succumb to claims that there are failure-proof ways through the messiness of everyday organizational life. Ways that will give them the ability to foretell and control what will happen. And that will ensure success. But any such promises are illusory. It is, of course, a natural human desire for us to be able to control the events that appear to define our lives. Or, if we can't, to have confidence that those in authority in any particular instance are capable of doing so on our behalf. But it does no favours to managers (or anyone else) to collude with this fiction. Claiming that specific concepts, tools, and techniques – and/or a certain combination of personal attributes – will put managers in control, simply perpetuates the myth.

Crucially, too, it fuels unrealistic expectations of what those in formal leadership positions can reasonably achieve independently of the actions of everyone else. By virtue of their formal roles, managers are relatively powerful participants in the organizational process. However, this "heroic" view of leadership practice – especially when applied in headline-catching ways to those in the most senior roles – sets them apart from those whose contributions they are seeking to mobilize. It positions them as extraordinary individuals, rather than as ordinary people who are seeking to participate skilfully in the organizational process, in ways that encourage, assist, and enable themselves and others to perform *extra*ordinarily well (however defined). As we know from our own day-to-day involvement, and as we'll explore more fully in the forthcoming pages, work gets done through the ongoing interactions of many, many people. People, that is, who are inextricably involved in the *ongoing process and practice* of organization.

Taking organizational complexity seriously

So where does this leave us in relation to organization and management practice? To begin with, even where managers (and others) act with deliberate intent and methodological rigour, they still can't be sure what will happen in practice. As David Collins puts it,[3]

> . . . understanding that the social world is inherently complex and difficult either to comprehend or manage, must be the first step to understanding what can be.

If we follow Collins's lead, and resolve to take organizational complexity seriously, we first need to accept that managers can't design, organize, and control what is going on in the ways that orthodox management theory suggests that they can. 'If you do this, you'll get that' prescriptions simply don't cut it. However sophisticated (or indeed simple) the formal structures, systems, and technologies might be, these are only physical manifestations of much more fundamental dynamics, to which none of the conventional prescriptions refer. It is therefore not credible to acknowledge that the dynamics of organization are complex and uncertain and then, at the same time, to claim that the use of a particular set of concepts, tools, and techniques will lead to success. As suggested above, these might help to simplify any unnecessarily complicated aspects of the *formal* organization. Or provoke new insights. Hopefully they will. But the complex social dynamics of organization will continue unabated.

Against this background, I have set out below a view of organizational dynamics and management practice which is firmly rooted in the real-world messiness of organizational life. As such, what follows privileges people's ongoing conversations and interactions, ahead of the usual focus on the formal trappings of organization that dominate mainstream theories and management models. This opens up the possibility of reframing our understanding of organization and management practice, *in ways that resonate much more strongly with our own and others' everyday lived reality*. So, in line with Collins's "first step", above, we need to begin by clarifying why the dynamics of organization are inherently, unavoidably, and *irreducibly* complex.

Order and knowability

It is probably safe to say that most of us would struggle to explain the inner workings of the various physical technologies that we encounter each day in our working lives. As well as in life more generally. As each day passes, new technological discoveries and developments make the gap between expert knowledge and end-user understanding wider still. We might consider such technologies to be complicated at best and impenetrable at worst. Nevertheless, we can say with confidence that these are *knowable*. Relevant experts would be able to explain, with accuracy and precision, how the specific equipment, tools, and technologies are supposed to work; how the various technological systems are designed to operate; which processes are intended to do what; and so on. It also means that issues arising directly in relation to these technologies lend themselves to "techno-rational" solutions. That is to say, any such solutions would be based – quite properly – on assumptions of linear cause-and-effect relationships and the skilful use of known protocols. Braden Allenby and Daniel Sarewitz describe such technologies as,[4]

> in effect, cause-and-effect machines, linking a human intent to a particular consequence via the embedded function of the technology, and often doing so with very high reliability . . .

However, as soon as we add people into the mix, we enter uncharted – *and un-chartable* – waters. The process becomes *unavoidably complex* and the effects of its use *ultimately unknowable*. It's here that orthodox approaches to management practice tend either to ignore or dismiss this complex reality, by persisting with these same mechanistic assumptions in the social arena. Or else, as we've seen from the opening example, the claim is made that such complexity can be reduced or eliminated altogether by deliberate management action. In contrast, as we'll explore more fully in later chapters, complexity in human affairs is ever-present. That is to say, organizational complexity is not a design parameter. It is a natural characteristic of everyday human interaction. It is through this ongoing process that organization is continuously (re-)enacted, and from which all outcomes – good, bad, and indifferent – continuously (re-)emerge, in the detail of people's day-to-day being, and in their ongoing practice. To put this starkly; even in what appear on the surface to be quite straightforward situations, such as two or three people interacting informally, the ways in which things will turn out are *never fully knowable*. This applies even more so to any wider effects that might emerge from their exchanges. People display all of the frailties, idiosyncrasies, and diverse characteristics that are the 'stuff' of being human. And this means that nothing is merely simple – or even complicated – when people are involved. The only obvious thing that we can say about it is that it is *unavoidably complex*. People behave in a multitude of different ways, at different times and in different circumstances – always doing so from positions that reflect different interests, diverse beliefs, distinct perspectives, fluid power relationships, shifting emotional states, and so on.

Added to this, individuals participate in constantly-shifting networks of relationships in every sphere of their lives. Some of these relationships are formal, others informal. Some are openly acknowledged and others covert. Some occur intentionally, whereas others arise incidentally. Some matter crucially to those involved; others less so. Some are rooted in conflict while others stem from a history of co-operation and mutual support. At all times, people try to handle these competing demands in ways that preserve their sense of integrity, self-worth, and identity; and which, at the same time, sustain each of the relationships in a desired state.[5] They do this both with conscious intent and out of habit. All of this means that, as soon as people become involved, technologies, systems, and procedures become inextricably interwoven with the complexities of everyday human interaction. Or, to put it another way, the complex reality of everyday life. We might, of course, have a sense of what is likely to happen in our immediate context, and put our trust in the technologies, structures and procedures which increasingly dominate our day-to-day lives. Also, if we happen to be in a position of formal authority, we might strive to achieve order for ourselves and others in those things in which we are engaged. Despite this, though, we cannot foresee, understand, or control with any degree of certainty what will result overall from our own and others' participation. Whilst familiar patterns of response might well be the norm, and the pure technological aspects of the process might be operating close to certainty, the potential always exists for novelty to emerge and unexpected outcomes to arise.

Not everyone accepts this position. Dave Snowden for example, whose popular Cynefin framework[6] is positioned as a tool for leadership decision-making, argues, "By classifying everything as complex we not only make a series of category errors, but we also miss opportunities to stabilise that which can be stabilised".[7] My response to this claim was – and remains – an unequivocal, "No we don't – on either count". As regards categorization, classifying a particular process as either clear or complicated, say, and approaching them in different ways (as suggested in the Cynefin framework), is not a statement of objective fact. Rather, it is a matter of interpretation, practical judgement, and emergent practice. It does nothing to negate the complex social dynamics of organization through which the future (including the natural human desire to establish order and predictability) is being continuously created in the present. In relation to stabilization, much of this ongoing, sense-making-cum-action-taking activity[8] is itself directed towards efforts to 'stabilize' the inherent complexity and uncertainty.

Crucially, *all* situations that involve people are complex and uncertain, regardless of how simple the context or content of their involvement might appear to be. It is therefore important not to confuse a description of the *unavoidably complex* dynamics of everyday human interaction, which exist *regardless of context*, with the diverse range of responses that one might deliberately seek to make *according to context*. And according to one's practical judgement at the time. The latter might well be usefully informed by the domains of the Cynefin framework, or similar classifications that have been developed over time.[9] Provided, that is, that such frameworks are seen as facilitative and/or provocative (in the lateral thinking sense of stimulating movement), rather than fixed and prescriptive. Even less so that they are thought of as describing an objective reality. In whatever ways these might be formulated, they are necessarily incomplete and provisional abstractions from the complex social reality of organization.[10] With this in mind, if we want to embrace the complex nature of organization, we need a fundamentally different way of thinking about what's actually going on. As well as some fresh insights into what this means for management practice, organizational performance, and policy formulation more generally. We also need to consider how such shifts in practice, performance, and policy-making might usefully be pursued. This is the essence of what follows.

The wiggly world of organization

Over 50 years ago, philosopher Alan Watts illustrated the world as a wiggly line.[11] On top of this he drew a net, which ". . . 'cut' the big wiggle into little wiggles". In this way, he argued, humans have sought to impose order on chaos. In a similar way, we can usefully describe the organizational world as "wiggly". It, too, is messy and complex.[12] This is represented by the wiggly line in Figure 1.1.

Sticking with Watts's imagery, the conventional view of the manager's task can similarly be seen as one of seeking to 'catch' this wiggliness in a metaphorical 'net'. In this way, managers strive to create order in the world, by putting things in place that are designed to provide them with the ability to stabilize, predict, and control what's going on. The net is woven from the 'straight-line' concepts, tools, and techniques of conventional management, such as formal strategies, structures, systems, procedures, programmes, projects, rules and regulations, etc. This is illustrated in Figure 1.2.

Figure 1.1 The wiggly world of organization

Figure 1.2 'Catching' the wiggliness in a 'net'

What is supposed to happen – organization by design

So, let's take a look at how things are supposed to work, if managers follow this established view of organization and management practice. That is, if they put their faith in management orthodoxy, and 'weave their nets' accordingly. This is sketched-out in Figure 1.3 and discussed below.[13]

Insofar as there is an identifiable starting-point to this process, it notionally begins with meetings, workshops, and other structured approaches, aimed at defining and communicating the sought-after organizational designs and intentions. In reality, of course, there is no definable starting-point, since today's actions are always situated within (and therefore affected by) everything that has gone before. It is not possible to "start with a blank sheet of paper". Regardless of this, the official narrative is likely to identify a clear beginning, based on the initiation of formal, structured decision-making processes. So we'll begin there, too. For now. The formal outputs from these activities tend to include such "must haves" of conventional management practice as, statements of mission, vision, and values;

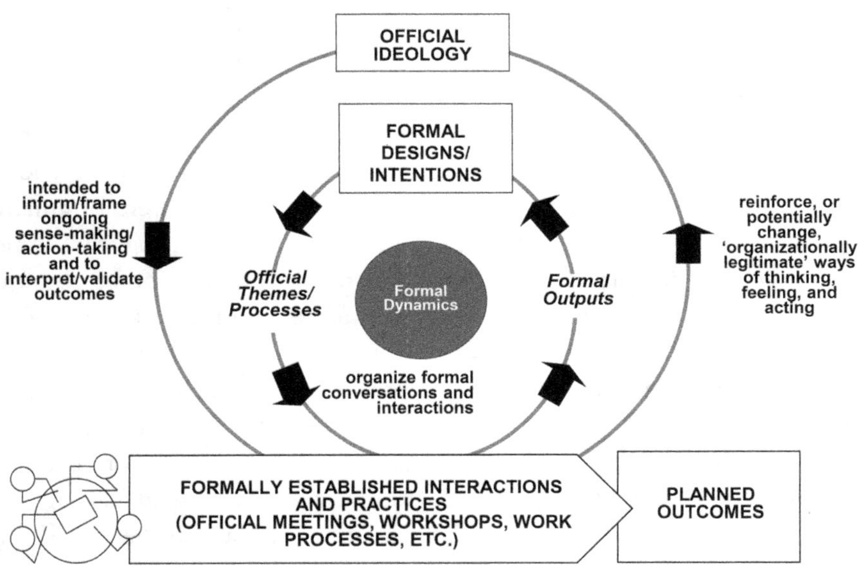

Figure 1.3 What is supposed to happen – organization by design

clear business strategies and organizational structures; the latest designs of management systems and business processes; operationally excellent operating models, procedures, rules, and regulations; and so on. Since the 'excellence movement' of the 1980s, this 'do it better and get it right', view of organization and management has increasingly been imported from the private sector into public-sector institutions.

When formally introduced, these designs provide tangible expressions of the officially endorsed themes that are intended to govern people's ongoing practice. That is to say, these are meant to organize the ways in which people interact and perform overall. Part of this will involve the development of derivative themes and processes, including such things as official roles and relationships; performance objectives; plans, programmes, and budgets; meeting structures; reporting requirements; and other protocols designed to organize and control people's day-to-day behaviour. Provided that everyone acts in line with their prescribed roles, and that their individual performance is at the required level, it is assumed that the planned outcomes will be achieved in an orderly and successful fashion. The particular organizing themes that are formally endorsed in the original design, and which are consistently repeated in public settings and published documents, come to define and reinforce the official ideology.

Such provisions carry the weight of formal authority and, in principle at least, are given voice (actually or by inference) by those currently in charge. These take the form both of official statements and physical artefacts, such as publications, structures, methodologies, tools, and so on. In this way, such themes retain the possibility of influencing interactions and outcomes well beyond those settings in which they were originally formulated. Depending on the material nature of what is produced, some of these provisions (such as buildings, infrastructure, and other physical assets) might have a more significant and more enduring effect on what happens. This is because they continue to provide people with cues and clues as to how they should behave. And/or they tend to enable, constrain and shape behaviour through their very existence – although not always in the ways envisaged by those who designed and implemented them originally.[14]

The official ideology serves to legitimize people's individual and collective activities, as well as providing the means by which their resulting actions and outcomes can be interpreted and validated. The presupposition is that a coalition of co-operative effort will form around these themes, as people behave rationally in pursuit of the specified objectives and act in line with the prescribed approaches. In reality, some people might instead be motivated to follow the intended course by factors other than willing co-operation. For example, they might feel coerced into compliance. Or else calculate that it's best to be seen to go along with formally established norms of behaviour to secure other ends, such as positive performance ratings, enhanced prospects of advancement, higher remuneration, and so on.

'Weaving the net' of management orthodoxy

The implicit assumption in all of this is that managers can in some way 'stand outside' this ongoing flow of human interaction and choose the optimum way to manage the situations in which they find themselves. Also that, having made that choice, people will willingly follow (or can be made to follow) the chosen path and the sought-after benefits will be realized. In this way, the felt need for clarity, certainty, predictability, and control is dealt with. This construction of reality contains within it the expectation that shortfalls will sometimes occur during implementation. And so, on those occasions when the sought-after benefits fail to materialize, this is most often blamed on poor implementation rather than unsound thinking. Perversely, then, failure confirms the validity of the dominant management discourse. It is part of what managers take for granted and 'know' to be true. By adopting this stance to implementation, failure is rationalized as a shortfall in execution. And so, the flawed assumptions remain to fight another day.

This perceived ability to plan, predict, and control outcomes, despite the acknowledged complexity and uncertainty, is further reinforced through the clichéd language, textbook practices, and 'if you do this you'll get that' logic that managers habitually use. Examples include such taken-for-granted notions as:

- knowing which *levers to pull* and which *buttons to push*;
- using *scorecards*, *dashboards*, and *traffic lights* to monitor and control what's happening;
- *steering* the organization in the desired direction;
- using transformation *engines* to *drive* change into the organization in line with *step-by-step models*;

- seeking *commonality of structures, systems and procedures*, across the diverse areas of organizational practice;
- *designing* and *building* a *common, shared culture;*
- transferring *universally applicable best practice* between units;
- *getting the message across*, so that everyone is *'on the same page'*;
- *leveraging Big Science and Big Data* to *eliminate surprises;*
- *future-proofing* the organization against future disruptive demands;
- claiming to base decisions on supposedly *evidence-based* principles and practices; and
- *"rolling out"* centrally determined initiatives to *ensure organization-wide consistency* of understanding, behaviour, and outcomes, in line with a formally established organizational *blueprint.*

Managers are exhorted to set about 'weaving their nets' in line with this dominant discourse, which essentially positions organizational management as a scientifically rational practice. In doing so, it emphasizes approaches that are rooted in such concepts as:

- knowability;
- clarity, accuracy and precision;
- analysis and rigour;
- structure and formality;
- physical and intellectual detachment;
- impersonality;
- objectivity and impartiality;
- procedural logic;
- discoverable cause-and-effect relationships;
- matter-of-factness;
- abstract models;
- universally generalizable rules; and
- a global (e.g. "organization-wide", "whole system", or "holistic") perspective.

Tor Hernes also speaks of this general tendency in terms of the desire to create a more predictable world, through *attempts* at stabilization that I referred to earlier.[15]

Provided that managers adhere to the prescribed approach – and that those they are managing comply with the specified requirements – the basic proposition is that the 'wiggliness' (seen here as a sign of dysfunction and the result of poor practice) will go away. This will allow them to get on with their sophisticated management task, free from the unwelcome and disruptive effects of messiness and uncertainty. John Clarke *et al*[16] argue that, viewed in these terms, management itself is a particular ideology, *managerialism*, "which proclaims the value and necessity of management for organisational, economic, and social progress, and establishes the foundational claim that, to be effective, managers must have 'the right to manage'". They then identify a "repertoire" of "discourses and devices, texts and techniques, roles and resources" from which managers might (in my terms) weave their nets in an effort to catch the wiggliness and render it controllable. This repertoire includes such things as:

- imperatives and injunctions – 'do this . . .';
- concepts and discourses – strategy, mission, culture change, etc. ". . . now often parodied as 'management speak'";
- analytical and empirical justifications – 'research', 'success stories', 'evidence', etc.;
- devices for transforming behaviour – incentives, targets, etc.;
- tools, techniques and technologies intended to bring order;
- identities and identifications that characterize the formal roles and relationships of people and places;
- scripts that establish the type of encounters and interactions that should take place.

When assembled, these further define the formally legitimate, as-designed organization, through which managers are meant to be able to achieve the sought-after certainty, predictability, and control. In other words, these are also used to cement the official ideology of formal organizing themes that are intended to circumscribe everything that happens (as illustrated at the apex of the diagram in Figure 1.3). Importantly, too, as Clarke *et al* further point out, it can be very difficult for managers to operate overtly in ways that run counter to the above repertoire of devices, etc., since adherence to them tends to be used as a proxy for 'businesslike performance' and 'managerial excellence', etc.

As we shall see later (in Chapter 3, for example), this last point is particularly relevant when we ask ourselves why it might be that people continue to talk about organization and management practice in ways which fail to reflect their own lived reality of everyday organizational life. More so too, perhaps, given that senior managers are themselves subject to this same ideology.

Real-world wiggliness

So where does this leave us? In spite of this much-heralded belief in managers' ability to achieve order by design, as Watts went on to say,[17]

> the real world slips like water through our imaginary nets. However much we divide, count, sort, or classify this wiggling into particular things and events, this is no more than a way of thinking about the world: it is never actually divided.

Nor is organization. Or rather the *complex social process of everyday human interaction* that is the essence of organization. This, too, slips through our imaginary nets of carefully constructed visions, strategies, structures, systems, and so on. Like life in the round, the everyday lived reality of organization is unstraightenably wiggly! If managers reflect on their own understanding of organizational life – as "walking case studies of these dynamics in action" (as I described it in the Preface) – they will know this to be the case. They will recognize that they are continually making sense of what's going on and taking action in the currency of their ongoing interactions with others. Acting into the world as this is emerging from their own and others' participation. They're also doing so officially and unofficially; in structured events and in the corridors; by design and by chance; for organizationally legitimate reasons and self-interestedly; with conscious intent and habitually. Some of the interactions that they are involved in occur in planned settings with structured agendas and people acting out their formal roles and relationships. Most though take place informally, whether with prior intent or spontaneously.

These informal conversations might themselves relate to specific formal events (such as people agreeing positions in advance of a meeting or discussing what they really think about things during breaks in the formal proceedings). At other times, they will just reflect the general life and everyday small talk, of organization, such as that expressed in informal working relationships, social cliques, informal networking, political influencing, chance interactions, private one-to-ones, and so on. Such small talk exists everywhere. And, although none of these dynamics are reflected in organization charts, reported in official documents or discussed in formal meetings, they powerfully influence what actually gets done, how it gets done, and what outcomes arise in practice.

As Gunnar Ekman points out,[18] leadership is constructed in everyday small talk. Formal organizing texts, if referred to at all, always require interpretation. In some instances, these might be "disqualified" altogether. Such interpretations are negotiated 'on the ground' and draw heavily on people's perceptions of the actions and inactions of those seen by others as role models, irrespective of their positions in the formal hierarchy.

Viewing organization in conversational terms inevitably brings gossip into focus. And gossip, like other aspects of small talk, is often dismissed as an irrelevant or, worse still, destructive component of the conversational mix. Which it can be, of course. However, Frank McAndrew identifies a number of potentially positive aspects of gossip,[19] including:

- the trust implicit in sharing gossip with another person;
- the bonding effect of sharing secrets with others;
- a means of learning the unwritten rules of social groups;
- an efficient way of reminding group members about the importance of the group's norms;
- a way of deterring deviant behaviour and of punishing anyone who breaks established norms; and
- being one of the most straightforward ways we have for comparing ourselves socially with others.

In other words, he points out that gossip is part of the forming of our identity and an important aspect of effective group performance. As regards group dynamics, it also reinforces power relationships and so goes some way towards establishing and sustaining 'in groups' and 'out groups'. Importantly, too, engaging in gossip helps people to find their way through the ambiguities of everyday organizational life. From a wiggly-world perspective, as McAndrew similarly argues, it would perhaps be more helpful to view the practice as a social skill rather than a character flaw. The skill exists in knowing when, where, with whom, and about whom to engage in the practice. Those who indulge in too much, indiscriminate gossiping are likely to earn themselves reputations as people who can't be trusted. Whereas a refusal to become involved is, as McAndrew suggests, a shortcut to social isolation.

These dynamics will not go away, however 'well' (in conventional terms) managers might set about their task. Or however determined anyone might be to get rid of them. I was once told by a senior client that the CEO of the company had naively said that they must put a stop to people's corridor conversations!

More significantly, as James C. Scott points out,[20]

> Formal order . . . is always and to some considerable degree parasitic on informal processes, which the formal scheme does not recognize, without which it could not exist, and which it alone cannot create or maintain.

In his critique of the established belief in the ability of the formal trappings of organization and conventional prescriptions on management practice to bring about social change, he illustrates the above point by reference to the tactic of working to rule in response to an industrial relations dispute. As was commonly experienced in the UK in the 1970s, by performing precisely in line with the formal rules, regulations, job descriptions and so on, employees can ensure that work will slow down dramatically or be brought to a halt entirely.

All of this means that, in spite of our craving for clarity, certainty, predictability and control, the real-world dynamics of organization are unavoidably ambiguous and paradoxical, uncertain, unpredictable, and complex. As these always have been, of course.[21] Importantly, too, the inability to predict and control outcomes and to pinpoint the causes of particular events is an *ever-present* dynamic of people interacting together. It is not something that only happens now and again. Or only in some (assumed to be poorly managed) organizational settings and not in others. It exists all of the time. In all organizational contexts.[22] So what is really happening?

What's actually going on – the complex social process of everyday human interaction

Further to the formal, structured view set out in Figure 1.3, the messiness of 'human being' and 'human doing' (i.e. 'real life'!) intervenes to affect the ways in which the formal designs emerge and how these are enacted in practice. To begin with, regardless of how precisely such design intentions might be specified, they will always be subject to interpretation by *specific* people, at *specific* times and in *specific* circumstances. How people make sense of what's going on, individually and collectively, and how they act into the situation as they perceive, interpret, and evaluate it, is therefore pivotal to what actually happens moment by moment. And hence, to what emerges overall. Crucially too, the meaning that people take from formal initiatives, and how they respond to them, are – like everything else – mediated through their ongoing interactions with others.

Even in a so-called "command-and-control" regime, where planned changes are imposed from on high with little or no formal involvement of those affected, these conversations continue apace. People are continuously immersed in their own, 'local' (i.e. small-group and one-to-one) interactions,[23] which take place before, during, and after the formally acknowledged exchanges. It's through these conversations with others (directly, via written texts, and through self-talk) that they make sense of pronouncements from on high; express their feelings and concerns; and are motivated to act. Or not! Overall outcomes then emerge from the ways in which the themes generated locally are endorsed, modified, embellished, contradicted, or otherwise taken up in countless other conversations 'organization-wide'. Importantly, neither managers nor anyone else can control this process. It is self-organizing. That is to say, there is no outside agent, objectively observing what is going on and controlling the thoughts, emotions, and actions of others from an external vantage point. I'll say more about this in Chapter 2. This basic process is illustrated in Figure 1.4, which extends the earlier discussion to take account of the hidden, messy, and informal, "shadow-side" dynamics of organization.

We are all familiar with these real-world aspects of organization, which frequently contravene and take precedence over formal policies, rules, and procedures. This is both because we have been on the receiving end of the shadow-side behaviours of others, *and because we constantly engage in them ourselves.* These are natural – and essential – dynamics of everyday human interaction. For better and for worse.

"Shadow side" refers to those elements of organizational practice that have a significant effect on what actually happens *but which are not spoken about openly in formal settings.* Although familiar with these dynamics throughout

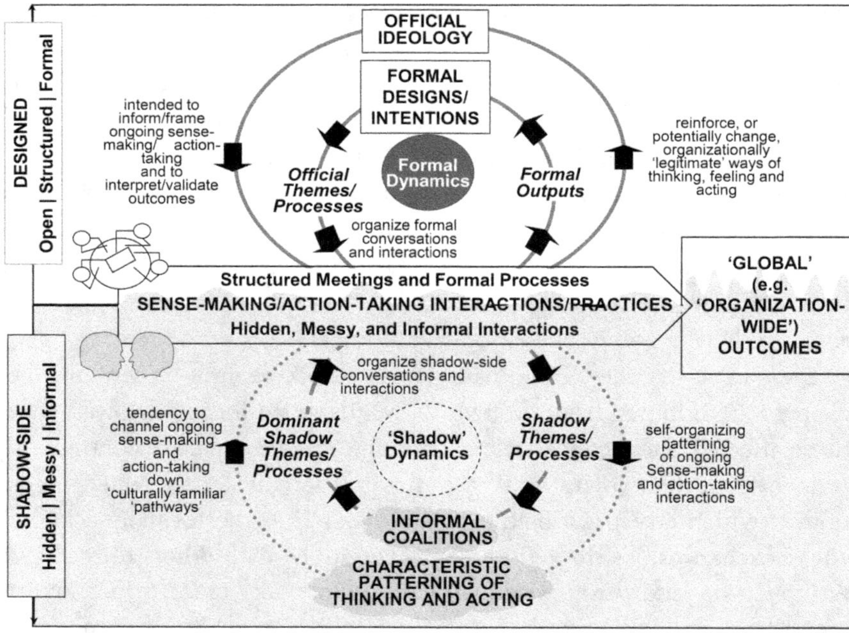

Figure 1.4 Impact of shadow-side dynamics

my working life, I first came across the term itself in the mid-1990s, when Gerard Egan used it in his book, *Adding Value*.[24] The concept resonated strongly with my own experience as a practising manager. Egan equates this with such things as informal, 'get the job done' relationships, which cut across the official lines of communication; social cliques; political activity; organizational culture; and individual idiosyncrasies. Although the term "shadow-side" tends to conjure up an image of negative behaviour, I believe that it usefully conveys the sense that any action will necessarily generate shadow-side activity – in the same way that shining a light on an object will always cast a shadow. You can't have the light without the shadow. Nor can you have an officially endorsed action without its shadow-side effects. Or, as we'll see later, its shadow-side origins.

There is an often-quoted story from the Nasrudin series, in which the Mulla has lost his keys inside his house but is found searching for them outside "because there is more light here". Managers are similarly encouraged to look for the 'keys' to organizational success in the supposed light provided by best-practice prescriptions and rationalized accounts of what's going on, rather than in the 'shadows' of real-world organizational practice. However, *as we know from our own experience*, it is not only the dysfunctional stuff that arises from the hidden, messy, and informal dynamics of day-to-day organizational life. Much of the productive work is done there, too. What happens in practice is heavily conditioned, for instance, by people's informal networks and social relationships; their exercise of power and political activity to influence outcomes; the characteristic patterning of interactions, which imperceptibly channels ongoing sense-making and action-taking along culturally familiar pathways; and so on. These are often the undiscussables of organizational life – the secrets that everybody knows. But simply ignoring – or, worse still, denying – these shadow-side dynamics is not a helpful way to progress. We've been told so many times, and in so many ways, what 'proper' management and organization look like that, for the most part, we've stopped looking at *what's actually going on*.

Instead, we continue to mask the unavoidably disjointed and fragmentary nature of our day-to-day experience with the managerially 'correct', politically acceptable, and unequivocal language of management orthodoxy. Like the photographs in magazines that present an impossibly perfect impression of the human form, this airbrushed view of organization bears little resemblance to managers' everyday lived reality. Yet it persists. Judging by many of the most popular posts and articles on social media, as well as the bookshop best sellers, there is little sign at present of this thirst for simple answers having matured into something more credible. Instead, we need to pay deliberate attention to the hidden, messy and informal aspects of organization – *in which we are all participating* – and not believe that organizational outcomes are determined by the 'set piece' events that ordinarily dominate the thinking of managers, consultants, policy-makers and others. Chris Argyris (1992) pointed out that such aspects of organization are not only undiscussable in formal meetings and published documents, but their undiscussability is also undiscussable. So, let's discuss them . . .

We'll begin by working our way around the bottom half of Figure 1.4. This illustrates that it is not only the formally acknowledged outputs that arise from the structured design and implementation processes. Other themes emerge at the same time, as a result of the shadow-side dynamics. How these shadow themes are taken up by people significantly influences their ongoing practice. This includes both *the extent* to which they embrace those principles, processes, and practices that have been formally endorsed, and *the manner* in which they do so. As these shadow themes emerge, people tend to coalesce informally around those that dominate their local conversations, and which 'ring true' to them. Or which otherwise align with their interests.[25] Where the dominant conversational themes are in tune with the formally stated intentions, it is more likely that the latter will be realized in practice. However, where shadow themes emerge which run counter to the official ideology, and which come to command sufficient informal support, other outcomes will inevitably arise.

Even if policies and processes could be stated unambiguously and were interpreted in the way intended, it is also important to recognize that some of the resulting political activity would be directed towards changing these formally established ends and/or means, not simply accommodating them. Where proponents of a particular shadow theme are able to mobilize a sufficiently powerful coalition of support for it, this is likely to emerge from the shadows and be put forward as a formal proposition. *This is how the elements of today's official ideology, and the themes and processes arising from it, were initiated, adopted as policy, and developed in the first place.* Mobilizing such a coalition of support behind a proposed shift in strategy, structure or practice will itself involve the use of hidden, messy, and informal interactions – and associated small talk (above) – alongside those involved in the formally constructed design process. As a familiar illustration of this, I was once having lunch with a client when we were joined by a member of the central Organization Design team. He and his colleagues had been working to develop a revised organizational structure, in support of the shift in strategy that had been settled upon some weeks earlier. He was decrying the fact that, after having developed a new structure based on rational design criteria, he was now on his "seventeenth iteration", following a series of meetings with managers whose departments would be affected by the changes. As we all know in practice, this is par for the course.

Some of the shadow themes that resonate strongly with certain people will nevertheless fail to attract a sufficiently powerful coalition of support for them to be raised as formal policy propositions or to influence the official design process. And, in any event, that might not have been the intention. Although remaining in the shadows, these will still continue to shape the local practices of those who take them up – perhaps decisively so; reflecting the continuing indifference, opposition or only partial alignment of those involved to the official story and related design changes. Shadow-side behaviours might also help people to sustain what I called in *Informal Coalitions* their personal frames of reference.[26] This exercise in the art of 'organizational plate-spinning' enables them to fit in; to maintain important relationships (within and beyond those relating to people who are currently present); and to be seen by personally significant others to be acting competently and 'playing the game'.[27]

The emergence of organizational culture

The final shadow-side dynamic at play here is illustrated by the outer loop in the bottom-half of Figure 1.4. This reflects the fact that, whilst the detailed interactions and overall outcomes that emerge are unpredictable, other aspects of the process are more amenable to what Richard Jenkins calls "everyday predictability".[28] This *sense* of knowing what to expect arises from the practices that people continuously (re-)enact, and the narratives that they share, as they engage with others in their various day-to-day contexts. In particular, a generalized tendency emerges for people to think and act in characteristic ways that reflect (and thus reinforce) those *locally established* patterns of thinking and acting that have emerged through past sense-making-cum-action-taking. This means, for example, that the more we make sense of things and act in particular ways, the more likely it is that we will continue to make similar sense and act in similar ways going forward. It also explains how particular ways of thinking and acting are imperceptibly sustained, further strengthened, and tend to become institutionalized over time.

Importantly, it is this patterning process that enables people to go on together, by creating expectancy that things will progress in certain ways and not others. Without it, they would have to think afresh before each and every (inter)action; making organization – and what we think of as normal life – impossible. At the same time, shifting these habitual patterns of thought, feeling, and action can be difficult, since this same self-organizing process tends to inhibit novelty and change. This means that, in the normal course of everyday organizational life, other possibilities tend to remain unseen – unless and until the characteristic flow of interaction is interrupted in some way. This might arise, for example, from an unexpected turn of events; a mistake in 'processing' that exposes a previously taken-for-granted way of thinking and acting (such as might occur when someone new joins a team); or through deliberate attempts to 'shift the pattern'.

This characteristic patterning of interaction is what most managers and other practitioners think of as organizational culture.[29] Importantly, this is an *ongoing, iterative process* of interaction between people. It is not a pre-determined 'thing'. The term describes the self-organizing, pattern-forming and pattern-using dynamic of people interacting together on a continuing basis. This also explains why culture is necessarily fragmentary rather than uniform. Even though some characteristic aspects of people's interactions are likely to be observable across a broad population, the overall patterning of their thoughts and actions will be highly conditioned by their local interactions – many of which might be geographically and/or functionally specific. Understood in this way, culture cannot be designed and built as a deliberate act of management. Although, by virtue of their formal roles, managers will be relatively powerful participants in this everyday co-creation process. By way of illustration, Figure 1.5 recasts the earlier (open and shadow-side) dynamics of organization in terms of organizational culture.

At the top of the diagram is the idealized view of what's going on. This suggests that, if managers were formally asked to describe organizational culture, it is likely that they would base their response on the contents of official publications and other intentional design criteria. The former might draw on such things as published statements of the sought-after culture (such as behavioural norms, for example); declarations of mission and vision (or their equivalents); extracts from Annual Reports; publicly available policy documents; press releases; and so on. The latter might refer, for example, to symbolic aspects of building design, and office layouts. Together, these are described in the diagram as the "Culture as Stated". This is concerned with the way that things are officially supposed to happen – or "the way things are done around here" (as this is popularly – and simplistically – described). That is, it is based on the *principles* that are supposed to govern people's attitudes and behaviour.

However, the extent to which this idealized state is realized in practice depends on how these official artefacts are made sense of and acted upon in the detail of people's day-to-day interactions with others. That is, on the basis of their everyday, lived experience. If people were asked to describe

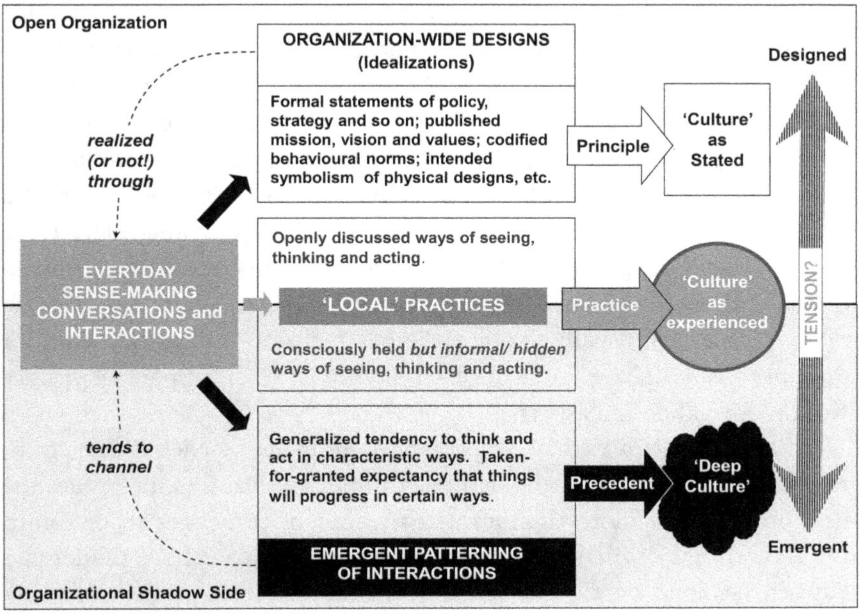

Figure 1.5 The dynamics of organizational culture

organizational culture based on this evidence, they might well mention some of the openly acknowledged ways of thinking, feeling and acting that matched the official line. However, the privacy of their small talk would also draw on some of the shadow-side aspects of their local experience. That is, ways in which they and their colleagues thought, felt, and acted that strayed from – even ran counter to – the stated norms. These would relate to local power relationships, as well as immediate conditions, customs and practices of which they were fully aware, but which they would not openly acknowledge in formal settings. This visceral understanding of organizational culture is referred to in the diagram as the "Culture as Experienced". It is rooted in people's day-to-day *practice*.

However, this still fails to account for everything that's going on. There is a further dynamic in play, which has the most fundamental impact on what happens in practice. This is the generalized tendency for people to think and act in characteristic ways, as they participate in particular contexts and relationships. This embodied, context-specific patterning of interaction tends to channel their ongoing interactions, without conscious intent, down well-trodden pathways. It is this deeply embodied, taken-for-granted and self-organizing patterning process that creates a sense of expectancy that things will progress in familiar ways. Or, as Jenkins describes it above, "everyday predictability". I've referred to this aspect of the overall process as the emergence of "Deep Culture". It arises from – and tends to strengthen further – what has gone before; that is, it is based on *precedent*. Mapping this onto the earlier representations of the ongoing interactional process, the "Culture as Stated" is a product of deliberate design; whereas "Deep Culture" continuously (re-)emerges in people's ongoing interactions. Where, as is usually the case, there is a tension between the two, it is the latter that will have the strongest influence on what happens in practice. Not the formal design aspects.

This is consistent with an important point made by Nick Chater, in his recent provocation about the nature of mind. Within this, he argues that past precedent is more significant than a set of principles in determining how things ordinarily play out in practice.[30] This echoes the ideas of Edward de Bono on the mechanism of mind and the practice of thinking. I have referred to his writing on this for many years; seeing it as a rich source of analogy for the self-organizing and patterning dynamics of organization. The focus of De Bono's and Chater's work is primarily on the internal mechanics of brain functioning and how people's thoughts and actions emerge from this process, when triggered by sensory inputs of various kinds. In the context of organization, much of this stimulus comes from people's interactions with others, both in person and via various other means. The latter include such things as recalling past conversations; reading their written words; acting within processes and systems that they have devised; inferring what they might say, and how they might react, in relation to whatever might be going on; feeling the effects of their actions; and so on. Also, whatever the nature and extent of people's conversations with others, they are always talking to themselves (i.e. thinking). In these ways, people are always engaged in a social process, even when they are physically alone.

Acknowledging the mess

Overall, then, the ways in which people take up the various shadow themes in their everyday practice serves to reinforce, modify, or reject the formally endorsed ways of thinking, feeling, and acting that comprise the official ideology. In this way, organization continues to (re-)emerge, in a never-ending, self-organizing process of conversational interaction. In light of these dynamics, nobody can predict or control what will flow overall from people's ongoing exchanges. This is not least because everyone else is similarly participating in their own local, conversations and doing so in line with their own intentions, prejudices, and assumptions. This is always the case – even though power relations are often significantly skewed in favour of those who have formal authority in a particular situation. Most of the mainstream literature and media commentary on the nature of organization and management practice majors on the formal aspects of organization and tends to adopt a matter-of-fact, "if you do this, you'll get that" view of the management task. However, as illustrated above, it's not as simple and straightforward as that. It's wiggly. *As our own experience tells us*, what's actually going on is *unavoidably* messy and fragmented. It's in the immediacy of people's in-the-moment interactions with others that they make sense of, and act into, the world. A world that is emerging continuously from their own and everyone else's participation in it.

To use a sporting analogy, this 'open play' of everyday organizational life is interspersed with 'set-piece' meetings, forums, and workshops. These provide for the formal input to, and official endorsement of, decisions that are heavily influenced by informal practices. Practices that are aimed at mobilizing collective action in support of one particular construction of reality, rather than another. It is in this way that the formal designs and intentions illustrated in Figures 1.3 originated. And it is these same dynamics that are at play in determining which of these formally endorsed designs are taken-up by people in the course of their ongoing practice – and in what ways. As illustrated in Figure 1.4, then, what happens *in practice* is heavily affected by the shadow-side dynamics that are always at play whenever people interact together. Crucially, too, these dynamics are unavoidably political, power-related, and partial:

- First, they *always* embody the differing interests, ideologies, identities, and so on of those taking part. Interactions are never neutral and matter-of-fact, they are always political.
- Secondly, they *always* reflect the differing and shifting power relations between those involved in any interaction, some of which become

institutionalized through people's ongoing enactment of their formal role relationships, policies, and procedures, etc. This means that nothing happens – 'good', 'bad' or 'indifferent' – except through the power relationships at play in the moment of people's interactions with others.

- Thirdly, they are *always* partial, in the sense both of being biased (for better or worse) towards a particular conception of what's going on and what might be required, and incomplete as regards the full range of possible perceptions, interpretations and evaluations of the specific situation.

Much of this process takes place informally. And, as set out above, many of the themes that emerge in conversation remain hidden and undiscussable in formal organizational arenas. Also, whilst a lot of interactions appear to be formally planned and structured, the most significant exchanges often occur spontaneously and/or are improvised between people informally – before, during, and after the set-piece events. Far from being impersonal and emotion-free, therefore, personal concerns and feelings are always in play in these encounters. So are the personal idiosyncrasies of the people involved. Ultimately, then, what matters is not awareness of the so-called "facts" of a situation (which might often be broadly shared) but rather people's perceptions, interpretations, and evaluations of what's going on. And these emerge in the moment of their local interactions. These contrasting dynamics are illustrated in Figure 1.6, below.

Recognizing the as-designed state

To aid explanation, I've discussed the as-designed view of organization separately from the hidden, messy, and informal dynamics that we experience every day and in all contexts. However, both aspects are socially formed, and *intimately intertwined*. As we saw earlier, the conversational mix includes both official and shadow themes. The former invariably originate in, and come to gain momentum and formal legitimacy through, the shadow-side dynamics. In challenging management orthodoxy, by deliberately exposing the wiggliness of real-world organization and management, I'm inevitably going to focus primarily on the implications of the latter for the ways in which things happen in practice. However, it's

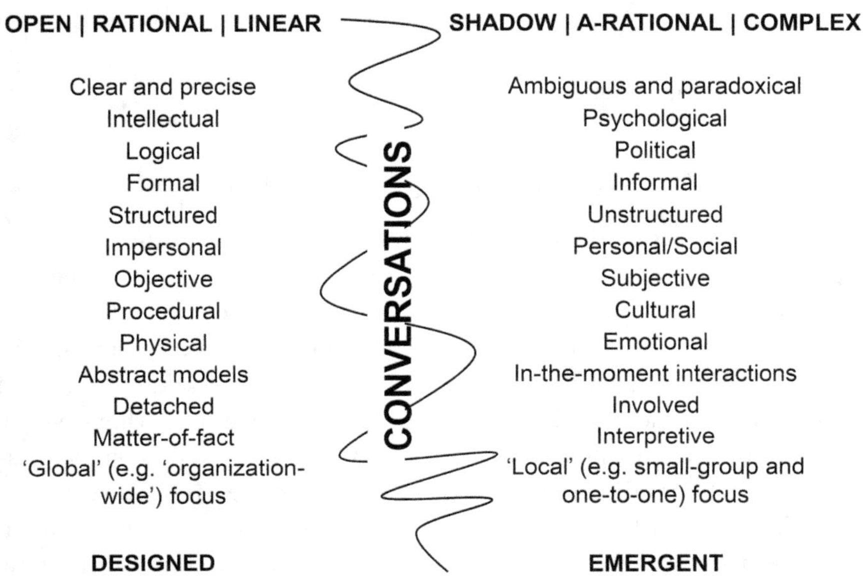

Figure 1.6 Open and shadow-side dynamics

important to recognize that the 'as designed' aspects of organization have a significant effect on how people behave and on what emerges overall – even if this is not always in the ways intended, or that their proponents expect.

As we discussed in relation to Figure 1.3, the formal trappings of organization play an instrumental role in setting out the official 'rules of the game' and providing the support infrastructure that is designed to realize these in practice. These officially endorsed themes, strategic structure and set-piece events reflect the formal design intentions and power relationships at play in a particular setting. As such, they also provide important sense-making-cum-action-taking opportunities, such as: marking key stages of particular planned developments; relating seemingly disparate initiatives to an overall 'story' of what's going on and what's supposed to be happening; helping people to frame their understanding of, and reaction to, emerging events; focusing attention on formally agreed priorities; highlighting and brokering significant interdependencies; introducing new concepts; surfacing any latent issues that become apparent from people's ensuing reactions; and so on. At the same time, seeing these formal, structured and as-deigned aspects as reflective of organization and management in the round falls well short of the complex reality.

Managers are in charge but not in control

Within the levels of their delegated authority, managers can 'command' specific actions such as the above to take place. However, they can neither control the ways in which people make sense of such commands and take action, nor the effects that these have on organizational outcomes. As outlined earlier, regardless of how powerful they might appear to be in formal terms, what actually happens will depend on the ways in which people take-up those commands in their everyday practice. As well as on the decisions and actions taken by countless others beyond their immediate sphere of influence. That having been said, the natural dynamics of organization provide managers with a degree of social control, by constraining how people behave in public. Whether intentionally or otherwise, the official ideology and various structural artefacts offer clues as to the language, attitudes, and behavioural norms that people are expected to demonstrate, in formal organizational arenas, if they are to survive and thrive.

As pointed out by Stacey[31] these act as a form of disciplinary power (after Foucault). That is to say, they enable those managers who are formally in charge in a particular setting to 'control' – at least in public settings and in outward appearance – the minds and bodies of those they are managing. This is because those affected become aware that observed compliance with the prescribed norms of behaviour provides the basis for such things as job selection; everyday acknowledgement and inclusion; formal recognition and reward; future advancement; and so on. Establishing such norms is therefore one of the ways in which managers, *who are themselves subject to these same dynamics*, seek to "catch the real-world wiggliness in a net". This is the case, even though many of the currently popular design provisions (such as the notion of "shared values") are usually spoken about in the positive language of "organizational transformation" rather than as instruments of control and compliance.

Against this background, it is important for managers to recognize that they are both *in control* (in the sense of being in charge) and, at the same time, *not in control*. This is a natural dynamic of organization, not a matter of choice. The challenge then becomes one of embracing this paradox; understanding and actively participating in the messy reality of everyday organizational life, rather than seeking to deny or somehow eliminate it. At the same time, none of this means that people can simply do as they please. Or that everything is a matter of chance. Quite the opposite, in fact. Everyone is both enabled and constrained in everything they do – and their practices are shaped – by the actions, inactions, and interactions of everybody else. Within this, the ways in which managers exercise their own contribution of 'being in charge' is also important. For example, establishing norms as an instrument of disciplinary power is not, in itself, bad or ineffective. Any more than a supposedly "values-led" approach is necessarily good. It depends on the nature of the established norms, how these are derived and how they are applied. And on the extent to which these resonate with the *personally held* values that are also motivating and guiding people's behaviour.

In the context of performance in the sporting arena, for example, Sir Clive Woodward's 'Black Book' approach to managing performance is often cited. In his management of the England Rugby Union Team's victory in the 2003 World Cup, he and his coaches began by establishing a number of key themes to do with team discipline. The players themselves then developed what became known as "Teamship Rules" for achieving these through their everyday behaviours. In the same field, the New Zealand All Blacks have formally developed and adopted a number of "mantras", to help guide their day-to-day behaviour. The mistake would be in seeing the ritual codification of such matters as 'job done'. As discussed earlier, it is the individual and collective interpretation of such artefacts, and their re-*presentation* in everyday practice, that carries the most weight. And this happens through people's everyday small talk, as also informed by their observation of the actions of those whom they view as role models – both formal and informal. Social organization – especially on a large scale – necessarily requires people to behave in line with certain norms, if the process is to continue to function coherently and a necessary degree of mutually beneficial order is to be achieved. And, in the context of teamworking, the emergence of a "We identity" can contribute positively to collective performance. What can be unhelpful though, is attempts to disguise the exercise of disciplinary power, and the associated dynamics of constraint, compliance, and control that this involves, as characteristics of something that should be met with willing and unquestioning engagement. Something, that is, which is enthusiastically and universally shared rather than imposed.

Managers are 'on the pitch, playing'

Managers, like everyone else, participate in this constantly shifting network of conversations, out of which organization emerges. That is to say, they, too, are 'on the pitch, playing'. They are not, to continue the metaphor, 'sitting in the dugout'; observing and directing other people's actions from a position of detachment and objectivity. This is not to say that they can't, at the same time, strive to take a detached view of what's going on within and around them. Clearly, they can. And they should. Ronald Heifetz and Donald Laurie,[32] for example, refers to the desired state as one of "standing on the balcony". My concern is that this phrase might evoke the image of their setting themselves apart, watching and commenting on other people's actions from a wholly detached vantage point. Rather than recognizing that they, too, are unavoidably participating in (and contributing to) the messy reality of organizational life. A better description of the sought-after state might be the paradoxical one of "detached involvement" (after Elias). Not in any sort of mystical sense. This simply recognizes that, by virtue of their formal role-relationships with others, managers are always involved. For example, they cannot *not* communicate. Everything that they say and do – *and everything that they don't say and don't do* – 'sends messages' to people about such things as the sense of direction that they are expected to pursue; what's important and what's not; the sought-after behavioural norms; and so on. These interactions provide what I described in *Informal Coalitions* as "moments of leadership truth".[33]

As we'll discuss in Chapter 6, expert practice in this involves managers adopting a more reflective and reflexive approach to their own and others' participation *in the midst of this ongoing flow of interaction*. Paying attention, in the moment, to the movement of their joint sense-making with others; identifying and exploring dominant themes; challenging clichéd responses (in the sense of actions as well as words); provoking shifts in perspective; and so on. This is a paradoxical relationship between involvement and detachment, not an either-or choice. However much a manager might wish to stand back from the action, take stock, and control what's going on from on high, their actions (including where their 'standing back' is observable by others) will affect the ways in which people perceive, interpret, and evaluate what's going on, and how they behave. It's also important to understand that managers are always participating in this process through their own local interactions. Even if they are dealing with organization-wide issues and/or other matters that have global impact, they can still only lead and manage via their local conversations. That is, in small-groups and one-to-one interactions. This is a fundamental dynamic of organization. An important corollary of this is that it's not what managers settle upon and announce formally that determines what happens. It's how people *make sense* of what they see and hear, in their own, local interactions. And how they find themselves and others acting in practice. In the social process of organization, it's the *meaning* of things that matters, not the things themselves.[34] And meaning does not reside with any one of the participants. It is co-created in the moment of the local interactions that are taking place constantly *between* people.

As we saw in Figure 1.3, some of the themes that emerge from this process enter the formal organizational arenas as explicit propositions. The formally stated intent is then one of bringing about outcomes that are intended to be organizationally beneficial. However, the political nature of the process means that this might well not be the sole – or even the primary – purpose of all of the people involved. After 'due process', including any modifications considered necessary to accommodate the needs and wants of others, these provisions are adopted as policy. Or maybe not, of course. It all depends on whether or not a sufficiently powerful coalition of support can be mobilized in support of the proposed changes. Other themes remain in the shadows. The aim, here, might be to further or frustrate the formally established policies. Or to initiate shifts in practice, in pursuit of altogether different intentions. Such conversations relate both to the openly acknowledged and formally designed aspects of organization (i.e. the metaphorical 'net' that managers have woven in an attempt to 'catch the wiggliness') as well as to the informal, shadow-side dynamics. Despite the hold that the former has on the established ways in which we talk about organization and management, it is the latter that continue to 'slip through the net' and powerfully shape what happens in practice. Contrary to mainstream prescriptions, it is to these hidden, messy, and informal aspects of organization that managers need to direct much of their attention. Stacey captures this beautifully, when he describes strategic management as, "actively participating in conversations around important emerging issues".[35]

A sobering thought for managers in all of this, though, is that they are not party to the vast majority of conversations that take place amongst members of their team. Or to those engaged-in more widely, both 'at work' and elsewhere. *And it's out of the widespread interplay of these myriad, local conversations (as earlier defined) that whatever happens, happens.* However, even though they might not be physically present in most of these conversations, the 'imprints' of their past interactions with some or all of those present, and the power relationships that these imply, will necessarily affect the nature, content, and outcomes of those later interactions. To what extent they do so, and whether this helps or hinders from a particular perspective, is not within the manager's gift to control. It depends on how those interactions were perceived, interpreted, and evaluated by those who happened to be involved in – or merely observing – the original exchange(s). Any imprints left by such conversations will reflect both the immediacy of the interactions themselves, and any subsequent conversations that those directly involved might have had with others. So, the patterns of interaction that managers have had in the past will continue to influence the ongoing sense-making and action-taking of those people, whether or not the manager happens to be present. The ways in which this plays out – and the tangible effects that it has on what happens in practice – is wholly contingent on what takes place in the moment of those subsequent interactions.

So, what can managers *do*? . . . Taking experience seriously

What, then, are the implications of this wiggliness for managers – from CEO (or equivalent) to the front line? What can they actually *do*? Especially if they recognize the reality of their being "in charge but not in control".

To begin with, there are no simple, 'if you do this you'll get that' formulae. Nor, despite what many academics and practitioners claim, is it possible to provide evidence which demonstrates that a generic prescription will work at this *specific* time, in this *specific* situation, with these *specific* people. Inconvenient though this might be, in a world in which we have been brought up to value clarity of process, certainty of outcome, and proof-before-action, the craving does not make these socially complex and uncertain dynamics of everyday interaction go away. As in all things complex, what happens depends on situation, circumstance and the 'path to now'. The idealizations of management orthodoxy remain an illusion. Despite this, managers continue to be surrounded by messages which suggest that what I'm describing here as the wiggliness of organization is a sign of dysfunction and/or poor management practice. If they search the internet to discover ways through the mess, they will not be disappointed. Although they might be by the results that they get should they decide to follow the readily available, 'do this and you'll get that' prescriptions. Sadly, these serve only to divert managers' attention away from the messy reality of organizational life. *Messiness that they experience and unavoidably contribute to every day.* Instead, they are directed towards the abstract conceptions of an imaginary world that they supposedly have the ability to control,[36] provided that they and others follow the prescribed ways forward and 'do things right'. As we'll discuss more fully in Chapter 3, even those who are perhaps more attuned to what's really going on, and to what it is that they are actually doing in practice, are nevertheless likely to find themselves accounting for their actions and events in ways that fit-in with the established expectations of certainty, predictability and control.

Getting real

Acknowledging this gap between established thinking and the real-world wiggliness of organization is not a cause for despair or a call for inaction. On the contrary, it offers managers and consultants an escape route from the fantasy world that is reflected in many business books, development programmes, website offerings and policy formulations. It calls on them instead to pay attention to their own and others' *everyday lived experience* and the implications that this has for their ongoing practice. Rather than requiring them to collude with the view that it's all measurable . . . all controllable . . . and all predictable, this allows them to take seriously the complex social reality of organization and better understand their contribution to it. In particular, it recognizes that, as outlined earlier, they are not objective observers and controllers of other people's actions. They are involved contributors to whatever is happening. As we'll discuss in some depth in Chapter 4, they will then be better placed to acknowledge *what they, like everyone else, are actually doing in practice.* That is to say, they are muddling through the unavoidable wiggliness of organizational life, as they act forwards, moment-to-moment, into a continuously emerging and unknowable future. The challenge then becomes one of muddling through with *purpose, courage*, and *skill*.[37] And it's to the practicalities of doing this that we'll turn our attention in Chapter 6.

This does not mean managers abandoning any sense of intention, setting aside all notions of formal management practice, or abdicating responsibility for results. Far from it. But it does mean doing all of these things without any certainty as to what might ultimately emerge. Most importantly, it means focusing on the here-and-now of people's everyday conversations and interactions, through which they and others are continuously making sense of what's going on, taking action and co-creating whatever outcomes emerge. This also means recognizing that the ongoing, conversational process of organization is fundamentally *a*-rational, political, and interpretive rather than rational, politically neutral, and matter-of-fact. In short, it means accepting, with humility and curiosity, this state of not knowing – understanding that questions might generate yet more questions, rather than producing seemingly definitive but ultimately illusory answers.

To conclude this chapter, I'd like to return briefly to my opening remarks. There, I argued that we need to begin by *taking complexity seriously*. To illustrate the problem, I used a quotation that positions "complexity" as just another of the variables that managers can manipulate and control. I'd like to end it with a couple that challenge this simplistic view of organizational dynamics. The first is again by Allenby and Sarewitz, in which they conclude that we should,[38]

> Stop trying to think our way out of what is too complex to be adequately understood, and seek the sources of rationality and ethical action in our uncertainty and ignorance about most things, rather than in our knowledge about and control over just a few things.

The second is from what might seem an unlikely source of support for the notion of organizational wiggliness and the muddling-through nature of real-world management practice: the US Marine Corp's *Warfighting*.[39] In describing the nature of war, it says,

> Individual causes and their effects can rarely be isolated. Minor actions and random incidents can have disproportionately large—even

> decisive—effects. While dependent on the laws of science and the intuition and creativity of art, war *takes its fundamental character from the dynamic of human interaction* [my emphasis].

For war, read organization. And, as regards the laws of science, we need to take particular account of insights drawn from the sciences of uncertainty and complexity. As mentioned in the Foreword to *Warfighting*, one of the reasons for updating the original, 1989 edition was "to emphasize war's complexity and unpredictability".

The following chapters explore in more depth what all of this means for our understanding of the dynamics of organization, before considering the implications of this for real-world management practice. Consistent, again, with *Warfighting*, "the book . . . requires judgment in application". And purpose, courage and skill, of course!

Notes

1 Flinn, K. (2018: 49) *Leadership Development*. Routledge.

2 This particular example is taken from an article published on the McKinsey *Insights & Publications* website (Birkinshaw, J. and Heywood, S., 2010): http://www.mckinsey.com/insights/organization/putting_organizational_complexity_in_its_place.

3 Collins, D. (1998:195) *Organizational Change – Sociological Perspectives*. Routledge.

4 Allenby, B. and Sarewitz, D (2013: 36) *The Techno-Human Condition*. MIT Press.

5 In *Informal Coalitions*, I described this as the art of organizational plate-spinning. The 'gravitational field' at work here, though, does not follow the straightforward laws of Newtonian physics! Instead, it comprises the conversational patterns that continuously (re-)emerge through our everyday interactions with others. These are affected by such things as the relative power that people have to command our attention, the personal importance of those relationships, the ways in which we each perceive, interpret and evaluate those interactions, and so on. In 'spinning our own plates', each of us also affects – to a greater or lesser extent – the dynamics of the 'plates' that are being spun by everyone else who is participating in our own relationship networks. As they do ours. As I described it at

the time, "This process is self-organizing. Nobody is sitting outside of these networks and orchestrating what is going on. There is no 'Great Plate Spinner in the Sky' – or in the Boardroom!" (Rodgers, C. (2007: 37) *Informal Coalitions*. Palgrave Macmillan).

6 The Cynefin framework (pronounced kunev-in) has been designed and developed by Dave Snowden. It is widely referenced by those who view organizations *as* complex adaptive systems – which I don't (see Chapter 2). The framework seeks to provide managers with broad strategies for intervening in situations according to the perceived nature of the context in which they are working at any particular time. The basic proposition is that there are ontological differences (i.e. distinct states of being) between the ordered states of "Clear" (previously labelled "Obvious" and, before that, "Simple") and "Complicated", and those that are seen as being unordered, i.e. "Complex" and "Chaotic". Each of these is represented by a separate domain on the framework, with specific decision-making approaches identified for each. The latter are based on the relationship between cause and effect that is assumed to apply in those circumstances. The boundary between Clear and Chaotic is drawn as a catastrophic 'fold', to suggest that complacency in the face of a seemingly obvious way forward might lead suddenly and unexpectedly to failure. A fifth domain, "Aporetic/Confused" (previously called "Disorder") is shown at the centre of the framework. This is intended to reflect the situation in which people cannot decide what type of causality exists or, as Snowden currently argues, provides the entry point into the sense-making process.

7 Dave Snowden's post from September 2015 can be found here: http://cognitive-edge.com/blog/on-the-value-of-order/.

8 I use the somewhat 'awkward' term, "sense-making-cum-action-taking," to emphasize that the ongoing conversational process of making sense and taking action is indivisible. People do not make sense of things intellectually and then take action in a linear, first-you-do-this-then-you-do-that fashion. Instead, they are immersed in an ongoing process of thinking and acting that is intimately intertwined.

9 Several frameworks have been developed over the years, which seek to differentiate decision-making strategies according to context. Most have commonalities with the Cynefin framework (above). For example:

- A chapter in Ansoff's *From Strategic Planning to Strategic Management* (Wiley, 1976) refers to a framework published by Charles Perrow in

1970. This adopts a sociological view of organizational analysis. In this, he seeks to define problem characteristics and prescribe solution processes based on whether a situation is analysable (or ordered, to use Snowden's term) or unanalysable (unordered); and on the degree of variation in the problems encountered (from low to high). This resulted in four domains (again, to use Snowden's term): Rote (Clear); Programme (Complicated); Judgement (Complex); and Construct (Chaotic).

- In *Putting Strategy to Work* (1995), Eddie Obeng looks at the world of project and programme management. Here, he distinguishes contexts on the basis on whether or not managers *Know What* they are trying to achieve and also whether or not they *Know How* to achieve it. When both the what and how are known, he refers to this situation as "Paint by Numbers". Where the necessary knowhow exists but the best way of deploying this is unclear (i.e. those involved don't know where best to apply this expertise – "Don't Know What"), he describes this as "Making a Movie". Where the What is known but how to achieve it isn't, Obeng calls this "Going on a Quest". As he suggests, under these conditions, you might never realize the full extent of what you set out to achieve. But you might achieve some valuable learning along the way. Finally, where neither the What nor the How is known, he describes this as "Walking in the Fog".
- In the second edition of his textbook, *Strategic Management and Organisational Dynamics* (1996), Ralph Stacey introduced what has since become known as "The Stacey Diagram". In it, he sought to identify differences in circumstances (and hence implied response) according to whether people were operating close to, or far from, certainty; and close to, or far from, agreement. When conditions were considered to be both close to certainty and close to agreement, Stacey suggested these called for single-loop learning (after Argyris) and required managers to use what he termed, "ordinary management" (Order: Clear and Complicated). As the levels of uncertainty and disagreement increased, this called for double-loop learning and what he called "extraordinary management" (Complex). Under conditions that were far from certainty and far from agreement (Chaotic), he posited anarchy, no learning, and avoidance as the likely result. Although this diagram remains widely referenced, and is popular with

'complexity-aware' consultants and managers alike, Stacey himself now argues strongly against its use.

10 In *Complexity and Organizational Reality* (Routledge, 2010), Ralph Stacey describes such models and frameworks as "second-order abstractions" from the complex reality of in-the-moment interaction, in which we are all immersed.

11 Watts, A. (2009: 59) *The Book on the Taboo Against Knowing Who You Are.* Souvenir Press Ltd. Watts originally published this in 1966.

12 Even Jack Welch, the supposed embodiment of mainstream management principles and practice, said in his autobiography, *Jack*, that, like the kitchens in the best run restaurants, all business is messy and chaotic. Sadly, his later descriptions of his time in GE rendered this 'mess and chaos' largely invisible, as he defaulted to a more rationalized explanation of events. See Chapter 3, to find out why that might be – and the consequences of this.

13 It is important to recognize that the dynamics of organization means that any diagrams that purport to show what's going on are necessarily abstractions from the complex reality. This includes all of those in this book. However, these are offered as aids to sense-making and to provoke fresh thinking. They are not intended to be used as 'if you do this you'll get that' prescriptions.

14 This has some resonance with psychologist James J. Gibson's notion of "affordance". An affordance is a property of an object, or a feature of the immediate context, that suggests how one might interface with that object or feature. A car, for instance, *affords* movement from one place to another. Crucially, from the perspective I'm putting forward here, it might afford other things to those observing it. Such as a potential target for theft; a status symbol, a hiding place, or whatever. How people take-up the particular affordance *in practice* ultimately determines what it means for them. That is to say, its meaning and utility (as originally described by Gibson) is relational and contextual. Its use is contingent on the particular circumstances of the moment, and on the needs, perceptions, and capabilities of the potential user.

15 Hernes, T. (2014) *A Process Theory of Organization.* Oxford University Press.

16 Clarke, J. *et al* (2015:98) *Making Policy Move.* Policy Press.

17 Watts, A. (2009: 59) ibid.

18 Ekman, G. (2001) *Constructing Leadership in Small Talk* in Sjöstrand, S-E, *et al Invisible Leadership.* Thomson Learning.

19 McAndrew, F.T. (2008) *The Science of Gossip.* October 2008 edition of Scientific American Mind.

20 Scott, J.C. (1998) *Seeing Like a State.* Yale University Press.

21 There is much talk in current management texts, development programmes and consultant offerings about our living in a so-called VUCA world. That is, one that is characterized by volatility, uncertainty, complexity and ambiguity. The term was introduced by the US military in the mid-1980s and has been increasingly adopted as part of the mainstream management discourse. This is used most often to suggest that managers (and the rest of us) are having to deal with a step-change from the conditions of the past. A past that was, presumably, stable, certain, simple and clear! It is also often positioned as a particular concern for those whose formal roles relate to the policy and strategy arenas. In reality, life – everybody's life – is and always has been volatile, uncertain, complex and ambiguous. If the acronym helps, fine. But be wary of its use becoming a fad.

22 Crucially, this underscores the role of local interactions in determining what happens in practice. And, equally importantly, it opens up the possibility of thinking afresh about "context". Rather than seeing this as an all-powerful, externally imposed state of affairs, it exposes the fact that this is similarly co-created through people's local interactions *in which they themselves are participating.* The proper focus of reflection and reflexivity is then on the dynamics and content of these interactions that take place continuously between people, and on the contribution that they themselves make to the outcomes that emerge from the process.

23 All interactions are necessarily 'local'. That is to say, they take place one-to-one or between a small number of people. Such interactions might take place between people who are thousands of miles apart geographically (e.g. via a phone call or online) but the number of participants is necessarily limited in the moment of people's interaction. It's also important to recognize that these conversations take place everywhere and address a diverse range of themes. The term "local" is not meant to convey any sense of hierarchy. Even those conversations that take place in and around the Boardroom, and which ostensibly relate to 'organization-wide' matters, take place locally, as the term is used here.

24 Egan, G. (1993) *Adding Value.* Jossey-Bass.

25 My book, *Informal Coalitions* (Palgrave, 2007) is dedicated to this topic.

26 Although I refer to this as a "*personal* frame of reference", it is important to remember that this imaginary construct is continually formed and re-formed through individual's everyday interactions and experiences. That is to say, it is continually in the process of social construction. This affects the way in which they continue to interact and make sense of their ongoing experiences.

27 Culbert, S. (1996) *Mind-set Management.* Oxford University Press.

28 "This [everyday predictability], it must be emphasised, does not imply 'objectively' accurate predictability: it is, rather, predictability for practical purposes and, even more important perhaps, the comforting *sense* of predictability.#" [emphasis is in the original]. Jenkins, R. (2008: 150) *Social Identity (Key Ideas) 3Ed.*

29 Related ways of describing this general tendency include Pierre Bourdieu's concept of habitus, as in *The Logic of Practice* (1992, Polity Press) and George Herbert Mead's notion of the generalized other, as in *Mind, Self and Society* (1934, The University of Chicago Press). Habitus refers to the physical embodiment of cultural capital; that is, the deeply ingrained habits, skills, and dispositions that people possess as a result of their life experiences. The generalized other relates to a particular group of organized social relationships within which an individual interacts on a continuing basis, and which gives them their sense of unity with that group. It is in this way that the ongoing interactional process between such individuals influences their behaviour.

30 Chater, N. (2018) *The Mind is Flat.* Allen Lane.

31 Stacey, R.D. (2012) *Tools and Techniques of Leadership and Management.* Routledge.

32 Heifetz, R.A. and Laurie, D.L. (2001) The Work of Leadership. *Harvard Business Review.*

33 Rodgers, C. (ibid: 105).

34 Some conceptions of organization include the proposition that physical and material elements of organization also have the capacity to act into specific situations. But, as I will explain in Chapters 2 and 3, I believe that this shifts attention away from the interactive, conversational nature of the dynamics of organization. Whilst agreeing that "matter matters", I will suggest that, in the context of organizational dynamics, *this is only the case to the extent and in the ways that these are taken up by people in their ongoing interactions.*

35 Stacey R.D. (2000) *Strategic Management and Organisational Dynamics, 3Ed.* FT Prentice Hall.

36 Despite this, management education continues to encourage managers to think about the 'big things' of organizational life – strategies, structures, systems, etc. – as though these come into being and are sustained through processes that have little or nothing to do with people's day-to-day interactions. Indeed, the latter are often presented as distractions from – or barriers to – managers' sophisticated task, rather than being seen as the very essence of their leadership practice.

37 As we will discuss further in Chapters 4 and 6, "muddling through" most accurately describes what managers do in practice, as they act forward, moment-to-moment into a continuously emerging and unknowable future. The challenge then becomes one of knowing how best to apply their judgement and otherwise engage with the process, within the specific conditions that they are experiencing – at *that time*, in *that situation*, and with *those people*. It's here, in the practical reality of people's ongoing interactions, that managers can strive to make a difference – using formal and informal interactions, joint sense-making conversations, political acumen, and purposeful provocation in an effort to shift their own and others' practice in ways that they judge to be both organizationally beneficial and ethically sound.

38 Allenby, B. and Sarewitz, D. (ibid: 12–13).

39 US Marine Corps (1997: Ch1., 18) *Warfighting*. Marine Corps Doctrinal Publication 1.

2

UNDERSTANDING THE WIGGLINESS

THE COMPLEX SOCIAL DYNAMICS OF ORGANIZATION

"The beautiful, ugly truth" is how the leader writer in a mid-2014 issue of *New Scientist* headlined the argument that it is "better to see the cosmos as it is, rather than as we'd like it to be". Suggesting that scientists have come to expect truth to be beautiful – and symmetrically structured – the article argues instead that "the cosmos makes more sense if it's not quite perfect". This provides a lead-in to the cover story, which exposes the "ugly fact" that we live in an inelegant universe. "Perhaps", the writer suggests, "It's time we stopped trying to find the truth through beauty, and instead try a bit harder to find beauty in the truth of ugly facts". I'm arguing much the same here in relation to the nature of organizational dynamics and management practice. That is, that practitioners, academics, politicians, and other commentators would do well to see the beauty in the truth of the ugly facts – what I'm calling the "wiggliness" – of organization. That is, in the *unavoidably messy* reality of organization and the muddling-through nature of management practice as they actually experience it. So, what "beauty" might we find in these "ugly facts"? And why should we bother looking for it?

In Chapter 1, we looked at the basic arguments as to why and how the organizational world is wiggly. That is, why things don't operate in the neat straight lines implied by management orthodoxy and how organization is enacted in practice. I argued that the ways in which we think and talk about what's going on – and, in particular, what we have come to think *should* be going on – fails to take seriously the complex and uncertain nature of organizational life *as we actually experience it*. The established view on the nature of organization and management practice either ignores these dynamics altogether or sees them as signs of dysfunction that 'proper management' will cure. Mainstream prescriptions therefore remain rooted in the assumption that there is nothing inherent in the situation, or the nature of organization itself, that prevents managers delivering the sought-after results with confidence and repeatability. It's simply a matter of their following the latest model, demonstrating the particular set of personal competencies that are put forward as the epitome of professional practice, and ensuring that people do what they are supposed to do. That is to say, the focus is on 'getting the content right', according to the ideological stance being adopted, rather than understanding and engaging with the underlying dynamics of organization. Furthermore, it is the contradiction between these real-world dynamics and the idealistic view of what managers are supposed to be capable of doing that accounts for many of the perceived ills of organization that regularly dominate the news headlines.

When managers delve more deeply into what's actually going on, *drawing on their own lived experience*,[1] they have little difficulty in recognizing and relating to these otherwise unacknowledged aspects of organizational life. This is not surprising. They (like each one of us) are continuously living through, participating in – *and unavoidably contributing to* – these dynamics. This is the case whether or not they are consciously aware of this at the time. In their (and our) defence, the ability to escape from the grip of the established ways of thinking and acting – should they recognize the need to do so – is never wholly within their gift. This is the case irrespective of their formal position. Nevertheless, cultivating a raised awareness of these dynamics offers the opportunity of participating in a more insightful, meaningful, and savvy way. It makes them better placed to shift their own and other's understanding and practice towards something more useful. They can also take comfort in the fact that, despite this inability to predict and control events in the way that conventional theory dictates, patterns of behaviour emerge from these same dynamics that provide an *everyday sense of predictability and control*. This means that, for much of the time and in many ways, things do proceed broadly as expected. Organizational life – and life in general – would be impossible if this were not the case.

So, what are the underlying dynamics that we are talking about when we describe organization as wiggly? And what implications do these have for managers, as they go about their day-to-day business?

The 'in-betweenness' of organizational dynamics

Not long after the publication of *Informal Coalitions*, I accepted an invitation to give a brief, after-dinner talk on organizational change to a group of senior managers in the oil industry. As it turned out, the intention was to punctuate the dinner with a number of mini inputs on domestic matters, together with my guest contribution. My task was to fill the gap between the main course and pudding! On reflection, it seemed to me that speaking in-between courses was highly appropriate. And I used this as an opportunity to get people to focus on what I called the 'in-betweenness' of organizational dynamics. That is, on the things that don't appear on the 'printed menu', so to speak, but which have a major effect on what happens in practice.

Where we have starters, mains and puddings at dinner, we have strategies, structures, processes, and the like in organizations. It's these 'things' that mainstream management tells us to focus on. Instead, I asked the managers to think for a few minutes about what is going on *in-between* these familiar trappings of organization:

... what, for example, is going on *in-between* the structured meetings used to design and organize the formal plans, programmes and projects?

... what's going on *in-between* the set-piece announcements of new strategies, structures and systems?

... what's going on *in-between* the setting of official policies, processes and procedures and the formal carrying out of these by people 'on the ground'?

... what's going on *in-between* the highlighted issues and events that form the basis of official records, reports, and other communications of what's going on?

... and so on.

By in-betweenness, I mean the everyday interactions that take place continuously in all organizational contexts – within, beyond, and across what we might think of as formal organizational boundaries. It's here that whatever happens, happens. This also includes the seeding and bringing into being of those headlined activities, artefacts and events of formal management practice that are routinely joined-up, after the fact, to form the official accounts of what happened and to provide the accompanying rationale.

So, what is the basic nature of this in-betweenness of organization and management practice?

Basic proposition

The basic propositions that underpin everything in the book are that:

- Organization is a continuous and indivisible *process*.
- Organization is a *social* phenomenon.
- Organization is inevitably and irreducibly *complex*.

It is the coming together of these processual, social, and complex dynamics of everyday human interaction that accounts for the nature of organization (and life more generally). Importantly, too, this process is fundamentally played out in the conversational interactions that take place within and between people. Put simply:

- Organization *is* conversation.

These defining elements of the wiggly world of organization are explored below. This provides the technical underpinning for the basic description of organizational dynamics outlined in Chapter 1. It also draws out some important corollaries and implications for management practice that flow from them.

Organization is a *process*

To begin with, when we refer to organization, we are talking about the *active process* of organiz-*ing*. That is to say, the ongoing process of everyday human interaction. This is in stark contrast to the established view of organization as a tangible entity ("the organization"), which has the capacity to act in its own right. This tendency to reify organization – and to imbue it with the capacity to think, feel and act in some way independently of people – is especially prevalent amongst those who advocate certain forms of systems thinking. But, as Yvan Allaire and Mihaela Firsirotu put it, organizations are,[2]

> figments of participants' interpretation of their organizational experience; they have no external reality but are merely social creations and constructions emerging from actors making sense out of ongoing streams of actions and interactions.

Tor Hernes echoes this point, whilst acknowledging that the notion of organization that emerges from these streams of interaction has a felt sense of entity-like reality, even though this is an imaginary construct:[3]

> A unit is not an entity . . . but it is talked and acted into existence as an imaginary-yet-felt-as-real entity.

This sense of dealing with something real and tangible is the basis of conventional thinking on organizational dynamics and of prescriptions for management practice that flow from it. It is also a taken-for-granted (and linguistically convenient) part of everyday conversation to talk *as if* "the organization" exists independently of people's everyday interactions. What tends to be forgotten, though, is the 'as-if-ness'. Talking about organization in this way diverts attention away from the *interactional* and *socially constructed nature* of the organizing process. That is, from what's actually going on between people, as they interact with each other on a continuing basis. It also reinforces the fiction that organizations *do* things. They don't and they can't. People do.

A continuous and indivisible process

Organization, then, is the ongoing and indivisible process of communicative interaction (essentially conversation) between human beings. This process is continuously (re-)enacted by people in their 'local' (i.e. small-group and one-to-one) exchanges – whether these occur in the boardroom, in workshops and offices, in the corridors, or in myriad other forums. Whilst the focus, content and scope differ in each interaction, the underlying dynamics of the process are the same. And, whether these are played out skilfully or not, what happens 'overall' (however defined) emerges from the widespread interplay of all of these local interactions. This process is not designed. It has no beginning and no end. Nor does it exist in a stable state that is punctuated by periodic changes from one state to another. Instead, it is in constant flux.

The process is boundaryless

The interactions through which organization is being continuously (re-) enacted do not respect formally defined boundaries. There are no insides and outsides. No nested systems of levels, such as the individual, the team, and the organization on which managers can operate independently. And no external environment that exists in any way 'outside' this continuous flow of interaction. As Taylor and van Every point out,[4]

> there is no ontological difference between the macro and micro levels of organization. What we call "the organization" is generated in the same conversation where individual actors find their identity.

This also draws attention to the fundamentally social nature of identity. Like organization, this continuously (re-)emerges in the process of our ongoing interactions with others. But more of that later.

All that exists beyond people's immediate conversations are more conversations. There is no limit as to how far these might spread or who might become involved (whether directly or indirectly). And everything that happens does so at the level of these 'local' interactions. At the same time, an *imaginary construct* – "the organization" – does emerge from this process. It is the continuous re-enactment and re-emergence of this which gives people *a sense* of collective identity and boundaried existence.

The process is historically situated, path-dependent and context-specific

How the process plays out is always historically situated, path-dependent and context-specific. The characteristic patterning of people's interactions, in any particular setting, becomes institutionalized over time; tending to channel thinking and action ever more in line with past sense-making and action taking. The 'path to now' is also highly significant. Today's interactions continue to be affected by the multitude of interactions that have gone before, through their continued existence in the form of structures, systems, procedures, informal customs and practices, and so on. Thirdly, nothing happens "in general". Everything depends on the specifics of each situation. As such, ideas and practices that appear to have been successful in one context always need to be translated into the new circumstances. They cannot simply be transferred from one setting to another, with the expectation that similar results will be achieved.

Taken together, these aspects of the process of organization also mean that the point at which people enter into the interactional process crucially affects the ways in which they perceive, interpret and evaluate what's going on; how they act into the situation – at that time, with those people and in the particular circumstances; and what emerges overall.

The formal and shadow-side dynamics of organization are intimately intertwined

Earlier, I referred to the notion of the shadow-side dynamics of organization. These are those aspects of day-to-day activity that have a powerful effect on what happens in practice but which are not spoken about in official forums, publications and so on. They include unofficial, get-the-job-done relationships, social links, political activity (see below), cultural dynamics, and so on. Various shadow themes emerge from the wide range of informal interactions through which these dynamics are realized in practice. And the ways in which people take these up in their own practice serve to reinforce, modify, or reject the official ideology. Or, in some cases, to help mobilize coalitions of support for alternative routes forward.

As discussed extensively in Chapter 1, these hidden, messy, and informal dynamics are intimately intertwined with the formal, as-designed aspects of organization. Both are socially formed through people's everyday interactions. And both have a significant effect on how people behave and what emerges overall. Indeed, the as-designed elements of organization originate in shadow-side conversations, and come to gain momentum and formal legitimacy through them. At the same time, the shadow themes that emerge reflect people's interpretations of the official ideology and its perceived application in practice. Against this background, people are continually seeking ways through this diverse mix of formal and informal interactions that preserve their sense of self-worth and enable them to be seen by others as performing competently in their various social and professional roles.[5]

In sum

When we talk about organization as being a "process", we are drawing attention to. . .

... the continuous and indivisible dynamics of organiz*ing*, rather than to any sense of organization as a tangible entity ("the organization") . . .

... the '*boundaryless*' state of human interaction . . .

... the nature of organization as a *temporal* rather than spatial phenomenon, which is being (re-)enacted continuously through people's ongoing interactions . . .

... the *historically situated, path-dependent and context-specific* nature of everything that happens . . .

... the interweaving of the 'legitimate' (as designed) aspects of organization and the hidden, messy and informal (*shadow-side*) dynamics.

Organization is *social*

The second anchor point in our understanding of the process of organization is that it is enacted by people. That is to say, it is a *social* phenomenon. As stated above, the distinctive patterning of individual behaviour and collective practice that we tend to think of as "the organization" emerges from people interacting with each other on a continuing basis. As they do so, they are seeking to carry out their various role(s) and to 'go on together' in ways that both enable them to perform competently in that setting and, *at the same time*, to sustain their important relationships in various other aspects of their lives.

Human characteristics are always in play

There is a fundamental difference between the dynamics of organization and those that govern the workings of the natural and technological worlds.

Organization is an expression of human interaction. It involves the coming together of myriad people with differing interests, intentions, interpretations, ideologies, identities, and so on. It reflects personal idiosyncrasies that affect the ways in which people live and interact. People also display varying degrees of energy, emotion, expertise and levels of engagement, etc. These diverse and dynamic aspects of human being will have a major impact on what emerges overall. Most particularly, as discussed extensively above, recognition of the social nature of organization foregrounds the critical importance of 'talk' (in all of its forms) as its central currency. Alongside this, power and politics are ever-present dynamics of human interaction that are often conspicuous by their absence from mainstream texts and consultant offerings. As set out more fully below, nothing happens in the social process of organization – good or bad – other than through the exercise of power and political action.

People are interdependent

A large swathe of management guidance is based on a view of organization in which people are assumed to act autonomously, within the limits of their defined roles, responsibilities and relationships, to achieve their formally designated tasks. This reflects a first person, 'I' perspective of organizational dynamics. Counterposed with this is the systems viewpoint, in which "the organization", is viewed as having the capacity to act as an integrated whole. As such, it is thought to consist of various sub-systems (Divisions and Departments, for example) sub-sub-systems (Business Units and Teams, perhaps), and so on. Ordinarily, the boundaries of the organization and its sub-systems are taken as being co-terminus with the formally designed organizational and sub-system boundaries. In turn, the organization is considered to exist as part of a wider environmental supra-system, with which it interacts – again as an entity. This represents a third-person, 'it' perspective.

Crucially, both of these views fail to take proper account of the *locally situated* and *interactional* nature of human dynamics. From a wiggly world perspective, everything that comes about – formal and informal, structured and unstructured, planned and spontaneous, etc. – emerges in the ongoing process of everyday human interaction. Central to this is recognizing that people are *inter*dependent. That is to say, they are always thinking, feeling and acting in a social context, even when they are physically alone. This might be reflected, for example, in the attention that they pay to the gesturing and responding of specific others; the generalized patterning of their thinking and acting that has arisen from – and continues to be sustained by – their ongoing interactions with those people and relevant others; the fact that other people are taking action too – or have done so in the past – that affects their ability to think and act in particular ways; and so on. This is a second-person, '*You and I/me together*', intersubjective perspective. As part of this, people's 'internal conversations' and their seemingly self-directed actions always draw on the broader themes and patterns of interaction in which they are participating on a continuing basis – whether explicitly, and with conscious awareness, or not. In this regard, Ralph Stacey emphasizes what he describes as the irremovable interdependence of individuals,[6] drawing on the social conception of mind reflected in the psychosocial theories of Norbert Elias and George Herbert Mead. Central to this is Elias's notion of the individual as the singular, and the group or society as the plural, of *inter*dependent people.[7]

Everyone is always enabled and constrained by what others do and don't do

An important corollary of people being *inter*dependent is that everyone is perpetually enabled and constrained in what they can do by the actions, inactions and interactions of other people. It is, of course, true that the personal attributes of individuals, including their inherited characteristics, psychological tendencies, physical capabilities, psychiatric disorders, personal idiosyncrasies, and so on, will affect the patterning of those interactions and associated behaviours to a greater or lesser extent. The current psychological and emotional state of those involved will also affect the emerging dynamics. And some individuals might be more predisposed than others to respond in particular ways to the circumstances in which they find themselves. But we are fundamentally social beings. As a result, who we are, what we think and feel, and how we behave is largely shaped by the interactions that we have with other people – as, at the same time, who we are, what we think and feel, and how we behave shapes those interactions.

This applies as much to the psychosocial dynamics of organization as it does to other aspects of our being and doing. Any characteristic patterning of our thoughts, feelings and actions that might arise during our lives is therefore the product of our own relationship history – both those of which we are aware and others about which we have no awareness at all. This means that such patterning is both uniquely personal and, at the same time, communally social. One of the implications of this is that who we are, how we see the world and how we behave, constantly shifts according to whom we happen to be interacting with at any particular time, and in what context. Interdependence, interaction, and interpretation are therefore fundamental dynamics of organization; and hence of society at large – for better and for worse.

Participation is diverse, distributed and enduring

Organization is continuously (re-)enacted through small-groups conversations, one-to-one exchanges and related self-talk, in the present moment. This process is limited neither by geography nor formal membership and it involves a diverse range of people. These not only include current members, but also past employees whose 'presence' and influence continue in the ways in which their past contributions (formal and informal) live on in policies, practices, procedures, structures, rituals and routines, etc. A wide range of other stakeholders who are thought of as being 'external' to the notional unit of organization that is currently in focus also influence what happens. These might include, for example, managers and colleagues in other areas of the business, policy-makers, customers, suppliers, competitors, regulators, commentators, neighbours, family members, friends and so on. To a greater or lesser extent, the thoughts, words, and actions of these people will affect the nature, content, and patterning of people's day-to-day interactions. As well as the outcomes that emerge. Sometimes decisively so. This is the case whether or not they are physically present; and whether or not they are consciously aware, in any sense at all, of the effect that their words and/or actions are having.

Co-creation is a natural and ever-present dynamic of organization

Over recent years, it has become increasingly common for the word "co-creation" to be used to describe a *deliberate* act of collaboration within and/or between organizations. Whilst structured collaborative approaches can be valuable, seeing co-creation wholly in these terms can obscure a fundamental aspect of organizational dynamics. That is, that co-creation takes place spontaneously. Through their everyday interactions – physical and virtual, formal and informal, actual and imagined, overt and covert, etc. – people continuously make sense of what's going on and act into the future as it is emerging. In doing so, they – along with everyone else – are perpetually constructing this future together in the currency of their present interactions. They are doing this both intentionally and habitually; in official settings and elsewhere; and for diverse purposes that go well beyond those implied by their formal roles and relationships.

This means that *all* meanings and outcomes are co-created, as people perceive, interpret and evaluate things in the natural give-and-take of organizational life; through the conversations that they have with themselves (i.e. thinking) and those that they have with others. Importantly, this doesn't just happen where the formal position is arrived at through participation and involvement. *It applies just as surely where 'command and control' is the order of the day.* In short, co-creation is not something that happens if managers choose to act in a particular way and not if they don't. It occurs continuously and spontaneously, as a natural dynamic of everyday human interaction.

In sum

When we talk about organization as being "social", we're drawing attention to . . .

... the *centrality* of *uniquely human* characteristics, which distinguish the dynamics of organization from those that govern technological systems and the 'living systems' of the natural world . . .

... the fact that people are always participating as *inter*dependent social beings . . .

... the fact that *everyone is both enabled and constrained* in everything they do by their ongoing interactions with other people, both within and beyond the formally stated boundaries of the group in focus . . .

... the *diverse, distributed and enduring nature of human interaction*, embracing real-time, in-the-moment exchanges with other people 'in the flesh';

other, technology-mediated forms of communication; and aspects of past interactions that continue to affect why, what and how things happen today . . .

. . . *co-creation as a natural dynamic* of the interactional process.

Organization is *complex*

The final anchor point, in our understanding of the wiggliness of organization, is recognition that this social process is *complex*. Always and irreducibly so. That is to say, organization is characterized by the dynamics of self-organization, emergence, non-linearity, and a lack of certainty, predictability and control.

Self-organization

As we've seen, what we speak of as "the organization" is perpetually (re-) constructed (and thereby both sustained and changed) in the widespread interplay of people's local interactions. It does not exist in any way 'outside' those interactions. This process is self-organizing. That is to say, there is no-body (such as the manager) and no-thing (such as "the system") sitting outside those interactions controlling what is going on. At the same time, everyone is both enabled and constrained in everything they do by the actions, inactions, and interactions of everyone else. So, no-one can simply do as they please, however powerful they might be in terms of their formal authority. It is also important to recognize that whatever happens doesn't do so simply by chance. It emerges in the coming together of the differing intentions and actions of many, many people – both present and past. Such intentions reflect people's individual and collective interests, diverse ideological stances, habitual ways of thinking and acting, and so on. The result of this flowing together of intentions is the continuing emergence of a future that no-one planned, no-one predicted and no-one can control. Crucially, though, it is precisely because of this self-organizing dynamic that social order emerges. Where new insights, actions and motivations emerge through this process (that is, when pattern-switching occurs), conversations tend to self-organize around the newly emerging pattern (such as a new perspective and/or new way forward). And, because this process is also self-maximizing, the new pattern tends to take over completely. In doing so, it provides the basis of new narratives around which people coalesce, whether broadly in pursuit of the dominant line or running counter to it.

It is important to recognize that self-organization is a natural dynamic of this interactional process. Too often, the term is used to describe a supposedly more enlightened approach to organization and management practice, involving the formal adoption of 'flatter' structures and more widely devolved decision-making. That is, as a synonym for self-management. This usage has become so pervasive that, despite the fundamental importance of its meaning in the context of organizational dynamics, it can seem tempting to give up on efforts to preserve this and adopt alternative expressions – such as local interaction. However, to imply that self-organization is a design choice diverts attention from this fundamental aspect of everyday human interaction. In particular, it risks missing the point that this dynamic is just as much at play in an unalloyed 'command and control' regime, as it is in one that fully embraces the notion of empowered self-management. Adopting what might be thought to be a more empowering and enabling approach to work might well be a choice that is open to managers. Designing out the complex dynamics of human interaction is not!

Outcomes emerging in local interaction

People make sense of what's going on and take action in the midst of their ongoing interactions with other people. And it is through the widespread interplay of these 'local' (i.e. one-to-one and small-group) interrelationships that overall outcomes emerge and come to be recognized as such. People participating in this process might be acting deliberately, or simply through habit. Some of their interactions will be planned. Others will happen spontaneously. Throughout, they are likely to be anticipating and responding in the moment to the situation as it is emerging. What happens overall, though, is not within the ability of anyone to predict or control. This means that the essentially form-*less*, wiggly world of everyday human interaction leads to actions, outputs, and outcomes that are co-created by all of the people involved – both within and beyond the notional boundaries of the formally recognized group, organization, industry, country or whatever.[8] In all of this, it's important to recognize that what we think of in terms of outputs, and outcomes are simply points in the ongoing flow of interaction. Points which come to be seen as worthy of specific note and comment. Although transient and selective, these have an important part to play in the ongoing construction of meaning. As well as in the retrospective process of accounting for what's gone on, how things happened, and what people's role in that might have been.

Non-linearity

In the complex and uncertain reality of everyday (organizational) life, people are always acting forwards, moment to moment, into a continuously emerging and unknowable future. In doing so, they and everyone else are also perpetually constructing that future together. Whilst certain aspects of this, such as technology-based tasks, will be amenable to a techno-rational approach, we saw in Chapter 1 that the ongoing process of organization follows a different dynamic. This can't be reduced to the linear, 'if you do this, you'll get that' logic that is so prevalent in the management literature and consultant offerings. It is this realization that led Alan Watts to represent the world at large as a wiggly line, and why I've adopted the term "wiggly" to describe the fundamental dynamics of organization.

The non-linearity of this process means that there are no simple cause-and-effect relationships that can be drawn upon to explain what's going on. Or to predict what is likely to happen in apparently similar situations going forward. As we'll see in Chapter 3, though, our felt need to explain what's going on – to ourselves and others – leads us to construct after-the-fact explanations. Although these can provide us with insights and situationally contingent 'rules of thumb' that help to guide our own and others' 'next steps', we should beware of treating such explanations in any way as scientific truths, from which we can derive and apply universally applicable actions.

Inability to predict and control what emerges

As a result of the above dynamics, no individual or group of individuals is able to predict or control outcomes. This is the case irrespective of their formal organizational role.

In sum

When we talk about organization as being "complex", we're drawing attention to . . .

... the '*local*', *self-organizing patterning* of the everyday interactions through which those people make sense of events and act forward into the future . . .

... outcomes *emerging in the widespread interplay of local interactions* . . .

... the *non-linear dynamics of interaction*, in which causal links are untraceable. . .

... the fact that *no individual, or group of individuals, is 'in control' of what emerges from it.*

Bringing it all together – organization as the *complex social process* of everyday human interaction

Unknowable

As discussed extensively in Chapter 1, *all* situations that involve people are unavoidable and irreducibly complex and uncertain. This is the case regardless of how simple the context or content of their involvement might appear to be. As soon as people become involved, the related technologies, systems, and procedures become inextricably interwoven with the complexities of everyday human interaction. As such they become ultimately unknowable. This state of not knowing is fundamental to the socially complex nature of organization.

Pattern-forming, pattern-using . . .

The everyday process of human interaction provides the medium through which conversational themes continuously (re-)emerge in a particular context and organize themselves into locally meaningful patterns of thoughts, feelings and actions. This creates expectancy that things will go on in ways that people recognize and come to take for granted. Even though they remain consciously unaware of the deepest manifestations of this patterning process, it just feels natural for them to behave in certain ways within certain relationship contexts. As mentioned in relation to the dynamics of culture in Chapter 1, this means that the more that people make sense of things and behave in characteristic ways in a particular setting, the more likely it is that they will continue to make similar sense, and act in similar ways, going forward. Strengthening this tendency still further. It is in this way that people gain a sense of meaning and everyday predictability in their lives. The notion of organization would be impossible if this patterning dynamic did not exist. It is this that enables people to go on together. At the same time, this tendency to think and act in characteristic ways also constrains behaviour, by reducing the likelihood that new possibilities will emerge.[9] However, since this is an iterative process, in which small shifts occur during each encounter, pattern-shifting can still arise through this same interactional process. This happens naturally in a variety of ways, including through disagreement, confusion, mistake and misunderstanding. As well as arising through deliberate challenge.

This tendency for people to repeat and reinforce what has gone before, places precedent ahead of principle, when it comes to determining what is likely to happen in practice.[10] Importantly, this *is inherent in the self-organizing, patterning nature of the interactional process itself*. It is not – and cannot be – governed by any outside agency. It applies in all human contexts.

. . . and paradoxical

One of the most fundamental aspects of organization concerns the *irresolvable* tensions that exist in every aspect of organizational life. This further exposes the flaw in approaches that view clarity, predictability and control as the epitome of organization and management practice. Embracing (in the sense of accepting and taking up) the paradoxical nature of organization leads to quite a different understanding of what's going on – and what this means in terms of practice – from that which dominates conventional management thinking. Amongst other things, this means that:

- The characteristic patterning of people's thoughts and actions emerges from their ongoing interactions with others (that is to say, it is **formed by** those interactions). *At the same time*, this patterning tends to affect the form that those interactions take going forwards (**forming**).
- This self-organizing, patterning process creates expectancy that things will happen in certain ways and not in others (**sense of predictability**). *At the same time*, how things will actually turn out overall is ultimately unknowable (**unpredictability**).

- The tendency is for the currently established patterning of interaction to be replicated – and, hence, reinforced – in today's conversational exchanges (**stability/continuity**). *At the same time*, iterative shifts in the ways in which this patterning is taken up by people, in the moment of their interactions, means that the capacity always exists for pattern-switching to occur and novel outcomes to emerge spontaneously (**instability/change**).
- The process of organization is necessarily co-operative in nature, as people participate in the rituals and routines of everyday, conversational interaction through which outcomes emerge (**co-operation**). *At the same time*, the coming together of differing personal self-interests and emotions, diverse ideological stances and necessarily diverse organizational agendas, etc. make the process contentious and potentially conflictual (**competition**).
- People are enabled in everything that they do by the actions, inactions and interactions of everyone else (**enabling**). *At the same time*, they are constrained by these same interactional dynamics (**constraining**).
- Individuals' interests, intentions, interpretations, ideologies, identities, individual idiosyncrasies and so on influence the patterning, content and quality of their interactions with other people, as do the levels of emotion, energy, engagement, expectation, etc. that they express at a particular time (**individual**). *At the same time*, the factors that characterize individuals' behaviours in a particular context are themselves shaped through their interactions with others (**social**).
- Being formally in charge, managers (from CEO to the front line) have the authority to 'command' the actions of others, whether by imposition or involvement (**in control**). *At the same time*, they cannot determine how people will perceive, interpret, evaluate and act upon those 'commands' in the immediacy of their local circumstances; nor the effect that decisions and actions by others beyond their sphere of influence will have on the actions and outcomes that emerge (**not in control**).

In *Informal Coalitions* I also identified several examples of what I referred to as everyday organizational paradoxes. These are often experienced as mixed messages, in which managers and others are faced with satisfying a range of contradictory demands. For example: innovate *and, at the same time*, avoid mistakes; increase quality *and, at the same time,* minimize costs; take time out to develop yourself *and, at the same time,* deliver results now; use your initiative *and, at the same time,* stick to the rules; put the team's interests first *and, at the same time,* meet your own performance objectives; look for opportunities *and, at the same time,* avoid risks; play to your strengths *and, at the same time,* demonstrate a common set of personal competencies; commit to action *and, at the same time,* keep your options open; be yourself *and, at the same time,* fit in; and so on.

Paradox is endemic in all organizational contexts. Each aspect of organization is defined by its polar opposite, with both poles being simultaneously present. Each one has potential value, as well as complementary downsides. If either is overplayed, success can easily turn into excess. "Embracing paradox" means recognizing these unavoidable tensions and contradictions whilst, at the same time, striving to make them liveable for people.

Partial, power-related and political

This ongoing process of interaction between people is *always and unavoidably* partial, power-related and political. First of all, the process is partial in the sense that whatever transpires is necessarily incomplete as regards the full range of perceptions, interpretations, evaluations and actions that might have emerged. Also, because of the self-organizing patterning and precedent-based nature of organization, people's interactions tend to be channelled imperceptibly along previously established pathways of understanding, feeling and action. Strengthening these still further. That is to say, the understanding that emerges in interaction is prejudiced, *in the literal sense of being pre-judged*. This means that, *as a natural dynamic of everyday human interaction* (and hence, of organization – in all of its forms) people become predisposed to pre-judge other people and situations. It is through this self-organizing process that certain patterns of thought, talk and behaviour come to appear natural in specific settings, whilst others remain suppressed or out of awareness altogether. Crucially, this allows people to go on together in a particular social context, *which is essential for the functioning of organization* (and society more generally). At the same time, this dynamic carries with it the possibility that patterns of response might emerge, and become increasingly taken for granted, which are unjustifiably discriminatory – excluding or demeaning people and perspectives on the basis of factors unrelated to the matters in hand. Awareness of this dynamic demands that managers (indeed, all of us) remain alert to the emergence and institutionalization of such taken-for-granted patterns of understanding and behaviour. Especially where these lead to clichéd responses to organizational issues and/or deny the dignity, worth and creative potential of particular individuals or groups through acts of exclusion or other socially unjust responses.

Besides all interactions being partial, in the ways set out above, these also reflect the power relations that exist between those involved. Clearly, in most organizational settings, the prevailing power relationships privilege those in formal management positions. And the words and actions of managers typically have a broader 'reach' than those of other participants. However, the practical effect of a manager's formal power (i.e. their authority), in any particular circumstance, is always affected by the day-to-day relations that those involved have with others in their teams and more widely. These latter interactions are also power-related; reflecting unofficial hierarchies, situationally relevant capabilities and so on.

As well as being partial and power-related, the process of organization is necessarily political. That is to say, people's differing – and potentially conflicting – intentions, interpretations, interests, ideologies and so on are dealt with in the playing out of their everyday interactions. This is likely to manifest itself in a fluid mix of co-operative, competitive and sometimes collusive activity; with people tending to coalesce informally around those emerging conversational themes that resonate most strongly with them, and which help them to maintain the integrity of their personal frames of reference.[11]

Organization as conversation

To maintain that organization is a process might not seem to be too radical a proposition. After all, the phrase "process re-engineering" was on every manager's lips in the 1990s. Even today, the structured approaches to organizational design, development, and change invariably include "processes" as one of the components of organization requiring specific management attention. However, what's being spoken about in those instances are *formally designed* management and information processes, etc. Processes that, taken together, define "the organization". In contrast, what I'm talking about here is much more fundamental. Rather than this entity-based, design-and-build notion of organization, the essence of the wiggly world view is that organization emerges in the ongoing process of conversational interaction between interdependent human beings. This view of organization as conversation is central to everything that I've said so far. It is a position echoed by Richard Dunford and Ian Palmer,[12]

> Organization is conversation. That is to say, conversation does not just occur about organizations; conversations constitute organizations. Organization is not independent of conversation.

This position is similarly encapsulated in Stacey and his colleagues' description of organization as the "complex responsive process" of relating.[13] And, within that, the notion of organization as a *social* object,[14] rather than, as referred to above, a physical object that exists somehow independently of people's interactions.

Talking the organizational world into existence

We are all continuously immersed in this uniquely human flow of conversational interaction – even when we are alone. We each act, moment to moment, into an unknowable future. A future that *is emerging continuously from our own and everyone else's participation in it.* The nature of our interactions is, at one and the same time, an amalgam of deliberate intent and habitual response; continuity-maintaining and change-inducing; co-operative and conflictual; formal and informal; structured and spontaneous; self-reflective and other-directed; and so on. Although each interaction reflects the power relationships that exist between those involved, at that time and in that situation, nobody can predict or control what will emerge. That is to say, *every conversation is a co-creation forum.* Together, *we talk the social world into existence* – at all times and in all of its forms.

All interaction takes place 'locally'

The second point of note, here, is that all of these interactions take place 'locally'. That is, they occur as one-to-one or small-group conversations between *particular* people, at *particular* times, and in *particular* places (however far apart people might be physically). In many cases, of course, whatever arises from these local conversations will, over time, have a wider impact than simply on those who are immediately involved. Often much wider. This is because the themes that emerge from one conversation will regularly be taken up, embellished or challenged in others, as people move from situation to situation, and interaction to interaction. In an organizational context, managers might ordinarily have 'first-mover' advantage, of course. And what they say and do – *or, more particularly, other people's' perceptions, interpretations and evaluations of what they say and do* – might be taken up more widely and/or be more enduring than the themes put forward by most of the others involved. But they, like everyone else, can only participate in this process through their own, local interactions.

Where sufficiently powerful coalitions are mobilized in support of particular conversational themes that emerge through this process, these might come to be formally adopted as part of the official ideology and/or its various artefacts. That is, they might be 'woven into the net' of policies, strategies, structures, systems, and so on that are designed to 'catch' the inherent wiggliness and make it more manageable. Many other themes remain in the shadows. These shadow conversations bring to the fore the emotional intensity, personal nuances, political dynamics and so on, which are typically designed-out of official set-piece events and formal narratives. Tuning-in to those underlying themes that are organizing people's participation suggests the need for managers to shift the main emphasis of their attention and involvement from arms-length directing (formal and structured) to local interaction (informal and unstructured).

Identifying the 'Big Dots'

As people seek to make sense of their experiences, and explain this to others, various happenings along the way come to take on particular significance. These break-up what is an undifferentiated and improvised flow of human activity into meaningful, historically situated, and communicable episodes of activity ("Big Dots"). This reflects what Stacey refers to as the paradoxical relationship between people's immersion in the continuous flow of interaction of which they are part and, at the same time, their need to abstract from it if they are to make sense of what's going on.[15] As I described earlier, this is a self-organizing, patterning process. The ways in which people continue to make sense of what's going on, and the actions and interactions that they find themselves engaged in, are not shaped solely by their immediate circumstances. These are also powerfully influenced by their own and others' past sense-making-cum-action-taking conversations, as well as by governing narratives that have grown up and become institutionalized through this same process (such as managerialism, for example[16]). I'm not suggesting by this that sense-making is always deliberate, reflective, and well-thought-through. Far from it. For much of the time it will be emotion-laden and instinctive, with action being based on little in the way of formal logic or conscious intent. Often, the governing factor will be Robert Caldini's notion of "social proof",[17] based on the actions of significant others – or significant numbers of others. However, given the centrality of this process to the dynamics of organization, managers need to pay attention to the ways in which they and others participate in it and contribute to its effects.

As we shall explore more fully in Chapter 3, people's conscious attempts to explain what happened in terms of Big-Dot outcomes and events takes place after their in-the-moment, immersed experience. As a result, explanations tend to omit the experienced wiggliness. Especially where people are required to account formally for their actions, these are likely to reflect a more neatly packaged, 'managerially correct' and politically acceptable view of what constitutes professional practice. All of which tends to ingrain the established narrative still further.

Participation and patterning

People participate in this conversational process with widely differing degrees of intensity, purpose, and quality of engagement. In some cases, conversations become stuck in repetitive patterns. Fixed, clichéd, and unchanging. At the other extreme, interactions can become frenetic and chaotic, with minimal concession made to the give-and-take of meaningful conversation. Such interactions lack real engagement, with many 'pseudo-conversations' taking place simultaneously, as participants fail to connect with each other or with the supposed purpose of their interactions. Neither of these conditions is conducive to effective organizational performance or personally meaningful participation. Nor, for that matter, do they further the progressive conduct of wider society, to which events around the world attest. These nevertheless continue to account for many – maybe most – of the conversations through which organization (and life more generally) is enacted and from which whatever happens, happens.

In contrast, where conditions of genuine give-and-take exist, conversations can become more meaningful, animated, and engaging. In this state, people are more able to feed off, and build on, each other's contributions in a dynamic and (multi-)purposeful way. From a 'wiggly world' perspective, stimulating and participating in this more dynamic form of conversation around emerging issues is an important part of managing skilfully. At the same time, it's important to remember that each manager is only directly involved in a small number of the conversations through which organization is enacted by members of their teams and from which outcomes emerge. So, even when managers are particularly skilled in the practices of coaching and dialogue, for example, the overall process of organization will reflect the full spectrum of interactional dynamics, from stuck, through lively-and-engaging, to chaotic.

It is also important to recognize that, of itself, the quality of people's participation says nothing about the underlying dynamics of the conversations. So, a lively and engaging exchange might be rooted in mutual dislike and deep-seated conflict. Similarly, a conversation that is stuck in repetitive patterns of interaction might be seen as a very comfortable experience by those involved – such as the patterning of relationships in a client organization some years ago that was described by some of those involved as, "Like being in a fur-lined rut"!

Imprints of past conversations

As we'll explore more fully below, the past – in the sense that we 'know' it – is similarly a product of today's conversations. It is not fixed and unchanging. To begin with, we continually *re-member* the past. That is, we put it together afresh each time, in the context of our current relationships and as perceived from our present state of being. As part of the patterning of our current interactions, we've seen that we also continue to take up physical artefacts and ways of being, thinking and acting that have been carried forward from the past. These include, for example, formal strategies, structures, systems and procedures that remain current, as well as informal customs and practices, organizational folklore and so on that have become a taken-for-granted part of people's day-to-day practice. These remain as *imprints of those past conversations* through which they were first seeded, developed, adopted and subsequently put to use (whether as originally intended or not!). In this sense, we continue to be affected by the thoughts and actions of those people who have gone before us. Many long gone. Some of these 'imprints' are very enduring, such as physical structures, cultural patterning and so on. These carry forward the understanding and influence of past participants into present interactions, albeit moderated by the ways in which these are perceived, interpreted, evaluated, and acted upon in the currency of today's interactions. Others are more ephemeral and limited in their effects. This is irrespective of whether or not these continue to exist as physical artefacts.

Authoring the organizational story

In viewing organization as conversation, what I earlier referred to as the official ideology (Figure 1.3) can be thought of as the authorized version of the 'organizational story'. As we've seen, this takes forward into new conversations those themes that have been given this formal stamp of authority. However, in light of the natural political dynamics of everyday organizational life, it's important to recognize that the creation of this authorized version, and its subsequent dissemination, is itself likely to be affected more by the interests, intentions, ideological stances, personal identities and so on of those involved, than by the wholly rational analysis and systematic decision-making that is implied by the conventional narrative.

Leading as an emergent property – punctuation marks in the ongoing conversation

All of the above further underlines the fact that acts of leadership are not confined to an elite group of specially gifted people who have been appointed to senior management positions. More broadly, these occur as a natural and emergent property of the real-world wiggliness of organization. As such, anyone can demonstrate leadership through the nature and quality of their participation. In seeing organization as continuously (re-)emerging in the interactions between interdependent people, acts of leadership can be thought of as 'punctuation marks' in this ongoing process of conversational interaction. That is to say, these acts are experienced as brief interludes in the otherwise uninterrupted flow of organization. Pauses which facilitate meaning-making; signal shifts in intention and tone; enable those involved to take stock; provoke new insights and first-step responses; prompt (self-) reflection; shift the patterns of interaction; mobilize action in support of a particular way forward; and so on.

As the conversations change, so does 'the organization'

Since organization emerges in the natural course of people's ongoing conversational interactions, it follows that organizational change arises from shifts in the content and patterning of those interactions. In other words, as the conversations change, so does the (process of) organization.[18] As we've seen earlier, many of the most significant conversations reflect shadow themes that are not raised in formal organizational settings. This underlines the importance of managers and other practitioners receptively and creatively participating in the everyday conversational interactions through which organization is continuously being enacted and outcomes are emerging. Tuning-in to those themes around which people are coalescing and which are organizing their participation. It is important to recognize, too, that all organizational change plans which come to be formally adopted are seeded, and progressively shaped, in the detail of these informal conversational exchanges. So are people's diverse responses to any practical changes that might materialize from such plans over time.

In sum

To summarize this aspect, then, organization emerges in, and is sustained through, the continuous and indivisible process of everyday conversational interaction. It is a process in which we are all immersed. And it is through this same conversational process that continuity is sustained (pattern reinforcement) and change happens (pattern shifting). Throughout our waking hours we talk to ourselves. For a lot of the time we talk with others as well. It's through this ongoing process of communicative (essentially conversational) interaction that we make sense of our experience and act into the future. And it's in this way that the future is perpetually being constructed in the detail of our own and others' current interactions. As part of this, we continually abstract from the indivisible flow of our participation in the process, so that we can construct a plausible explanation of what's going on. We do this individually and collectively by 'connecting the Big Dots' between what we and others see as significant events, activities, and outcomes in this endless and unbroken flow of interaction.

As discussed above, and as illustrated in Chapter 1, our individual and collective sense-making tends to be channelled imperceptibly down well-trodden pathways of understanding and action; strengthening these still further. It's in this way that imaginary, but nevertheless 'felt real' constructs – such as "the organization", "the system", "the culture", and so on – are co-created and sustained in conversation. It's also why these come to be thought of as tangible entities, rather than simply as the characteristic patterning of interactions between people, which is continuously (re-)constructed in the ongoing process of everyday conversation. In this regard, James Taylor and Elizabeth van Every are others who point to the fundamentally communicative and interactional nature of organization:[19]

> organization emerges in communication (and nowhere else). It emerges, furthermore, in two distinct ways: as described, and thus an object about which people talk and have attitudes, and as realized, in its continued enactment in the interaction patterns of its members' exchanges.

Within this, organizational change arises from shifts in the nature and patterning of people's everyday exchanges, stimulated by acts of leadership that emerge as 'punctuation marks' in this ongoing flow of conversational interaction.

The principle aspects of viewing organization as the complex social dynamics of organization are summarized in Figure 2.1, below.

Related dynamics

Set out below are a number of dynamics of organization that flow directly from the complex, social and processual nature of human interaction set out above. Most of these run counter to the assumptions about organization that underpin mainstream thinking on organization and management practice. These are:

- the asymmetrical nature of the patterning process and the illusion of control;

- polarization and the dynamics of inclusion and exclusion;
- boundaries in the boundaryless process of human interaction;
- the nature of time and the "living present";
- personal 'frames of reference' and authored identities;
- . . . and on "being authentic".

Asymmetrical nature of the patterning process, and the illusion of predictability and control

There is a fundamental characteristic of organization that flows naturally from the self-organizing patterning of social interaction. This is the ability that exists, post-event, to explain what happened in logical terms, based on a linear view of cause and effect. Ironically, although this arises from the wiggly-world dynamics of human interaction, it serves to reinforce the illusion of linearity, control and predictability that sits at the heart of management orthodoxy.

On several occasions, I've drawn analogies between Edward de Bono's explanation of "the mechanism of mind" (which he describes as a

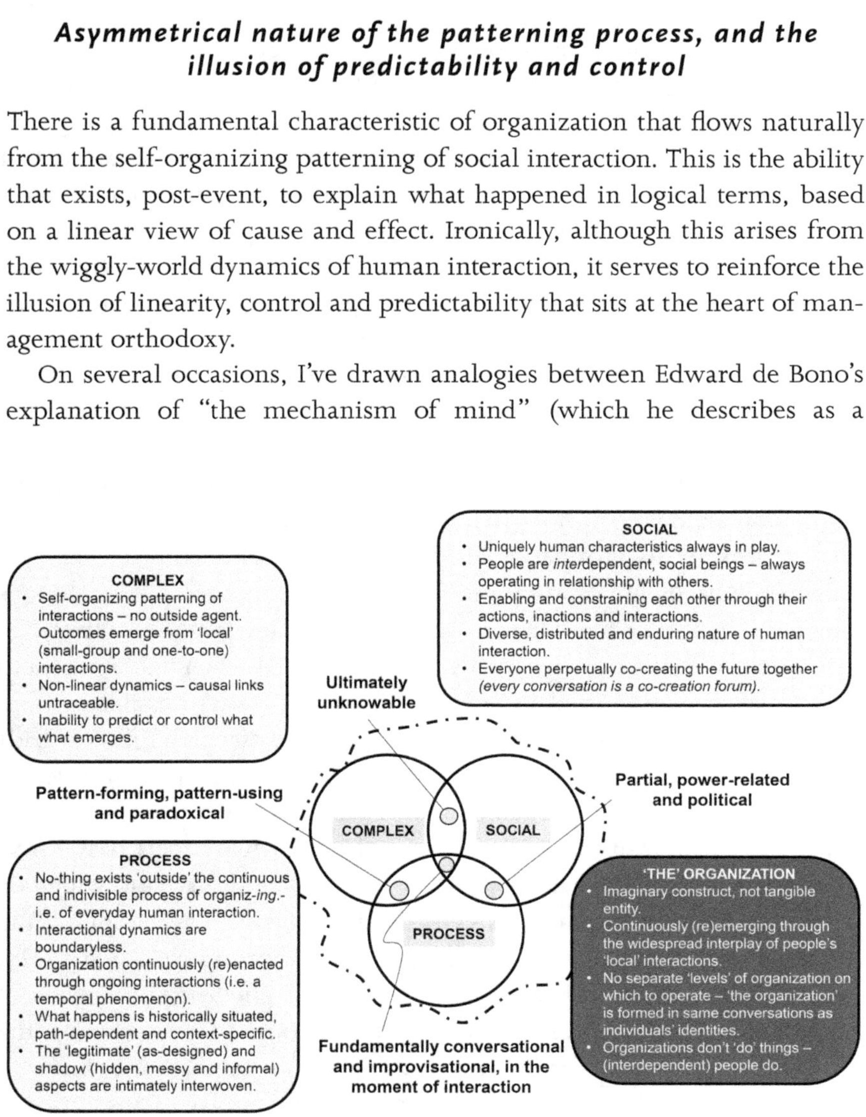

Figure 2.1 Organizational dynamics

self-organizing, patterning system) and the complex social dynamics of organization.[20] In relation to lateral thinking, he makes the point that solutions arrived at using his lateral thinking techniques always appear logical – even obvious – after the event. They would, he argues, be of little practical value if they didn't make sense to people. However, as he is also at pains to point out, this does not mean that those solutions could have been arrived at by applying logical thinking from the outset. The self-organizing dynamics of the brain tend to channel people's thoughts, feelings and actions along mental pathways that have been established previously. This reinforces these further; making spontaneous pattern-switching ever less likely, as alternative 'pathways' tend to be ignored or remain out of awareness altogether. Lateral thinking techniques are intended to interrupt this tendency, by provoking a switch to a novel pattern that otherwise is unlikely to have occurred by chance. Having landed upon an idea that makes sense retrospectively, the false conclusion might be drawn that this could have been arrived at using logic and rational analysis from the outset. It couldn't. The asymmetrical nature of this patterning process means that, although the solution is logical in hindsight, *it is not accessible using logic beforehand*.

In a similar way, sociologist Duncan Watts draws attention to a flaw in the commonly held view that we can predict and control outcomes, provided that we seek out all information relating to a particular decision and analyse this methodically. He captures this in the title of this book, "everything is obvious – once you know the answer".[21] Somewhat counter-intuitively, he also points out that this view tends to be reinforced when outcomes *fail* to match the prediction or plan. This is because it is always possible to work backwards to create a narrative that links the actual outcome (good or bad) to the starting condition. That having been done, it then becomes clear – or apparently so – that such-and-such a factor accounted for the observed outcome. Or that failure to take account of a particular aspect of the situation explains the shortfall. This is the same flawed thinking to which de Bono draws attention. And it mirrors the after-the-fact connection of 'Big Dots', above, to construct a supposedly explanatory narrative of what went on. That is, since we can *seemingly* link cause and effect after the event, it must be possible to do so in advance. As Watts himself argues, though, the inherent complexity of organization means that it is impossible to know in advance which of the unlimited number of factors at play in any situation might prove to be critical. These imaginary, after-the-fact rationalizations of 'the path to now' cannot be used as maps to guide future action, with any expectation that these will lead to similar outcomes. The self-organizing, patterning process that emerges in practice is asymmetrical. It is not characterized by, or amenable to, linearity, predictability and control.

Polarization – the dynamics of inclusion and exclusion

Another dynamic that arises in the complex social process of organization is the tendency for polarization to occur between different organizational groups and between the positions that they come to adopt on issues. This, again, is a natural characteristic of all self-organizing, pattern-forming and pattern-using processes. One pattern comes to dominate and others tend to be dismissed or ignored entirely, regardless of how similar, valid or useful these might be. This emerges in the interplay between identity, ideology and power relations, as these are continually reproduced and potentially transformed through the everyday politics of organization. The dynamics of inclusion and exclusion help to shape the identity of the 'in-group', such that members come to identify themselves ever more firmly with the collective and its ideology, interests and/or institutions. And, since identity is defined as much by difference as by sameness, there is a natural tendency for group members to magnify small differences that might exist between themselves and 'non-members', until these come to be seen as defining characteristics of the group. Once such distinguishing features and ideological stances have been established, these become self-perpetuating and self-reinforcing. Each (re-)affirmation of a particular position further strengthens the likelihood that the same or similar choices will be made in the future. The patterning process is further biased in favour of continuity by people's growing emotional investment in, and identification with, the favoured 'pattern' of understanding around which they are coalescing.

One of the most significant implications of this polarizing tendency – and one which can lead to dysfunctional behaviour – is an increased potential for "groupthink" to occur. This dynamic is one in which people strive to remain members of the in-group by coalescing ever more firmly and unquestioningly around the themes and viewpoints that they, severally and collectively, come to advance. When this occurs, contrary views tend to become increasingly marginalized, counter-arguments ignored and contradictory themes become undiscussable. This preserves the fantasy, by avoiding information that might otherwise undermine the perceived 'correctness' of the intended course or expose any ethical shortcomings. Groupthink is a concept that has been written about extensively since the 1970s. In a paper exploring the phenomenon amongst policy-makers, Irving Janis identifies what he describes as "symptoms" of groupthink.[22] These include:

- over-estimating the power and morality of the group, leading to riskier decision-making and ethically questionable choices;
- rationalizing and rejecting challenges to the group's assumptions, including pressurizing in-group members to conform and marginalizing the ideas and contributions of outsiders;
- illusions of unanimity arising from self-censorship amongst members of the in-group and the existence of what Janis called self-appointed "mind guards", to protect the group from adverse information and challenge.

Where the in-group in question includes the most senior managers, and interactions within it are characterized by groupthink, the tendency for contrary voices to be disregarded becomes more extensive and taken for granted (at least in formal arenas and official communications). And this lack of overt challenge can further blind such managers to any flaws that might exist in the actions that they are taking.

The tendency to behave in this way, and see it as normal, becomes further ingrained through the patterning process described earlier. And it continues to exist unless and until the prevailing pattern is disrupted in some way. This might occur through the mobilization of an informal coalition of support for change. Or it might happen where a call for change is precipitated, and the coalition building accelerated, by a major incident that cannot be ignored or hidden. In circumstances in which a powerful in-group has formed, it requires courage for individuals to take the initiative – even covertly – in seeking to mobilize action which goes against the grain of established practice, ideology and power dynamics. As a result, many practices remain unchallenged or, worse still, come to be replicated by others. In this way, the 'normality' of the behaviour becomes accepted and those advocating a different path can become increasingly sidelined or, in extreme cases, ostracized.

Understanding these dynamics, and seeking ways to encourage constructive challenge, is an important aspect of managing and leading from a wiggly-world perspective. This points to deliberate actions designed to cultivate diversity of background, thought and action, as well as paying attention to views and contributions that might, at first sight, appear marginal and/or heretical. Replicating and valuing the 'court jester' function, and openly encouraging the 'speaking of truth to power' also deserves particular attention.[23]

The question of boundaries in the boundaryless process of human interaction

We earlier saw how organization, as the ongoing process of human interaction, is boundaryless. Although people's interactions are not limited by the formally defined organizational boundaries, other important boundaries arise naturally from the polarizing and political dynamics of inclusion and exclusion. In their 1992 HBR article, Larry Hirschhorn and Thomas Gilmore talk about the then popular design notion of "the boundaryless company". In response, they argued that psychological boundaries would need to be constructed in place of those that had previously existed in the formal structure. In the context of 'boundarylessness by design', Hirschhorn and Gilmore draw attention to the need for,[24]

> new boundaries [that] are more psychological than organizational. And instead of being reflected in a company's structure, they must be 'enacted' over and over again in a manager's relationships with bosses, subordinates, and peers.

Although I'm suggesting that boundarylessness is a natural dynamic of organization, rather than a design choice, the 'psychological boundaries' to which Hirschhorn and Gilmore draw attention have some practical merit in the context of the complex social dynamics of organization. In brief, the boundaries that they suggest as being important are:

- the authority boundary – "Who is in charge of what?"
- the task boundary – "Who does what?"

- the political boundary – "What's in it for us?"
- the identity boundary – "Who is and isn't us?"

Hirschhorn and Gilmore's point concerning the continuing enactment of these boundaries as people relate to each other is particularly relevant. First, it reminds us that it is not the formally stated positions on authority, task, and so on that will determine what occurs, but rather how these come to be taken up by people in the midst of their ongoing interactions. Secondly, that what they are calling "psychological boundaries" do not exist physically anywhere. They are continuously (re-)created in the currency of people's ongoing interactions. That is to say, these are temporal rather than spatial. At the same time, there are two aspects of Hirschhorn and Gilmore's conception of this process about which I would express some caution. The first relates to their description of these imaginary constructs as "psychological". This suggests that they see them as originating in the minds of autonomous individuals. However, as we've seen, people are *inter*dependent with everyone else. As such, the 'answers' to their authority, task, political, and identity questions are continually being *socially* constructed *between* people in the playing out of their ongoing interactions. The second point of departure concerns their suggestion that the boundaries "*must be 'enacted' over and over again* (my emphasis)". This implies a degree of choice over whether or not this process takes place. But, from a wiggly-world perspective, these dynamics are continuously in play. As a final point here, it is important to recognize the inherent conflict and co-operation that are simultaneously present in the playing out of these boundaries.

The nature of time – the "living present"

Over 60 years ago, in speaking to managers at a conference in 1957, Peter Drucker explored the subject of decision-making.[25] He describes decision-making as, "essentially a time machine which synchronizes into one present a great number of divergent time-spans". As he went on to say, "Our approach today still tends towards the making of plans for something we will decide to do in the future. This may be a very entertaining exercise, but it is a futile one". Fast forward 60 years and the notion that decisions about the present and future are separated in time still dominates management thinking. As Drucker said at the conference,

> Decisions exist only in the present. The question . . . is not what we should do tomorrow. It is: what do we have to do *today* [my emphasis] to be ready for an uncertain tomorrow? The question is not what will happen in the future. It is, what futurity do we have to factor into our present thinking and doing, what time-spans do we have to consider, and how do we converge them into a simultaneous decision in the present?

He then added another important insight, that managers ignore at their peril:

> we can make decisions only in the present; the rest are pious intentions. And yet we cannot make decisions for the present alone; the most expedient, most opportunist decision – let alone the decision not to decide – may commit us on a long-range basis, if not permanently and irrevocably.

So, Drucker's idea of decision-making as a "time machine" recognizes that future outcomes are wholly products of the complex interplay of decisions made by people *in the present*. Also, that it is not only those decisions that are 'headlined' as strategic decisions that have potentially strategic implications for the organization. This sits four-square with the notion of organization as the complex social process of everyday human interaction. And, taking this further still, Doug Griffin challenges the taken-for-granted, seemingly common-sense notion that time is linear. That is, that it flows from the matter-of-fact past, through the transient present, towards a future that is waiting to be unfolded. Instead he refers to what he calls "the living present". Here, the present itself has a time structure that embraces the past and the future:[26]

> The past is not factually given because it is reconstructed in the present as the basis for action to be taken in the present. The past is what we re-member. The future is also in the present in the form of anticipation and expectation. It too forms the basis of action in the present. Furthermore, what we are anticipating affects what we remember and what we remember affects what we expect, in a circular fashion. In this way, the movement of the living present is experience, having a circular

time structure that arises simply because humans have the capacity for knowing what they are doing.

I've sought to illustrate this in Figure 2.2. In the notion of the living present, then, "the future, as expectation and anticipation, is in the detail of actual interactions taking place now, as is the past as reconstructions in this process of memory".[27]

What, then, can we take from these insights into the nature of decision-making and action-taking in an organizational context? First, although Drucker is advocating long-range planning as an aspect of management practice, he emphasizes the critical importance of focusing on the *futurity of present decisions* in carrying this out, not on future decisions. He also argues forcibly that it is not about forecasting or trying to mastermind the future, which he acknowledges is beyond the capacity of human beings. Instead, Drucker calls on managers to pay attention to those decisions – theirs and others' – that are taking place through interactions *in the present*. Similarly, from a complex social process perspective, the required emphasis shifts

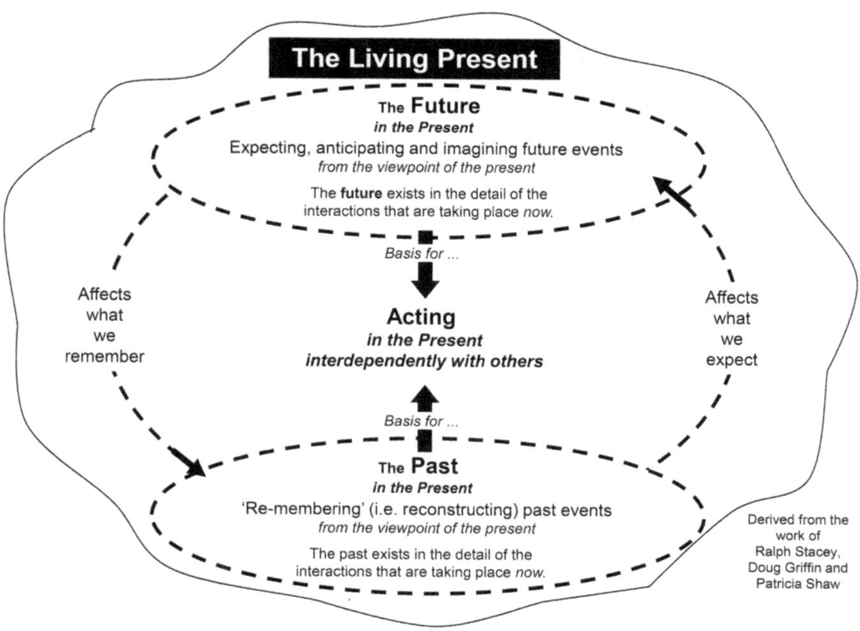

Figure 2.2 The living present

from one of making choices in and about the future towards the quality of participation in self-organizing conversations from which such choices and the responses to them emerge in the living present.[28]

So, both perspectives, five decades apart, underscore the importance of managers paying attention to, and engaging in, what's happening in the present. Importantly, this sense-making-cum-action-taking process will go on with or without their active involvement. The only real choice that they have, therefore, is whether or not to engage with this process in a deliberate way; with the aim of *improving the quality of their participation*.

Personal 'frames of reference' and authored identities

One of the important implications of viewing organization as a *social* process is the nature of personal identity that flows from this. Earlier I suggested that who we are and how we behave is largely shaped by the interactions that we have with other people – as, *at the same time*, who we are and how we behave shapes those interactions. This runs counter to the widely held idea that our identities comprise a wholly personal set of attributes; the manifestation of an internalized "true self" that sits at the core of our unique being. This latter notion is central to many aspects of organizational development, performance management, the pursuit of "authentic" leadership, and so on. So, I want to say a little more about the fundamentally social nature of individual identity, given the implications of this for management practice, personal development and organizational performance. In essence, like everything else in the context of human being, our identities emerge from the everyday conversational interactions that we have with other people. And from our inner dialogue with which these ongoing exchanges are intimately interwoven. They are not pre-existing and internal; waiting to be revealed to the world from the inside out. To paraphrase Taylor and van Every above, individuals find their own identity in the same conversation in which the notion of "the organization" is continuously (re-)formed. Or, as Griffin puts it:[29]

> Both the self and the social are the same process, with the only distinction being that the former is a private role play or silent conversation while the latter is a public 'game' and vocal communication.

Steph Lawler similarly challenges the widely held view that a person's "true identity" is somehow 'inside' them and fundamentally separated from the social world. Instead, she advances a radically social perspective, arguing that identity is produced and negotiated between people in relationship.[30] This means that identity is not a 'given', but something produced through the narratives people use to explain and understand their lives. Her focus on narrative challenges the notion of the atomized individual and replaces it with a concept of a person enmeshed in – and produced within – webs of social relations. Lawler's perspective on the nature and dynamics of identity sits four-square with that which is embodied in the radical, wiggly-world view of organizational dynamics and other relational standpoints. As such, although its focus is primarily on broad social and political issues, it necessarily places a number of question marks against important elements of mainstream thinking on organization and management practice. As she says,[31]

> Identity needs to be understood not as belonging 'within' the individual person, but as produced between persons and within social relations.

This notion of identity hinges on the paradoxical combination of sameness and difference: We are the same as ourselves (from birth to death) and the same as others – sharing some aspects of identity with them. *At the same time*, we are unique and, therefore, different from others.

As Lawler goes on to say, identities are (like all other aspects of our experience) 'made up' through crafting a story out of life: assembling various memories, experiences, episodes, interpretations, understandings, etc. through narrative. I've referred to this earlier as "joining the Big Dots". This narrative view of identity forms the core of her argument. We endlessly author stories about our lives, which we tell to ourselves and to others. And it is through such stories that we make sense of the world, of our relationship to that world, and of the relationship between ourselves and other selves. Importantly, these narratives do not reflect a given identity. Instead, they are "produced through the autobiographical work in which all of us engage every day".[32] Identity is therefore profoundly social. Insofar as we know ourselves (and others) we achieve this knowledge only through interpretation. Self-knowledge then involves a continuing act of self-interpretation. I have previously referred to this dynamic in terms of individuals personal frames of reference[33] – an amalgam of characteristics that we come to claim as our own. This is a continuously (re-)emerging construct that is socially formed through our ongoing interactions with others. At the same time, it affects the ways in which we continue to interact and make sense of our ongoing experiences. This sense of individual identity (I/me) is the personal analogue of the equally imaginary notion of "the organization" at a collective level (a we/us identity). It does not exist in any way separately from the roles that we are each continuously 'playing out' through the *diverse* relationships within which we are participating. Seeking to keep this frame intact – simultaneously across all of our important (and necessarily diverse) relationships – is an important factor in the ways in which we respond to actual and emerging shifts in a particular context.

. . . and on being authentic

Since our concept of self arises from our sensing of our own self *in relation to* specific and generalized 'other selves', it does not exist – indeed cannot exist – in isolation from the specific relationships of which we see ourselves being part. Or from the more generalized social patterns of thinking, feeling and acting that reflect the broader communities to which we see ourselves belonging. It is continuously (re-)developed though all of the interactions that we have with people throughout our lifetime – directly and indirectly, real and imagined, planned and spontaneous, etc. Or, as Lawler puts it, "we are both made and unmade by each other".[34] The ways in which we perceive, interpret, evaluate and talk to others about our experiences, in the immediacy of our interactions and through self-reflection, determines who we currently are in *our ongoing process of becoming*.

This does, of course, bring into question what we mean when we talk about someone "being authentic" in an organizational context. This is most often spoken about in relation to the actions of those people in formal management positions (i.e. managers with a capital 'M'). In particular, how they are seen to act when they are carrying out the leadership aspects of their role. It is usually taken to mean their acting in ways that are consistent with their "true self" – a condition which is assumed to be universally good and an expression of them at their best. However, if no such self exists, where does that leave us? And them? Thankfully, there is a clue in the word, *auth*entic. In understanding identity as a social phenomenon, being authentic implies that the stories that they *'author'* about themselves – and which they are seen to enact in their everyday lives – are congruent with those that others tell about them. Whether these are viewed as good, bad or indifferent.

The idea that individual identity is a function of people's interactions with others, and of the stories that they and others tell about them – rather than something that is inherent – can be a challenging notion. This is especially the case, perhaps, for those who have risen to great heights in an organizational context and/or in society more generally. But this relational and narrative view of identity flows naturally from the complex *social* process of everyday human interaction.

Ideology and the wiggly world of organization

As a critically important final point, seeing organization as continuously emerging in the complex social process of everyday human interaction provides an *ideologically neutral* description of what's going on. This means, for example, that the adoption of an unalloyed, 'command and control'/managerialist approach as well as one that reflects a more co-operative/'democratic' view of organization and management practice are *both* emergent outcomes of this same interactional process. The ways in which these play out in practice, and the feelings etc. that these invoke, will differ fundamentally. But *the underlying dynamics of interaction will be the same in each case*. This similarly applies to the emergence and application of societal norms, political philosophy and so on, regardless of where people sit on the 'loose-tight'/left-right spectrum. This descriptive, ideologically neutral nature of the complex social process (wiggly world) view of organizational dynamics is fundamental.

Notes

1 In Chapter 1, I drew a distinction between the "knowability" of technological products, systems, and processes, and the ultimately "unknowable" nature of situations in which people are involved (such as in the process of organization). As regards the former, insights gained in one setting (such as in the research, design, development, operation, repair and maintenance of a particular product or item of plant) can usefully be

applied with confidence to similar products and plant items being used elsewhere. That is to say, it makes sense to identify good technological practices and lessons learnt, and to apply these more widely. However, the same cannot be said for the complex social dynamics of organization (and life more generally), within which such techno-rational solutions are situated.

According to conventional practice, case studies setting out people's experiences in one organization are presented as prescriptions for use elsewhere and/or are seen as providing the raw research material from which 'best practice' guidelines can be derived. However, as will become clearer from later chapters of the book, from a wiggly world view of organization, this is not a credible way to proceed. As such, no case studies or so-called "best practice" templates are offered in this book. Instead, readers should consider themselves to be 'walking case studies' of these dynamics in action. That is to say readers can gain the most from this book if they similarly reflect on their own experiences of organizational life, when interacting with the ideas contained in it.

2 Allaire, Y. and Firsirotu, M.E. (1984: 208) Theories of Organizational Culture in *Organization Studies* 5(3): 193–226

3 Hernes, T. (2014: 55) *A Process Theory of Organization*. Oxford.

4 Taylor, J.R. and van Every, E.J. (2000: 171) *The Emergent Organization*. Lawrence Erlbaum Associates.

5 Culbert, S. (1996) *Mind-Set Management*. Oxford University Press.

6 Stacey R.D. (2012:99) *Tools and Techniques of Leadership and Management*. Routledge.

7 See Elias, N. (1939) *The Civilizing Process*, Blackwell and Mead, G.H. (1934) *Mind, Self, & Society*. University Press, Chicago.

8 At the time or writing, the coronavirus pandemic, COVID-19, is sweeping the world. This is similarly the result of the widespread interplay of local (i.e. small-group and one-to-one) interactions. As with people's conversational interactions, this does not respect national boundaries and no individual, or body of people, is in control of its spread or of the impact that it makes on people's individual and collective lives.

9 The dominant narrative on organization and management practice is one such pattern – a clichéd response to the complex social dynamics of organization that I'm setting out to challenge. My argument is that it is the mismatch between the experienced wiggliness of organization

and managers'/consultants'/writers' continuing pursuit of the myth of rationality, predictability and control that is at the core of many of the current dysfunctions of organizational life – and life in general!

10 I mentioned this in Chapter 1, in relation to the dynamics of organizational culture (as per de Bono and Chater).

11 As I discussed in *Informal Coalitions* (Palgrave, 2006), we each develop and try to maintain a personal frame of reference throughout our lives. This mental construct is continually formed and re-formed through our everyday interactions and experiences. In turn, this affects the way in which we continue to interact and make sense of our ongoing experiences. It enables us to find our way through the complexities and uncertainties of life in ways that preserve our feeling of personal meaning and self-worth. It also gives us our sense of identity, our perceived place in the world, and so on.

12 Dunford, R. and Palmer, I. (1998: 218) *Discourse, Organizations and Paradox*. In Grant, D. *et al* (Eds) *Discourse and Organization*. SAGE Publications.

13 See, Stacey, Shaw, and Griffin (2000), and Stacey and Mowles (2016), for example.

I ordinarily use the term "complex social process" to describe the dynamics of organization, rather than "complex responsive process", which is a phrase that was coined in the early-2000s by Ralph Stacey, Patricia Shaw and Doug Griffin at the UK's University of Hertfordshire. They settled upon the latter description to emphasize that it is through the responsive process of "communicative interaction" (essentially conversation) between interdependent people that organization is enacted "in the living present".

On the fundamentals of organizational dynamics, the perspective set out in this book differs only 'at the margins' from that advanced by exponents of the Hertfordshire 'school'. I believe that the terms complex responsive process and complex social process provide equally accurate descriptions of the socially complex dynamics of human interaction. At the same time, I would readily concede that the term complex responsive process more precisely describes the essentially conversational nature of these dynamics. That is to say, it reflects the fundamental point that meaning is not contained within an individual's act of communicating (the "gesture", after George Herbert Mead) but rather is co-created in the ongoing gesture-response process *between people*. However, I don't want to imply that my own views, and the practical implications that I draw from them, are wholly congruent with the carefully crafted theory of complex responsive processes. They are not. It would therefore be a distortion to use the label "complex responsive process" to describe my own thinking and practice. The term "complex social process" echoes the same themes, without misappropriating the Hertfordshire term. Also, the theory of complex responsive processes arose, and continues to be developed, in the context of teaching, research and reflection within a specialist department of a UK university. As such, it offers a comprehensive and coherent view of organizational dynamics, which is underpinned by a wealth of academic writing – not only in the field of complexity, but also embracing perspectives drawn from philosophy, sociology, and anthropology amongst others. In contrast, my use of the term complex social process arose primarily from my own observations of the complex social dynamics of organizational life, gleaned over many years as a practising manager, and further reinforced by my consulting experience and related interactions.

14 A social object does not exist as a physical entity. It exists solely in terms of the patterns of interaction between people. These are continuously reiterated over time; creating – and reinforcing - generalized tendencies for people to make sense and take action in similar ways, in similar situations, going forward. At the same time, given the need for people to particularize these general tendencies in the actual situations in which they find themselves participating, the potential always exists for new patterns to emerge through this same, interactional process.

15 Stacey, R.D. (2009) *Complexity and Organizational Reality*. Routledge.

16 This is discussed in Chapter 5.

17 Caldini, R. (2007) *Influence*. Harper Business.

18 See Patricia Shaw's *Changing Conversations in Organizations* (Routledge, 2002) for her particular take on this.

19 Taylor, J.R. and van Every, E.J. (ibid: 4).

20 De Bono, E. (1969) *The Mechanism of Mind*. Simon & Schuster.

21 Watts, D. (2012) *Everything is Obvious*. Atlantic Books.

22 Janis, I. (1971) *Groupthink Among Policy Makers*. In Sanford, N. and Comstock, C. (Eds.) Sanctions for Evil. Jossey-Bass (1971: 71–89).

23 See Edward de Bono, on the "court jester function", in *Lateral Thinking for Management* (Penguin, 1982); and John Higgins and Megan Reitz on speaking truth to power in *Speak Up* (FT Publishing International, 2019).

24 Hirschhorn, L. and Gilmore, T. (1992:5) *The New Boundaries of the "Boundaryless" Organization*. HBR (May–June 1992).

25 Drucker, P. (1986: 109 et seq.) *Technology, Management and Society*. Routledge.
26 Griffin, D. (2001: 206 et seq.) *The Emergence of Leadership*. Routledge.
27 Again, from Griffin, D. (ibid: 185).
28 See, for example, Stacey, R.D. (2007: 444) *Strategic Management and Organisational Dynamics, 5Ed*. Financial Times/Prentice Hall.
29 Griffin, D. (ibid: 154).
30 Lawler, S. (2008) *Identity: Sociological Perspectives 1 Ed*. Polity Press.
31 Lawler, S. (ibid: 8).
32 Lawler, S. (ibid: 13).
33 Rodgers, C. (2006) *Informal Coalitions*. Palgrave.
34 Lawler, S. (ibid: 149).

3

MANAGEMENT IN FIVE ACTS

SCIENTIFIC RESEARCH AND THE COMPLEX SOCIAL REALITY OF ORGANIZATION

A few years ago, I attended a brief presentation of some extensive academic research into leadership performance. Leadership here was taken to mean the contribution of the organization's 'top person'. So far as I could judge, the research had been carried out impeccably in terms of established academic rigour. But, in abstracting from the complex reality of organizational life on which the research was supposedly focused, the subsequent conclusions were, to my mind, seriously flawed. The research sought to draw causal links between the backgrounds of those in the most senior leadership positions and the comparative success of their organizations, as defined in the research. The central proposition was that those whose backgrounds satisfied the particular criterion identified would make the best leaders. Simple.

But none of this took account of the complex social dynamics of organization through which "success" (however defined) – and indeed "leadership" – emerges in practice.

Inferring causation from correlation

The basis of the researcher's conclusion was their discovery of a "statistically significant" correlation between one aspect of the leader's background and the chosen measure(s) of business success. That is, based on the data analysis, success occurred more frequently when one 'type' of leader rather than another was in post. However, the presence of one of these factors (either specified leader type or successful performance) was not always accompanied by the other. Success also occurred when other types of leader were in post, although less frequently. And it is impossible to say from the research that the latter caused the former, even when both factors were present.

Despite this, the link between successful performance and the preferred background characteristic was turned into a linear, 'if you do this you'll get that' relationship. The 'causal vacuum' was filled by the construction of a narrative that sought to identify why the defined condition might plausibly lead to success. Since this was presented in the form of a flow diagram, the necessarily tentative inferences that had been drawn from the data appeared to show clear directionality and causal logic. None of this, though, was a product of the research. Nor – if we take the complexity of organizations seriously – could it ever be.

Taking complexity seriously

As we've seen, in the complex social process of human interaction that we think of as organization, it is not possible to demonstrate links between cause and effect in anything but very limited conditions. In essence, these cease to have any meaning. As does research of the conventional kind. The scientific paradigm, on which such research is based, presumes that generalizable conclusions can be drawn from the analysis of data and applied universally. But this is not the case when it comes to organizational dynamics. Nor, therefore, can it be with business performance. For hard-pressed managers, though, such research appears to offer proof and certainty – pinpointing a sure-fire route through the real-world complexities that they face on a daily basis.

In a truly scientific context, of course, research of this kind is essential to the progress and wellbeing of humanity. Its purpose is to develop a clear body of evidence to inform future practice in a wide range of situations.

Medical and technological advances, for example, owe everything to rigorous scientific research. But organization is a continuously emerging, socially constructed phenomenon. As such, it is not amenable to rational scientific analysis, and to the presumption of linear causality and universality of application on which this is founded.

As I've argued in the opening chapters, organization is a *relational* phenomenon. It emerges in the self-organizing patterning of human (essentially conversational) interaction. Such sense-making-cum-action-taking interactions are always characterized by differing, and often conflicting, interpretations, intentions, interests, identities, ideologies, and so on. What we come to see as "outcomes" emerge from the widespread and indeterminate interplay of these local interactions. Interactions, that is, which take place between different individuals, who are nevertheless *interdependent*. As mentioned earlier, therefore, everything that happens is both uniquely personal and, at the same time, communally social.

I-opening research

One of the charges that is made when challenging the validity of using conventional, science-based research methodologies in a social context is that, if you reject this as a means of gaining (supposedly) greater awareness and understanding, you are left with nowhere to go. This is not the case at all. The conversations that comprise the organization take place one-to-one and in small groups. It's here, in this specific local context, that practitioners can begin by adopting a reflective and reflexive stance *in the midst of their ongoing interactions*. As well as researching their own experience "off line". This means looking to draw out the contextual factors, dominant conversational themes, prevalent thought and behavioural patterns (both characteristic and unexpected), governing assumptions, power relationships, personal biases, and so on that are currently:

- organizing their own and others' interactions and co-creating the outcomes that are emerging from them;
- both enabling and constraining their own and others' ongoing practice; and
- providing the basis for potentially beneficial shifts that they, individually and collectively, might seek to make going forwards.

Such practice-based research would be likely to open-up some of the 'I's that I mentioned above. By this I mean that those involved would seek to gain insights into the differing intentions, interpretations, identities, interests, ideologies, idiosyncrasies, interdependencies, and institutionalized practices, etc. that are in play – *at that time, in that situation and within those relationships*. These everyday politics of organizational life are simultaneously shaping *and being shaped by* people's ongoing interactions. As we've seen, this process is boundaryless. It is happening simultaneously everywhere. Throughout the world. *All that anyone can ever do* therefore, is to "act into" the future *as it is emerging* – using their practical judgement, moment to moment, as facilitated by a reflective and reflexive approach to their individual and (appropriately) collective practice.

So, what can we make of this?

To frame the discussion, Figure 3.1 sets out what I call the five acts of management. This is, of course, an abstraction from the complex social reality of what's actually going on. But, like other sense-making and descriptive (rather than prescriptive) frameworks, I believe that it offers a welcome challenge to the plethora of n-step models, assessment questionnaires, and similar tools and techniques that promise to deliver universally successful outcomes. Even when their advocates acknowledge the complex, uncertain, and ambiguous nature of what's actually going on.

So, what am I trying to illustrate here?

Act 1 – What we do in practice

Act 1 begins by describing what managers – indeed, all of us – *actually do in practice*. That is, they act forward, moment-to-moment, into a continuously emerging and unknowable future. In doing so, they are both enabled and constrained by the actions, inactions, and interactions of everyone else. Others are similarly engaged in seeking to shape what happens, in line with their own sense of what's going on now, what happened in the past, and what they hope, expect, and fear might happen in the future. All of this is taking place in the present moment, through their ongoing interactions with other people.[1] As such, they are always adjusting what they are doing, and how they are doing it, as they move from one point in time to the next. This is happening both with conscious intent and in-the-moment

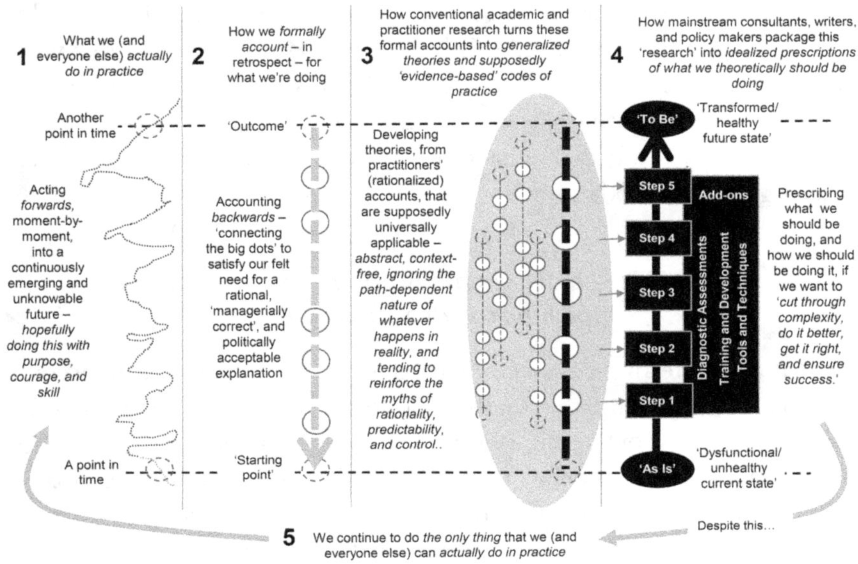

Figure 3.1 Management in five acts

awareness, as well as habitually. There is no start to this process. And no end. It is an ongoing flow of activity, represented in the diagram by a wiggly line.

Hopefully, as suggested in the diagram, managers will do this with purpose, courage, and skill. But more of that later. Whether done well or done badly, this is what they are all doing. All of the time. Each manager participates in this continuous flow of activity, which is very real, very tangible, but impossible to describe in any meaningful sense. Like everyone else, they are continuously immersed in 'the game'[2] of organizational life whilst, *at the same time*, abstracting from it to make sense of what's going on as a basis for their ongoing participation.

In Chapter 4, I describe this practice as "management by muddling through" and explore it much more fully. For now, it's important to understand that I'm not using this term in a derogatory sense – as might be inferred from its everyday use. Instead, I'm suggesting that *this most accurately describes what all managers actually find themselves doing in practice*. Improvising in the moment. Acting intuitively, on the basis of their embodied knowledge and practical judgement. Imaginatively making do, in the light of the situations they face, the sense they make of these, the resources available to them, others' involvement and so on. As we'll see later, this has a close affinity with what the French call "bricolage". Having acted in this way – in anticipation of, and response to, the circumstances in which they find themselves participating – managers are then faced with reconciling this improvisational and fragmentary reality with the need to communicate what's going on to others.

Act 2 – How we account, in retrospect, for what we've been doing

Act 2 is therefore an essential corollary of Act 1. It is how managers account, in retrospect, for what they have been doing. This is an important aspect of learning. It's about accounting backwards – "connecting the Big Dots", as I've called it – to provide a plausible explanation of their lived experience. Telling the story of what they and others are 'doing', and what they see happening around them, is an essential act of everyday living. And, as we shall see later, doing this well – that is, in ways that resonate with people, make sense to them and move them in some way – is a critical aspect of managing and leading skilfully. At this point, the uninterruptible flow of time is broken up into imaginary segments that are given meaning in terms of a notional 'starting point', felt-to-be-significant 'events' along the way, and a specific 'outcome'. This is an example of what Stacey refers to as "first order abstraction",[3] which is what I mean by connecting the Big Dots. This retrospective sense-making, and the conversations it provokes, is fundamental to organizational practice. It is also the basis of learning, as well as the 'unlearning' associated with new insights and innovation. However, this natural dynamic is distorted when managers (and others) are asked to account *formally* for what they are doing. There is then pressure on them to respond in ways that satisfy the felt need for a 'managerially correct' and politically acceptable account of their practice, in line with the scientifically rational assumptions of the dominant, managerialist view of what constitutes expert practice.

Acts 1 and 2, then, provide the basis of management practice in the wiggly world (i.e. complex social process) of organization. These reflect the dynamic interplay of in-the-moment, immersed, improvisation; ongoing sense-making; and post-experience reflection and commentary on what has taken place. However, as we saw from the opening story in this chapter, the dominant discourse on organization and management maintains that such practice can be studied in the same way as natural phenomena and technologies. That is, it assumes that generalized, 'scientific' principles can be derived from this process. Furthermore, that application of these principles will provide the sought-after certainty, predictability, and control that the wiggliness of the process supposedly obscures. I spoke of this in Chapter 1 in terms of managers seeking to catch this wiggliness in a metaphorical net . . . woven from the familiar concepts, tools, and techniques of conventional management practice. In Figure 3.1, this is reflected in Acts 3 and 4 of Management.

Act 3 – The part played by conventional (i.e. scientifically rational) academic and/or practitioner research

Act 3 illustrates how conventional academic and/or practitioner researchers seek to turn managers' *formal*, post-event accounts into generalized theories and (what are claimed to be) evidence-based codes of practice. They do this by developing theories based on managers' rationalized, after-the-fact descriptions of what they have been doing (i.e. 'Act 2-type') and the supposed effects that these have had. But this process results in even more abstract and partial representations of what are already abstract, partial, and 'polished' accounts of the messy reality. The error is then compounded by the suggestion that such theories can be applied universally. That is to say, they ignore the path-dependent and context-rich nature of what people are actually experiencing and doing in practice. These assumptions, of universal applicability and identifiable causal links, then serve to reinforce still further the myths of rationality, predictability and control that disfigure current understanding and the prescriptions that flow from them.

All of this presumes, first of all, that the scientific method is capable of discovering universal, 'if you do this, you'll get that' truths. Secondly, it takes for granted the idea that the same methodology can be applied to the complex social process of human interaction that is deployed in the technological and natural worlds. My argument has always been that conventional management wisdom falls down on the second point. That is to say, the dynamics of human interaction differ fundamentally from those involved in man-made technologies and the natural world. This remains the case. However, I was pleasantly surprised when I came across a book, by scientists Mike Fortun and Herbert Bernstein, which throws a different light on the nature of scientific method itself and the assumed truths that emerge from it.[4] In it, they argue that this is mistakenly predicated on the notion of a given, fact-based reality, which can be discovered and theorized upon through observation, measurement and calculation. A process in which indisputable pieces of this reality can be revealed and assembled into a theory that provides a perfect match with the world as is. This is the essence of Act 3, in which these supposedly "indisputable pieces of the real world" comprise managers' post-event rationalizations of their in-the-moment experience.

Fortun and Bernstein then set out to challenge these conventional accounts. They argue that we can no longer excuse the errors and simplifications on which such popular tales are based and no longer afford to have this view of the sciences circulate in the social and political realms. "The stakes", they say, "are too high". Central to their argument, then, are a number of points that resonate strongly with the ideas I am setting out here in relation to the established discourse on organization and management. For example, they maintain that the scientific method *produces* the facts that we take to be the truth, rather than discovering a given reality. Secondly, that the status of a theory as 'truth' depends less on the extent to which it reflects a pre-existent world, than on the "viability, strength, or robustness of a tangle of connections, or articulations". And, thirdly, that science is never neutral. As a result of the partial, power-related and political dynamics that we have discussed earlier, what we know, and what we think of as the truth, is always shaped and shaded by our interactions with others – formal and informal, real and imagined.

So Fortun and Bernstein set out to reposition our understanding of science and the scientific method in terms that are much more congruent with the complex social dynamics of organization and with the unavoidably human nature of those scientists and researchers who practise it. Despite this, claims that the scientific method is being used to define the nature and dynamics of organization and management practice continues unabated. And, in the context of the Five Acts of Management, things don't stop there. . .

Act 4 – Idealized prescriptions – with add-ons

Act 4 moves us into the realm of mainstream management consultants and writers, as well as that of policy-makers more generally. The former package this research (their own or others') into idealized prescriptions of what managers *should* be doing and how they should be doing it. More often than not, given the dominance of the established discourse, and the way that this particular form of managerialism has infected all corners of public-sector thinking, these flawed prescriptions then form the basis of policy statements and regulatory regimes that tend to institutionalize such thinking still further.

From this viewpoint, as discussed in Chapter 2, the ongoing and indivisible *process* of organization (i.e. organiz-*ing*) is viewed, instead, as an entity, "the organization", which can be worked on by managers to bring about a desired future state. This is often referred to as "To Be", or something similar. The starting point for this sought-after change – more likely to be referred to as a "transformation" – is presented as a currently dysfunctional and/or "unhealthy" state ("As Is"). By this stage, the issue-specific Big Dots that featured in the accounts of various managers in Act 2, and from which the generalized theories of Act 3 were derived, have now become firm steps and/or prescriptive elements in a formal change or development methodology.

To compound the error, arguments in favour of the newly prescribed approaches are often accompanied by overly precise figures in support of the recommendations. So, for example, it might be suggested that adopting a particular approach has been shown to lead to an increase of 11.35% in the likelihood of a successful outcome in relation to a sought-after performance factor. The use of such precision presents managers with the hoodwinking logic[5] necessary to assure them that what is being offered is scientifically based and a clear-cut way of delivering the sought-after results. At this stage, too, various 'add-ons' typically appear as part of the package on offer. These might include such things as diagnostic assessment questionnaires; pre-packaged training and development programmes; and a plethora of other derivative tools and techniques. All of these are based on generalizations, drawn from the aggregated experiences of managers whose actual practice is one of context-specific, situation-contingent and path-dependent behaviours, *arising in the moment of their local interactions with others.*

Act 5 – What's actually going on. . .

Presented with these neatly packaged explanations and prescriptions, and mindful of the high expectations placed on their ability to deliver the required outcomes, it is understandable that managers can find themselves drawn-in to a world that is defined by the logic and language of Act 4 Management. However, whether or not they officially adopt such approaches, they continue to do the only thing that they (and everyone else) can actually do in practice (Act 5). That is, they act forward, moment-by-moment into a continuously emerging and unknowable future. A future that they and everyone else are perpetually co-creating in the currency of their present interactions. This means that they have no option but to continue to participate in the everyday, wiggly reality of organization that I referred to earlier as Act 1 Management . . . and so it goes on.

Woven into this wiggly reality, of course, are those current and past 'oughts' and 'shoulds' of Act 4 Management that have been incorporated into the formally adopted ideology, designs and intentions (see Figure 1.3). Managers experience these as aspects of the continuously emerging and unknowable future into which they find themselves acting, but with an added sense of legitimacy and felt need to comply. In reality, it is the ways in which the formally endorsed positions are made sense of and taken up in people's local interactions that determine how these actually play out in practice. Nevertheless, as I noted in Chapter 1, it is very difficult for managers to resist the pressures to be seen to be acting to make the formally adopted prescriptions work. This is the case however far removed from the complex reality of their everyday experience some of these might be. Conventional role expectations and political considerations push managers towards endorsing these in their formal interactions, as well as describing their actions in these terms in official settings (Act 2 Management). All of which inevitably diverts their attention away from the conversational themes and patterns of interaction that are organizing their own and others' participation. And co-creating what actually happens – as they, and everyone else, act forwards, moment-by-moment. . . .

Notes

1 As described extensively in Chapter 2, "the present" is not a point in time between a fixed past and a yet-to-be-formed future. As Doug Griffin describes it, in *the Emergence of Leadership* (2002: 184) "It is in the present that we are continuously constructing the future on the basis of the enabling constraints developed over time as our past." Griffin, and his co-authors of the complex responsive process view of organization, refer to this as "the living present".

2 This is a term used by French Sociologist, Pierre Bourdieu, to describe the nature of social interaction; with each 'game' having its own rules, knowledge, and skills, etc. See, for example, *The Logic of Practice* (1992).

3 Ralph Stacey first introduced the notion of first- and second-order abstraction into his description of the dynamics of organization in *Complexity and Organizational Reality* (2010: 108 et seq.). In relation to first-order abstraction, he writes, "the conscious simplifying generalization of narrative does amount to abstracting from, that is, simplifying and generalizing, the detail of each uniquely experienced situation". He contrasts this with what he calls second-order abstraction. Here, he suggests, "we also frequently articulate generalizations/idealizations of the categories of experience as maps and models. . .". He sees abstraction as existing in a paradoxical relationship with our ongoing immersion in the "game" of everyday organizational life (to use Pierre Bourdieu's term). He goes on to say, "In our immersion . . . we are together meaningfully patterning our interactions by drawing upon both the first and second order abstractions which have evolved in our community and in so doing we are together changing the abstractions in our local interaction".

4 Fortun, M. and Bernstein, H.J. (1998) *Muddling Through*. Counterpoint.

5 "Hoodwinking logic" is a phrase that I first came across many years ago, in the poem, *Christmas Shopping*, by Louis MacNeice. He uses it to describe the tendency for goods to be priced at just below the relevant rounded-up figure – such as £199 rather than £200. Hoodwinking people into believing that they had secured more of a bargain than they had in reality. It seems to me to be an apt phrase to describe the tendency for organizational researchers to use overly precise numbers, in an effort to hoodwink clients into believing that their findings are more credible than they are in reality.

4

MASTERY, MYSTERY AND MUDDLING THROUGH

GETTING TO GRIPS WITH THE REAL-WORLD WIGGLINESS

A few years ago, I spoke briefly with a manager during the lunch break in a senior management conference. This followed a presentation by the Divisional MD, in which he had comprehensively overturned the performance projections that had been presented only a few minutes earlier by the local finance managers. This sudden about-turn had taken those present by surprise and sparked many such informal conversations during the break. I suggested to him that this latest intervention was just another example of the wiggly reality of everyday organizational life – both a product and producer of the ongoing messiness. And that, despite outward appearances, what he and his colleagues were actually doing was "muddling through".[1] By way of explanation and reassurance, I went on to say that we are *all* doing this. *All of the time*. It is the best that any of us can do, if we are to take seriously the complex and uncertain dynamics of organization – and of life more generally. Dynamics in which we are all participating, and to which we are all contributing through our actions, inactions, and interactions with everybody else. I was not meaning to suggest by this that managers were not applying themselves conscientiously and professionally to the challenges that they faced. Nor was I suggesting that they couldn't make a positive difference by their actions. Clearly, they could – and they did. Less still was I arguing that they should throw up their hands in despair. But I did remind him of what we'd discussed on a number of previous occasions: that is, that managers need to *pay attention to what they actually find themselves thinking, feeling, and doing in practice*, rather than being overly fixated by the formal structures, systems, and routines of organization.

Eighteen months on, I found myself at the University of Hertfordshire's Complexity and Management Conference, held each year at Roffey Park. That Saturday's programme was structured around inputs by Ralph Stacey, Chris Mowles, and Emma Crewe, as faculty members of the university's Doctor of Management (DMan) programme. The broad question that we were addressing was "Can leaders change organizational culture?" As usual, the semi-formal inputs were interlaced with small-group conversations around some of the themes that had emerged in the course of those 'presentations' and open-forum discussions. I would broadly express one such theme as, "What is it that those in leadership positions can do, if they can't change culture in the way that conventional management theory presumes that they can?". In response to this, I offered to initiate a small-group conversation based on the following proposition:

> 'Muddling through' is not something that managers do until they can find the optimum way to proceed. It's the very best that they can do.

Besides reprising my earlier, client-manager conversation, this also echoed similar sentiments expressed in a book that I'd recently come across by Braden Allenby and Daniel Sarewitz on "the techno-human condition". In it, they say,[2]

> importantly, muddling through is not a second-best process to be dropped when appropriate optimization techniques are developed: it is the best we can do.

An example of muddling through in action

Eventually, some ten of us settled down in a Roffey Park 'pod', to explore this notion of muddling through. At first, there was a mixture of agreement, curiosity, and some scepticism. Then, for 90 minutes or so, we enjoyed a rich conversation, which one of our number pointed out was itself an example of muddling through in action. By the end of the session, I think it is fair to say that the general proposition resonated strongly with most – if not all – of the participants.

A colleague from Norway spoke of how he'd had to cope (in a 'muddling through' sort of way) with the challenges presented by a particularly dangerous stretch of water off the Scottish coast, which he'd succeeded in navigating when sailing with some initially reluctant friends. He drew an analogy between this and the process of dealing with uncertainty and complexity in the day-to-day exigencies of organizational life. He also stressed what he saw as the critical importance that courage plays in this. Others discussed a variety of examples from their own experience as organizational practitioners of one kind or another, whether acting as in-house managers or external consultants. Despite some unease with the phrase itself, the general thrust of the discussion strongly supported the argument that muddling through accurately describes the essence of what managers do *in practice*. And that this is *all that they can do*, given the complex and uncertain nature of human interaction. At the same time, they acknowledged that those who pay deliberate attention to the quality of their own (and others') participation in that process are likely to become better able to muddle through in ways that facilitate more useful outcomes (however constructed). By "quality of participation" here, the general view was that this meant acting into the future with purpose and courage; and doing so skilfully. That is, as we'll discuss further in Chapter 6, applying practical judgement and other complexity-congruent capabilities in relation to one's own and others' actions as the future is emerging.

Finally, my point was acknowledged that, when outcomes are judged to be successful, it is always possible in retrospect to construct a rational (albeit fantasy-based) explanation of how such success was brought about. Indeed, given the established narrative, it is understandable why this might be a politically savvy thing to do. But we should not kid ourselves that this seemingly rational pathway through the real-world dynamics of organization would actually have worked in practice. Or that this offers the prospect of replacing muddling through with rational design and textbook management practices. We might be able to reverse-engineer technological products, processes, and systems to discover a replicable and ordered way forward (the "knowable"). But no such approach is possible when it comes to the complex social process of human interaction – however much advocates of mainstream management practice (and some complexity theorists) might suggest that it is. It's unknowable. Even though, as discussed in Chapter 2, everything appears obvious when you know the answer![3]

Managing in the real world

As we know, conventional management wisdom maintains that success arises from the disciplined application of structured methodologies that are supposedly evidence-based and politics-free. Approaches in which optimal decisions are translated seamlessly into step-wise implementation plans and programmes. From this standpoint, the management task is one of using what are seen as universally applicable models, tools, and techniques to deliver the sought-after outcomes with certainty, predictability and control (what I referred to in Chapter 3 as "Act 4 of Management"). However, given the complex social reality of everyday organizational life, this neatly packaged view of management practice bears little resemblance to managers' everyday lived experience, which is *unavoidably* messy and disjointed.

A more accurate and helpful way for managers to describe what they actually do *in practice*, therefore, is to acknowledge that they "muddle through". As Allenby and Sarewitz go on to say,[4]

> Progress, when it occurs, comes through trial and error, through learning what works in particular situations, through incremental change that incorporates such learning, and through the difficult process of political compromise that allows people to take the next step.

To reiterate, this is not a second-best response to the challenges that managers face. *It's the only thing that they can do.* As in all things, some will do this better than others. And everyone will do it better on some occasions than they do at other times. Doing it 'better' means managers paying deliberate attention to how they and others are participating, individually and collectively, in the *ongoing process* of organization. Acting forwards, moment-to-moment, into the continuously emerging and unknowable future, whilst striving to do so with *purpose*, *courage*, and *skill*. It also calls for perseverance, even when – *especially when* – well-intentioned actions fail to achieve the sought-after results. In a wiggly world, muddling through provides a reality-congruent response to the demands that this brings. It flows naturally from the unavoidable wiggliness of human interaction whilst, at the same time, contributing to it.

Seeking beauty in the 'ugly truth' of organization and management practice

In Chapter 2, I borrowed the phrase "The beautiful, ugly truth" from a leading article in the *New Scientist* magazine[5] to headline my explanation of the underlying dynamics of organization. The idea that people's everyday practice is characterized by muddling through sits uncomfortably with established thinking on how organization works, how performance is supposed to happen, and what managers are supposed to be doing. It seems to imply a lack of direction, confused thinking, and a haphazard approach. We are meant to be too knowledgeable and too sophisticated for this to be the case. Or, if we are not so ourselves, there are supposed to be others we can count on to lead us successfully through the mess, in a fully thought-through and methodical way. Without much – if any – critical thought, we tend to accept that things will turn out as planned. Provided, that is, that we (and/or those acting with us and for us) do things 'right'. We see this reflected in increasing calls for practice to be "evidence-based"; moves by representatives of professional bodies to standardize, prescribe, and certify all aspects of the roles of managers and other organizational specialists; the requirement for organization-related academic research to demonstrate a measurable benefit, if it is to be considered worthy of academic pursuit and to merit the label "research excellence"; the widespread application of ever-tighter, rule-based regulatory and reporting regimes, following high-profile incidents that occur in specific, local settings; the simplistic, "who is to blame?" framing of complex issues by media commentators and others, whenever outcomes fail to match the expectations of order, predictability and control; and so on.

Underlying assumptions

All of this presupposes, first of all, that the scientific method is capable of discovering universal, 'if you do this, you'll get that', truths about the world. Secondly, it takes for granted the idea that this same methodology can be applied to the complex social process of organization. This is not the case. Nor has it ever been. And, given the complexity and unknowability of everyday human interaction, out of which organization emerges, it never can be. Managers, development practitioners, policy-makers, and others therefore need to recognize and embrace the muddling-through nature of real-world management practice that flows from this. The words of poet John Keats, written in the early 1800s, capture the latter notion well. In coining the phrase "Negative Capability", he described this as, "when a man is capable of being in uncertainties, mysteries, doubts, without any irritable reaching after fact and reason".[6] Muddling through is precisely what we each do in practice, as we seek to find our way through the "uncertainties, mysteries, doubts" of everyday life, to which Keats alludes.

In Chapter 3, I referred to Fortun and Bernstein's critique of the application of science to human affairs. In their book, itself entitled *Muddling Through*, they set out to reposition our understanding of science and the scientific method in terms that are much more congruent with the wiggliness of the real world. And with the unavoidably human nature of those scientists and researchers who practise it. As they say,[7]

> we have to engage with the sciences as the kinds of activities they have always been, the *only* kind of activities they can be: muddling through.

In the same vein, we have to engage with organization and management as the kinds of activities they have always been, the *only* kind of activities they can be: muddling through.

Deliberately provocative

In many respects, the term "muddling through" might be considered to be an odd one to use in relation to management practice. I mentioned the initial unease of some people with the term in my earlier description of the Roffey Park discussion. In common usage it suggests a lackadaisical attitude to whatever's being done. That is clearly not what I'm suggesting here. In a similar vein, drawing on Lindblom's initial work on what he called "the science of muddling through", Stacey and Mowles disappointingly dismiss the term as a "kind of organised anarchy".[8] They describe it as "decision making without intention where outcomes arise by chance". This is wholly inconsistent with the idea and practice of muddling through that I'm describing here; most of which sits four-square with the dynamics of organization and management practice that they expertly set out in the rest of their writing.

Despite the potentially negative connotations of the words "muddling through" in common usage, I am deliberately sticking with the phrase. And, by way of provocation, doing so without, as Keats says, "any irritable reaching after fact and reason". I want to draw a stark contrast between what managers actually find themselves doing and experiencing every day, and the romanticized and heroic view of leadership and management practice that is central to most texts on the subject. As I said at the outset, my aim is to *provoke* people into thinking afresh about what it is they believe that they and others are doing *in practice*. That is, to "wake people up", as Picasso puts it. "Force them to understand that they're living in . . . a world that's not what they think it is".

Getting in a muddle over muddling through

With this in mind, I was intrigued by comments relating to muddling through in General Sir Richard Dannatt's autobiography.[9] In it, he is very dismissive of the practice. In essence, he sees it as incompatible with his notion of leadership. An approach that he considers to be "aimless". In his most damning comment, he uses the term to attack what he sees as an unwillingness of politicians to properly resource the tasks that it demands of the armed forces:[10]

> If you want to do it, you have to be prepared to pay for it – muddling through on the goodwill of our servicemen and women is immoral.

Strong stuff. Here, though, I think, we have a clue as to why he is so disdainful of the idea. It seems to me that he is using the term very much in an 'everyday' sense, in which, as I suggested above, it might well be taken to imply a lack of purpose coupled with muddled thinking. But, as

I've argued earlier, managers have *no option* but to muddle through. Striving to do so with purpose, courage, and skill is the *very best* that they can do.

So why is Sir Richard so derisive in his comments?

Early military experience

In his autobiography, he provides an interesting account of his distinguished army career, interwoven with aspects of his personal life. It covers the period from his first post-Sandhurst role in Northern Ireland in 1971, through to his retirement from the armed services, as Chief of the General Staff, in 2009/10. His formative experience in relation to his views on muddling through occurred in Belfast in 1972, in the aftermath of "Bloody Sunday". As a second lieutenant, he sought guidance from a visiting General on what to do in relation to a problem that they were facing between Catholics and Protestants in the area that they were patrolling. In response to his question about what they should do, Dannatt reports, the General, "put his arm on my shoulder and said: 'Well, Richard, we've got broad shoulders in the British Army – just muddle through!'". As he said, he learned a lesson from this, "which really shaped things for me later on". And so, on a number of other occasions in the book, he uses the term "muddling through" in a pejorative way. Saying, for example, that this is, "Something I have thoroughly disdained since Belfast in 1972". Or, "There must be a better way".

A "better way"?

So what is this "better way"? According to Sir Richard,[11]

> we need to divide our thinking into three levels, the strategic, the operational, and the tactical. It is at the strategic level where the big thoughts are thought, where the broad ideas are conceived, and it is at the tactical level where the rubber hits the road and bullets fly. However, it is the level in between that is so critical, for this is where ideas are turned into practicalities, where a plan is produced that transforms concepts into a series of steps that take you from thought to action.

All very neat – and un-muddled, of course!

Everyday lived reality

Despite this textbook recipe for success, the autobiography is replete with examples of General Dannatt's own muddling through *in practice* (in the sense that I am describing it here). These include those in his role as a commanding officer on the ground, in such places as Bosnia, Afghanistan, and Iraq; as well as his later challenges dealing with government ministers, Whitehall mandarins, and the press, when he was a service chief and then Chief of the General Staff. Given his descriptions of the military, political, economic, and social challenges that were coming at him from all angles, and his (sometimes frustrated but always purposeful) responses to these, he – like everyone else – had no option but to muddle through. That is, he was acting forwards, moment-to-moment, into a continuously emerging and unknowable future. And he was mostly doing so – or so it seems from the book – with purpose, courage, and skill. To conclude, he says tellingly at one point,[12]

> I suppose at the end of the day it is all about professional background and experience. I learnt a lot of theoretical stuff at Sandhurst about decision-making and leadership, but it is at the school of hard knocks in the operational field that a young platoon and company commander lays his foundations for high command. In difficult ground operations, among the civilian people you have gone to help and among your own soldiers who depend on you, there is no substitute for experience. Of course, no one has a monopoly of wisdom; but, at the top level, wisdom comes from practical, often harsh experience, not just from textbooks, military academies and the Staff College.

Exactly. In reality, Sir Richard – like managers everywhere – muddled through the situations he found himself facing, as the future emerged from his own and everyone else's participation in its co-creation.

A passionate 'muddler througher'

In contrast to General Dannatt's expressed disdain for the idea of muddling through, another ex-member of the UK military takes a different, more pragmatic view of his own and others' everyday practice. For many years, there was a weekly programme on BBC radio called *Paenar's Politics*, covering political matters of the day. In it, there was a section entitled "Backbenchers

Questions". The Backbenchers referred to here are those members of the UK parliament who neither hold office within the Government nor shadow those roles as members of the Official Opposition (the so-called "Frontbenchers"). On one such occasion, in April 2017, it was the turn of Conservative MP, Bob Stewart, to take the hot seat. In his earlier career, he had been a Colonel in the British Army.

At one point, the stand-in host for the day, Chris Mason, asked Stewart whether or not he was confident about the (then) forthcoming negotiations on the UK's exit from the European Union ("Brexit"). When his guest replied that, in the end, we always muddle through and get something, Mason challenged him as to whether muddling through was good enough. With a hint of incredulity in his voice that anyone should ask such a question, Stewart said, "That's what happens in life". And so it is. Muddling through is what happens in life. It's what all of us do. All of the time. Mason signed-off the section by describing Colonel Stewart as, "A passionate 'muddler througher'".

The conduct of war

To underline the fact that "mudding through is what happens in life", we can draw again on the organization of military affairs – typically held up as the epitome of order, structure, and control. In relation to the ongoing conduct of war, the US Marines document on warfighting describes the nature of what they call "maneuver warfare":[13]

> As part of our philosophy of command, we must recognize that war is inherently disorderly, uncertain, dynamic, and dominated by friction . . . For commanders to try to gain certainty as a basis for actions, maintain positive control of events at all times, or dictate events to fit their plans is to deny the nature of war. We must therefore be prepared to cope—even better, to thrive—in an environment of chaos, uncertainty, constant change, and friction.

Coming to terms with the complex and uncertain conditions of everyday practice, and seeking to limit the debilitating effects that these have as one finds one's way from one point to the next, is what muddling through with purpose, courage and skill all about. Whether we are talking about war, private enterprise, public and voluntary service, or life in general.

Interplay of intentions

Of course, as we go about our day-to-day lives, we don't just cross our fingers and hope. We think things through. We make plans. We use many of the existing structures, systems, rituals, and routines to give us a sense of order, predictability, and control. At least we do so some of the time. And for some of the time it 'works'. What we tend to forget is that other people are doing the same. They, like us, are acting into (and hence co-creating) the future that is emerging. And, like us, they're doing so according to *their own* interpretations; in pursuit of *their own* interests; guided by *their own* ideologies; and with all of the issues of identity and personal idiosyncrasies that come with being normal human beings. Also like us, what they find themselves doing is shaped by *their own* ongoing, in-the-moment interactions with other people. People, that is, who are similarly engaged in living *their own* lives. And so it goes on. . . .

Returning again to Fortun and Bernstein's take on this, they say,[14]

> Far from being indecisive, noncommittal, or blandly middle-of-the-road, muddling through is marked by perseverance: a dogged pursuit and relentless enactment of both pointed inquiry ("How do you know that?") and thoughtful social and political work ("Given *that*, let's try this . . ."). As a result, it does not imply muddle-headedness, but in fact the opposite.

As underlined here, this does not mean managers and others relying wholly on instinct. Though that plays a vital part. Nor is it about indecisiveness. Instead, it's about adopting a stance of flexible rigidity; remaining steadfast in pursuit of the broad direction of travel (for as long as it continues to make sense to do so) and, at the same time, being flexible and responsive to the practical realities of whatever emerges along the way. It is about constantly blending together the polar opposites of realism and reach.

Intellectual and emotional challenge

There remains the challenge of getting people to integrate these insights into their own practice – and way of life. On the one hand, since we are all walking case studies of these dynamics in action, we know that what's actually going on is far removed from the idealizations that dominate mainstream explanations and prescriptions. On the other hand, it might not seem immediately appealing to admit that we don't know what's actually going on. Nor what will emerge overall. It is politically much safer, and less anxiety-inducing, to go along with the myth. Or to couch it in less challenging terms, perhaps. For example, economist and *Financial Times* columnist, John Kay puts forward an argument for adopting a similarly "oblique" – i.e. indirect – approach to decision-making and practice. In his book, *Obliquity*,[15] he equates this to the idea of muddling through, which he bases on Lindblom's original, 1959 paper (see note 1) and a 1979 update.[16] In support of this, he has headed one chapter of the book, "Muddling through – why oblique approaches succeed". However, in referring to "the modesty of Lindblom's phrase", he argues that obliquity is the better term. I disagree. And, for the reasons outlined earlier, I'll stick with muddling through. Either way, Kay describes this as, "a process of experiment and discovery".

In adopting Lindblom's description of muddling through, if not its name, he states that this, "should not be equated with unstructured, 'intuitive' decision-making but rather be seen as a disciplined, ordered process". I share his view to the extent that, performed skilfully, muddling through is the antithesis of a 'just see how it goes' approach. At the same time, as discussed extensively in previous chapters, much of what is going on is necessarily informal, unstructured, uncertain, messy, and contentious. As such, managers (indeed, all of us) have no option but to muddle through life; even if they might be unaware that that is what they are doing. Or reluctant to say so, even when they're aware of it. This is about their imaginatively making do with whatever information and resources they are able to call upon – at that time, in that place, and in the specific circumstances in which they find themselves immersed. And the practical judgement that they apply will necessarily be infused with intuition and blend improvised actions with more structured responses. Most importantly, though, it is about their doing this with conscious awareness of the nature of their practice. Including having the courage to keep taking the next step – and mobilizing others to do the same – despite the fact that they can't predict with any degree of certainty what the combined effects of their own and other people's actions will be.

On ethics and muddling through

From a different angle altogether, Klaus Hoeyer and Anja M.B. Jensen, suggest that health professionals should embrace an "ethics of muddling through". As members of the Faculty of Health Science at the University of Copenhagen, they discuss the complex ethical considerations relating to organ donation. In a conference paper on the subject, they argue that this will enhance relevant reflections and stimulate a productive dialogue among health professionals.[17]

Reflecting on real-life situations rather than abstract principles

In pursuing their argument, they maintain that the moral problems in clinical decision-making relating to organ donation seem to be more akin to those of organizational decision-making in general. They say,

> Instead of assuming a moral 'evidence base', we might be of more help to health professionals by acknowledging the lack of universal norms and standard situations. A productive dialogue about the problems people actually handle must appreciate the basic ambiguities surrounding the situations doctors and nurses face as patients become donors. . . . *clinicians must reflect on real-life situations . . . rather than rest on presumptions about a point of total clarity at which the 'real' ethical decision was made* (my emphasis).

Hoeyer and Jensen sum-up by concluding that,

> the kind of dialogue that health professionals need is better facilitated by an ethics of muddling through – which does not presume clarity where there is none – than by a set of principles that they rarely get the chance to apply.

This is a situation in which "norms are constantly negotiated and challenged in the messy and complex context of everyday clinical decision making". For "clinical", as Hoever and Jensen themselves observe, we can readily substitute "organizational".

Although Doug Griffin doesn't describe management practice in terms of muddling through, Hoever and Jensen's comments strongly echo his position on the ethical dimension of the underlying dynamics of organization. For example, writing in relation to the global financial collapse and the ethics of those managers most directly involved, he says, "The ethical crisis is grounded in the way we have formalized ethics and divorced it from everyday life". He cites, in particular, the "reduction of ethics to universalist and principled thought before action", and the consequences that this has for leadership behaviour.[18] He goes on to suggest that an important factor in this is the taken-for-granted assumption – often stated explicitly in management writing and development programmes – that leadership is good in itself, rather than "ethically 'neutral'". That is, that it can in some way be separated from the everyday politics of organization, out of which it emerges. Instead, as he points out, leadership is recognized just as much by those involved in antisocial activities (such as terrorism, gang behaviour, and bullying, say) as it is in those settings that tend to feature in business best sellers and leadership texts. As such, he argues that we need to think about how these ethics are embedded in the everyday political negotiations of society, if we are going to make serious progress in relation to what he calls "the crisis of business ethics".

As we've discussed extensively, organization is a pattern-forming and pattern-using process. Within this, the tendency is for the existing patterning of interaction to be repeated and reinforced, even though expressed in subtly different ways. These subtle shifts occur as the generalized tendencies to think and act in certain ways are particularized in the moment and successively iterated. The ethical nature of people's behaviour is intimately and inextricably woven throughout this conversational process; emerging from the specifics of the current interaction and reflecting the individual and collective histories of those involved. This 'ethical thread' cannot be separated out. You can't 'do' ethics in the abstract. People's judgements of the rights and wrongs of particular courses of action (arrived at through this same conversational process!) are unavoidably partial and contested. Outcomes emerge, and come to be recognized as such, in the practical reality of people's ongoing being and doing – whether these are judged to be ethically sound, wholly unethical, or something in between.

Also writing on a medical theme, David Mechanic similarly recognizes the practical dilemmas arising in the rationing of medical services. As he notes, "Medicine is both a scientific activity and a cultural form. Most of the ways in which we ration care are invisible, obscured by cultural assumptions, political understandings, and economic realities".[19] In light of the "incredibly difficult" issues that this brings to the fore, he argues that it is better to proceed by honestly recognizing their complexity, the heterogeneity of patient populations, the imperfections of our tools, and the uncertainty of medical knowledge and treatment; maintaining that this requires "continuing engagement, flexibility, and humility". He argues that the fitting response in such circumstances is to, "muddle through, changing course as knowledge and experience guide us". Using a phrase borrowed from his colleague David Hunter, he concludes by suggesting, "If we are particularly thoughtful and lucky, perhaps we will be able to say that we have 'muddled through elegantly'". Whether elegant or not, muddling through provides an apt description of what those involved find themselves doing in practice, even where they have to find their way through the clinical challenges and ethical dilemmas that they face within the constraints of formally instituted policies and practices. As Mechanic also said, medical care is a process of discovery and negotiation, not simply the application of technical means. And so is management more generally.

Muddling through as the new politics

In the run-up to the UK 2015 General Election, as is ever the case, candidates of all parties were constantly asked by journalists and television interviewers to explain precisely what things would be like at the end of the five-year parliament, based on the pledges made in their party manifestos. In the main, they duly obliged (as politicians tend to do!). As things turned out, their inability to predict what would happen in the future was laid bare on election night itself. Politicians, pundits, and pollsters alike all expected the election to result in a so-called "hung parliament", with a coalition between the Labour and Liberal Democrat parties being the most likely means of forming a viable government. In the event, the Conservatives gained an overall majority and a triumphant David Cameron put together his government, with a seemingly unobstructed path ahead of him and his colleagues for the next five years. Barely one year later, the rest – like David Cameron's premiership – was history. In the ensuing five years, two further General Elections have been held; the UK has left the European Union; the Labour and Liberal Democrat Parties have each changed their leader more than once; and affairs have been turned on their head globally with the onset of the worldwide COVID-19 pandemic.

False concreteness

The issue here is not with the breaking of manifesto promises but with the making of them in the first place. The world is too complex, ambiguous, and uncertain to be dealt with in terms of abstract promises that are detached from the real-world demands of day-to-day governing. A sense of direction: yes. Supposedly cast-in-concrete commitments: no. Fitness to govern should carry with it acknowledgement of the ongoing state of not knowing – however inconvenient and humbling that might seem to be in the context of the dominant discourse that worships certainty, predictability, and control. Manifesto commitments and related pledges imply a 'false concreteness' to the governing (and living!) of everyday life that bears little relationship to the wiggly reality.

Reducing anxiety – but at what cost?

I would concede that glossy manifestos and the like can help to reduce people's anxiety, by providing a sense that 'those in the know', those formally in charge, are somehow 'in control' of events. The same can be said about strategic plans, annual reports and so on in a business context. However, like many other of the trappings of modern management, these distort and misrepresent the actuality of national (and corporate) governance. In reality, our understanding of virtually all of the issues of any significance in our lives is hazy at best. Our politicians and their advisers might be slightly better informed of the 'ins and outs' of some of the issues. At least we hope that they are. But that means that they should also be better informed about the uncertain, complex, and ambiguous nature of the issues with which they are grappling. Mismatches between one-time aspirations/expectations and the emergent reality is not a matter of incompetence – at least not usually or wholly so. It's a fact of life.

Co-creating the future

Filling a manifesto with unqualified policy commitments, promises, and pledges, and then using these as the basis for assessing the rightness or otherwise of the ongoing governance of the country, is nonsense. It ignores the contingent and interdependent nature of events across the world, and of the millions of local interactions from which these emerge. It perpetuates the myth that members of the government (of whatever political colour) are blessed with the ability to predict and control everything that happens 'on their watch' with accuracy and precision. In doing so, it also lets the rest of us off the hook, as regards the part that we unavoidably play in co-creating the future that emerges in practice.

Politicians don't determine the future, all of us do. And, at the same time, none of us do. It is therefore the Whys, Whats and Hows of this continuously emerging future with which we should be concerned. In a February 2014 article, *Financial Times* columnist Simon Kuper refers to the remarks of the University of Colorado's political scientist, Roger Pielke Jr.[20] He was commenting on one of the main political concerns of our time, climate change. As Pielke acknowledges, even climate change requires piecemeal solutions. This means trying out a range of potential initiatives and scaling-up those that look promising, rather than spending time in trying to develop grand solutions underpinned by some kind of global treaty. As Kuper observes, if we are to embrace this reality, we need a new approach to politics based on muddling through, rather than pursuing the fantasy of all-encompassing, once-and-for-all answers. Kuper is talking here about politics with a big 'P'. But the dynamics – and argument – apply equally well to the everyday politics of organizational life.

Bricolage

Muddling through, in the way that I'm describing it here, has strong resonance with the notion of bricolage. This is a French term, which means using whatever knowledge, skills, and resources one has available, to perform the particular tasks and demands one faces at that time. In the context of organization, Peter Stokes suggests that the word bricolage,[21]

> tends to be employed to portray, for example, a phenomenon, objects, elements, events or sets of issues that are pulled together in a manner that is diverse, improvised, experimental, and borrowed from a range of sources and places. It represents the creation or development of an argument, model, concept and/or understanding from an idiosyncratic collection of things – whatever is in hand is brought into play.

In relation to international development, Frances Cleaver argues that bricolage is "a sort of institutional 'do-it-yourself' . . . rather than the more explicitly conscious and rational form of institutional engineering or design".[22] As Yiannis Gabriel also observes, "bricolage is opportunistic, ad hoc, devious, creative and original, constantly re-defining tools into materials and materials into tools, while, at the same time, re-defining the task at hand in the light of the meanings attributed to the available resources".[23] This theme is further echoed by Frank Barrett, who uses jazz as his primary metaphor for thinking about the dynamics of organization:[24]

> many jobs in organizations . . . require bricolage – fumbling around, experimenting, and patching together an understanding of problems from bits and pieces of experience, improvising with the materials at hand. Few problems provide their own definitive solutions.

As he goes on to say, many organizational tasks frequently require people to,

> apply their own resourcefulness, cleverness, and pragmatism. They play with various possibilities, recombining and reorganizing, to find solutions by relating the dilemma they face to the familiar context that preceded it.

The ideas of resourcefulness, cleverness, and pragmatism fit well with the notion of muddling through, as I am describing it here, although I might be tempted to use the term "practical wisdom", rather than "cleverness". Also, drawing on Gabriel (above), Keith Grint similarly makes a link between the two themes in his discussion of so-called "wicked problems".[25] That is, problems which demand what he calls, "clumsy solutions". Bricolage, he observes, is about,[26]

> mak(ing) progress by stitching together whatever is at hand, whatever needs to be stitched together, to ensure practical success. This is not, then, the clean world of analytic models and rational plans for progress to perfection . . . The assumption that wise leadership can be reduced to this might strike the reader as rather inglorious, even mundane, a reflection also captured in Lindblom's ground-breaking claim in 1959 that most decision-making mechanisms were little more than 'muddling through'.

Finally, here, Karl Weick[27] underscores the critical point that bricolage is not a random exercise. He argues that the improvisation of new arrangements – through generalization, analogy, comparison and the like – calls on practitioners to have an intimate knowledge of available resources; carefully observe what is going on; trust in their intuitions; listen to others' views and perspectives; and recognize that whatever is formally adopted will continue to be adapted informally through people's ongoing practice.

Muddling through as a natural way of being and doing, not a design choice

The notion and practice of bricolage highlights many of the practical aspects of muddling through *skilfully*. However, this term is meant to describe an approach that managers might deliberately adopt, in the context of specific organizational tasks and challenges (as in Grint's formulation above, for example). In contrast, I'm arguing that muddling through is descriptive of what *everyone is doing, all of the time* – whether skilfully or not. That is to say, no one can choose whether or not to muddle through, any more than they can decide whether or not they want the world to be wiggly. It just *is* wiggly. And they *have no option* but to muddle through whatever they find themselves facing.

The challenge for everyone then becomes one of striving to do this as best they can, in the particular circumstances in which they find themselves at each specific moment. This means emulating the bricoleur, in seeking to match whatever knowledge, ideas, and resources happen to be available at that time to the diverse mix of constantly shifting demands. Doing this flexibly, creatively, and opportunistically. At times, based on the experience and practical judgement of those involved, those who are muddling through might draw on aspects of highly structured, procedurally straightforward, and scientifically rational approaches to particular issues, problems or situations. However, managers rarely if ever find themselves dealing solely with isolated, well-defined, and neatly compartmentalized issues. Issues that can be attended to one at a time, in a precisely prescribed, step-by-step way, using an unlimited and dedicated supply of resources. Nor is their attention likely to be confined to the single-minded search for a solution to a particular problem, whether "wicked" or otherwise.

They are always embroiled in an ill-defined set of issues and challenges. And these are never limited by the boundaries implied by their formally stated roles and responsibilities in a particular work context. Nor are their responses limited by the supposedly 'right way' to approach a particular issue.

Mainstream models and methods in muddling through

So where and how do mainstream models and methods fit in to the notion of muddling through?

In the early 1980s, I was responsible for resource planning, work management and budgetary control in a UK power plant. At the time, the power station was part of the portfolio of plants that formed what was then the Midlands Region of the publicly-owned Central Electricity Generating Board (CEGB). Managers in the Midlands Region saw themselves as being in the vanguard of continuing efforts to improve the commercial performance of the business, at a time when the privatisation of the industry and the need for rival companies to compete for business was no more than a glint in Margaret Thatcher's eye. As part of this, senior managers decided to explore the possibility of using Zero-Base Budgeting (ZBB) to determine and manage the budgets of the region's central departments. The manager of the local plant where I worked took an equally enlightened view of business. As he was continually looking for ways to improve the commercial management of the business, he immediately saw the possibility of applying the ZBB approach to the management of the station's activities and investments. Although this had not been part of the Regional Managers' plans, he nevertheless decided to apply its principles and practices during the forthcoming budgetary round. It fell on me to design the specific approach that we would use, and to orchestrate the resulting process.

The essence of ZBB is that budgets are considered afresh each year, rather than taking the previous year's budget as the starting point (hence "zero base"). This meant that managers had to justify each item of spend from scratch. To facilitate this, we developed forms that could be used to clarify proposed investments, and which could subsequently be used to score and rank the various proposals. When this had been done, the plant manager and I sat down and agreed the target level of aggregate spend that would align with our overall commercial objectives. We then "drew the line" at that figure. Our starting point was that any proposals which fell below that line would not be funded – unless compensating reductions could subsequently be found in those above-the-line activities that had won through this initial pass. At that stage, many prized activities were at risk of being rejected. And my colleagues were not slow to let me know what they thought of this new process! One in particular was distraught that what he considered to be essential maintenance work on a key item of plant would not be funded. "The process", he said, "Is rubbish. We've gone back years". He was so upset that his usually mild manner was replaced by strongly expressed(!) anger and a threat that he would refuse to attend the meeting of the senior management team that had been arranged to review the output and agree the final budget. I counselled him not to worry and to stick with the process. "There is no way", I assured him, "That this work will fall through the net when we sit around the table and talk. Everyone will insist that it's included; not just you. The only task then will be for us . . . together . . . to identify some other, currently funded work that can be dropped to make way for it." He was not reassured by this response! But he did turn up to the subsequent management meeting.

From my perspective, the pivotal part of the process was never going to be the formal ranking of proposed spend, using pseudo-scientific measures of worth. Its value would always depend on the quality and depth of the conversation that the initial listing provoked. In fact, I had originally suggested to the plant manager – only half-jokingly – that I would have been happy to have compiled the preliminary listing by drawing the proposals out of a hat! It would certainly have saved time to have done so! But, in an industry based on technical precision and (outwardly) rational decision-making, something was required which at least had face validity with engineers and other professionals. The ranking forms satisfied that need. And so, it was this formally ranked list that provided the starting point for our dialogue. As the meeting continued over several hours, the power of ordinary conversation to shape outcomes became increasingly evident. Importantly, of course, it wasn't only the technicalities of plant management, operation and maintenance that were 'in play'. So were the power relationships, interests, and identities of everyone around the table. Sometimes these were openly on display; at other times they were operating 'silently' (but nonetheless influentially) in the shadows. As revisions were made to the original list of planned activities and investments, these changes were affected by – and at the same time affected – the power relations, interests, and identities, etc. of those doing the changing.

When the time came to consider the fate of the 'rejected' item of maintenance work which had earlier provoked such rancour, there was universal acceptance of the need for it to be carried out. And, when looking for potential savings to accommodate its inclusion, one of the most dominant voices in the room was subdued by the combined force of his colleagues. The senior operations engineers argued that his annual investment in the overhaul of a particular item of plant added little to overall operational performance. He was stunned by this revelation. The latter planned maintenance was therefore eliminated from the list and funding released. At the same time, the previously omitted work was reinstated to a position well above the cut-off line. As we left site that evening, I walked to the car park with the manager who had earlier berated me about the worthlessness of the process. Now I couldn't shut him up about how wonderful it had all been. It wasn't the technicalities of the ZBB process that had restored his faith. Rather it was the opportunity that this created for meaningful dialogue to take place around issues that mattered to him and to the others involved. By "dialogue" here, I'm not suggesting that we used a formally structured approach to achieve "good" conversation. I'm simply pointing to the power of ordinary, everyday conversation to enable people to make individual and collective sense of issues and events; challenge their own and others' assumptions; and decide how they are going to go on together in the anything-but-straightforward world of organizational management. In short, by drawing on the practical judgement of those directly involved – and exploring differences 'warts and all' – we muddled through to what those involved agreed was a very satisfactory outcome.

Starting from where people 'are'

So what part did the analysis and ranking process play in this? As I suggested earlier, in the context of the technical world of power generation, the techno-rational nature of the assessment process provided face validity for the initial work involved and the preliminary ranking. This was a case of 'starting from where people are', so to speak, rather than assuming that they can readily abandon years of schooling in the importance of achieving order by design. It made sense to start from this position, before opening up a different 'interactional pathway' that they might usefully follow instead. Whilst helping to establish rapport, this can also reduce the anxiety that naturally arises from a perceived lack of structure and sense of not knowing. The desire to reduce anxiety is a common factor in the tendency for managers to default to prescriptive methods and models; rather than engaging directly with what they find themselves facing in practice. As part of my own consulting, I often introduce what I call sense-making frameworks (as opposed to prescriptive models) to bridge this gap between the 'shoulds' of management orthodoxy and experienced reality. In doing so, I want to encourage and facilitate a shift towards more spontaneous, participative and meaningful conversation, whilst still acknowledging the pull towards structure and the containment of anxiety. As in the ZBB process above, though, it is the nature and substance of the resulting conversations that matter, not the frameworks.

Power relations and the everyday politics of organization

Whilst reducing anxiety is one of the main reasons why managers tend to succumb to the 'do this and you'll get that' promises of mainstream management, there are others. Most particularly, as suggested in the ZBB story, the dynamics of power and politics are always in play. Given the taken-for-granted assumption that managers should know – and be able to control – everything that's going on 'under their watch', it is unsurprising that they might sign-up to measures and methodologies that promise to deliver an ordered, positive, and predictable future. Doing so even though such theories and prescriptions often bear little direct relationship to their everyday lived reality. As illustrated in Act 2 of the Five Acts of Management (Chapter 3), managers use established theories, post-event, to provide what they consider to be a rational, 'managerially correct' and politically acceptable explanation of their (muddling through) actions. This serves to cover over the messy reality of everyday human interaction with accounts that preserve the collective illusion of scientific rationality, predictability, and control. Importantly, too, it also adds legitimacy and authority to the role as popularly conceived, by drawing on claims of evidence-based validity for what they're doing and locating the actions of individual managers within a wider community of practice. Many managers will see this political act of 'getting their story straight' as an important ritual for them to perform, if they want to remain part of the managerial in-group – whether for reasons of power and influence, reward and recognition, career advancement, social inclusion or whatever. Others, of course, might not be consciously aware that they are doing anything other than reporting what actually happened.

Beyond this retrospective accounting for their actions, though, acting politically in the broadest sense is a crucially important aspect of management and leadership practice. This is about using power ethically, in search of organization-enhancing ways through the diverse, ill-structured, and often competing range of interpretations, interests, intentions, ideologies, and identities, etc. that determine what actually happens. Together with the related challenge of building coalitions of support for particular ways forward, this takes the notion and practice of muddling through beyond the 'mechanics' of bricolage into the hidden, messy, and informal dynamics of everyday human interaction.

Pragmatism and heuristics

Against this background, managers can – and do – find practical value in many of the ideas, models, and approaches that they come across in their work and elsewhere. Although, not always in the ways in which their originators intended. As mentioned earlier, all models are abstractions (what Stacey calls second-order abstractions[28]) from the complex social dynamics of organization. That is to say, they are all wrong. At the same time, provided that they are not taken to be absolute representations of what's going on, but rather used heuristically and pragmatically, they (or aspects of them) might provide stepping-stones to a way forward in a particular circumstance. From a muddling through perspective, it is more important for an idea to be useful in the moment of need than to be 'right', in an absolute sense. Although knowing the difference is important. In this regard, too many theories and prescriptions on organization and management are presented as absolute truths, rather than as rules of thumb or "proto-truths", as Edward de Bono usefully describes them.[29] That is, as temporary or contingent truths that we make use of until something better and more useful comes along.

In his very interesting and insightful paper on how organizational theories are used in practice,[30] Gabriel talks of these as recipes that "sophisticated consumers" see as inviting "improvisation and elaboration rather than copying and imitation". These provide "flexible routines" rather than, as is assumed in the established discourse, programmes or blueprints for stepwise actions (recall the commentary on Act 4 of Management in Chapter 3). He calls these "paragrammes". These he summarizes as, "basic stocks of ideas, routines, images and ingredients which may be selectively trawled, lifted and adapted to the situation at hand". This is, he says,

> the enemy of perfectionism or optimization, in every way, and the champions of 'good enough' pragmatism. Good and bad theories can become useful, once framed in a suitable way, just as 'beautiful' and 'grotesque' objects can become features of aesthetic display, once suitably crafted.

Peter Vaill makes the same general point in his coruscating attack on attempts to reduce the act of managing to a list of competencies. Referring to what he describes as a manager's (or other actor's) "practice theory", he suggests that this is, "a personal theory guiding his (sic) practice, bearing some relation to public, objective theories about organizational situations, but in no sense identical with them".[31] I agree with his further comment that "There is far more wisdom in practice theories than academic theory has yet begun to tap". In other words, as I've argued throughout, the challenge for managers is not one of 'correcting' their everyday practice, so that this more closely matches some theoretical optimum. Rather it is to reflect on and exploit their own and others' *practical* wisdom, to make best use of whatever knowledge, ideas, and resources happen to be available – at that specific time and in those particular circumstances.

Lost in translation – the importance of context

At one point, Gabriel talks in terms of *translating* ideas from one context to another. In his case, he's talking about organizational theories. In a similar vein, we can look at the ways in which official policy positions are taken up in practice. In earlier chapters I have described the ways in which managers try to stabilize the inherent wiggliness of human interaction by designing idealized organizational forms and setting out what they judge to be robust policy positions. Crucially, though, the ways in which the various design elements and ensuing policies are taken up in practice will vary significantly from context to context. And necessarily so. By definition, the principles underpinning the design, and the formally adopted policies relating to the various aspects of organization and management, are intended to be generalizable organization-wide. This is meant to be the case whether these have been arrived at by innovative design or by the cloning of what are considered to be the best examples of successful practice from elsewhere (so-called "best practice"). However, despite the apparent desire for consistency, the way in which such design principles and policy positions are taken up 'for real' is always people- and context-specific. This therefore differs from setting to setting. The ways in which those involved perceive, interpret, evaluate, and carry out the formally endorsed requirements is through the patterning of their own, local interactions and in relation to other factors particular to their own circumstances.

Clarke *et al*, similarly talk of this as an active process of "translation", rather than the passive enactment of a pre-ordained position:[32]

> When policy moves, it is always *translated*: that is, it is made to mean something in its new context. Policy is never a singular entity: it is put together – or assembled – from a variety of elements that are also in the process of being reassembled in new, often surprising ways.

This notion of the ongoing reassembly of elements in new and surprising ways echoes the earlier comments on bricolage. And, as they go on to say,[33]

> As [policy] moves from one place to another, from one site to another, from one level to another, it is revised, inflected, appropriated and bent in encounters of different kinds . . . policy is always subject to revisions and inflections, which opens up a politics of translation in which there are always possibilities at stake. Policy, then, is *necessarily unfinished* (my emphasis).

This accords fully with the muddling-through nature of organizational practice that I am setting out here. Principles, policies, and procedures that are introduced formally only exist to the extent, and in the ways, that these are taken up by people in their current (inter)actions. They then remain part of the conversational mix, in the form of 'imprints' of those past conversations (both formal and informal) in which they were initially conceived; developed into formal propositions; formally adopted and disseminated as policy; encountered, accepted, rejected, modified, and engaged with (or not) by others; and so on. As with all other aspects of organization, *de facto* policy continuously (re-)emerges in the ongoing process of conversational interaction.

Reframing management as muddling through

Drawing all of this together, muddling through can be thought of as the 'action thread' through which people stitch together the disparate and constantly shifting – that is, wiggly – demands of organization. In doing so, they arrive at what they judge to be a practical way forward – for better or worse. A way forward that is both a response to the wiggliness and a contributor to it. This embraces both in-the-moment improvisations and habitual responses, as well as thought-through but nevertheless tentative and provisional judgements that reflect the socially complex, uncertain and paradoxical nature of organization – and life more generally.

When I'm speaking to managers for the first time about these dynamics (in the way set out in Chapter 1, for example), many respond with a mixture of surprise, reassurance and, in some respects, discomfort. Surprise, because it goes against most of what they have been brought up to believe about organization and management practice. Reassurance, because it describes their everyday lived experience of what's actually going on. And various levels of discomfort because of the challenges it presents to their ongoing practice. Central to this is the recognition that they are both 'in control' (i.e. formally in charge and having the authority to command certain things to happen) and, *at the same time*, not in control of large swathes of what's going on in and around their practice. More often than not, this realization is accompanied by an intervention from one or more of those present along the lines of, "Even though we can't control these things, we can influence what's going on". Which, of course, they can. And they do – whether intentionally or otherwise. Power relations are often heavily weighted in managers' favour, in terms of the formally prescribed roles and relationships. Nevertheless, they are participants in – not controllers of – the process of conversational interaction through which organization is being continuously (re-)enacted and outcomes are emerging moment to moment.

Being both 'in control' (i.e. in charge) and 'not in control' at the same time is a fundamental paradox of management practice. Given the taken-for-granted view that being in control is what managing and leading are all about, realizing that this is only true to a limited extent can be disconcerting. In most cases, though, this initial feeling of discomfort is supplanted by one of relief. This more reality-congruent understanding of organizational dynamics validates what they know intuitively and provides assurance that how they find themselves operating in practice actually makes sense. It legitimizes their lived experience and gives them the language to talk about this in a more meaningful way. When managers are given the opportunity to confront the established discourse, there is widespread acceptance that neither they nor anyone else can control the shadow conversational themes and characteristic patterning of interaction that are organizing people's ongoing participation. Nor can they control the emotions, attitudes and behaviours that accompany them. Even less so can they determine the outcomes that will emerge from the complex interplay of these dynamics. So, whilst their role places them in charge of certain aspects of organization, they are not in control of what happens overall. It's wiggly. And they muddle through.

In my conversations with managers, few see this as a counsel of despair. Or take it as an excuse for inaction. On the contrary, they recognize that their contribution, individually and collectively, remains as crucial as ever to what happens in practice. Arguably more so. At the same time, they come to see this contribution differently. In particular, as I point out in *Informal Coalitions*, for managers, talk is action. Or, to put it another way, the conversations *are* the work. The challenge then becomes one of deciding how best they might participate more usefully in this process; leading and managing with the intention (though still not the certainty) of bringing about beneficial changes in activities, capabilities, and performance *that otherwise might not occur.*

In practice . . .

So how does all of this translate into managers' day-to-day practice? How can they set out to participate more usefully in the ongoing process of organization? And what shifts in practice might be implied by my contention that they need to strive to do this with purpose, courage, and skill? We'll look at the implications of this in detail in Chapter 6. For now, I just want to put a few stakes in the ground as regards the centrality of purpose, courage, and skill in practising muddling through as a conscious act of management.

Purpose

Muddling through with *purpose* underscores the no-nonsense nature of what I'm talking about here. It emphasizes that this is not about aimless meandering and passive acceptance of whatever happens to be going on. That is to say, it is not about simply muddling *along*. It is also the antithesis of muddle headedness. Instead, it's about muddling *through*. This points to managers' deliberate (on purpose), determined (purposeful), and contingently useful (purposive) engagement in the ongoing process of human interaction that we think of as the organization.

Muddling through with purpose also means pursuing a broad sense of direction, rather than a precisely defined destination. It is about managers acting into the future whilst stimulating, and engaging in, ongoing conversations about why they and others are doing what they are doing, and how they are doing it; as well as 'why, what, and how' they might usefully do things differently. The aim of this is not to produce a detailed plan or blueprint for the future. Instead, it's about encouraging, assisting, and enabling people to become so immersed in this conversational process that, when the 'real world' happens – *as the result of their own and everyone else's participation in it* – they might be better placed to deal with whatever emerges.

The challenge then becomes one of consciously setting out to find their way through the issues and events that actually arise; not those that were supposed to have arisen according to the assumptions contained in formal plans, programmes and other prescriptions. As regards their own aspirations, this is about dealing with the aforementioned tensions that exist between realism and reach. Muddling through with purpose also means their acknowledging that, despite acting with a sense of personal intent, neither they nor anyone else can predict or control what will actually happen in the specifics of their ongoing interactions with others. Such "others" include current 'in-house' participants; those from the past, whose influence lives on in the ways that I've described earlier; and people operating 'outside' the notional organizational boundaries.

Courage

As regards muddling through with *courage*, I agree with Stacey and Mowles, when they say that "the distinguishing feature of management is not control but courage to carry on creatively *despite not knowing* . . ."[34] (my emphasis). As social entrepreneur, Jonah Sachs, also points out, "While many pathways are open to us when we decide to break our old thinking patterns, we can't take the first step down any of them without the foundation of courage".[35] In this regard, I recognize that for managers to challenge the established discourse on organization and management practice – seeing organization as wiggly and their management task as one of muddling through – can itself require an act of courage. The felt need to conform to this idealized view of organization and management practice can evoke powerful feelings. As Mowles observes, even those who were past critics of it can find themselves needing to be seen to 'play the game', as they progress through the ranks:[36]

> To find ways of openly opposing what is going on then requires a good deal of courage potentially to jeopardise one's stake in the game.

Skill

Muddling through with *skill* is about managers and others applying their practical judgement and participating creatively in the specific conditions that they find themselves experiencing in the moment. It's here, in the everyday reality of their own and others' ongoing interactions, that managers can strive to make a difference – using formal and informal interactions, joint sense-making conversations, cultural insights, political acumen, and so on, in an effort to shift their own and others' practice in ways that they judge to be both organizationally beneficial and ethically sound. The focus is on what is emerging within people's ongoing interactions; the habitual and contingent themes that are organizing these conversations; and how the manager is participating in them. It's here, too, in the specific local context, that managers can research and develop their own and others' practice *in the midst of their ongoing interactions* – seeking to draw out and test the contextual factors, dominant conversational themes, prevalent behavioural patterns (both characteristic and unexpected), governing assumptions, and so on. It is these continuously emerging aspects of everyday organization:

- that are organizing people's interactions, and enabling and constraining their ongoing practice;
- out of which local and more widespread 'outcomes' are continuously co-created; and
- which point to potentially beneficial shifts that might be made in people's current sense-making-cum-action-taking interactions – both their own and other people's.

This recognizes that all that anyone can ever do is to *act into the future as it is emerging* – facilitated by a reflective and reflexive approach to their own individual and collective practice. As Douglas Board and Rob Warwick conclude in their discussion of the social development of leadership and knowledge,[37]

> Developing the practice of leadership needs to be done within the experience of practice. Abstract ideas of leadership traits, models and stories of great people have their place, but these are secondary to what people do in the dilemmas that they face as they work within a context that deeply matters to them.

To do so requires the application of what Stacey[38] calls "practical judgement" or others (such as Grint,[39] 2007, and Bent Flyvbjerg *et al*,[40] 2012) call "practical wisdom", after Aristotle's notion of phronesis.

In endorsing the practice of muddling through,[41] James C. Scott characterizes such practical skills "that underwrite any complex activity"[42] as know-how, common sense, experience, a knack, or metis.[43] As he goes on to say,[44]

> Any experienced practitioner of a skill or craft will develop a large repertoire of moves, visual judgements, a sense of touch, or a discriminating gestalt for assessing the work as well as a range of accurate intuitions born of experience *that defy being communicated apart from practice* (my emphasis).

Griffin similarly finds knack to be

> a useful concept in pointing to the local and emergent character of what we have come to understand as skills. It draws attention to the fact what we have come to locate as a skill in individuals actually only exists and changes in the social interaction.[45]

As suggested above, this is not about acquiring and deploying a particular set of 'muddling-through-type' competencies. That is, a generic list of skills that can be defined, taught, and assessed in the matter-of-fact way that informs much of the literature and practice relating to management and leadership development, 360° feedback assessments, and so on. As Vaill argues forcefully, in his attack on the idea of having sets of defined competencies, "You *can't* split consciousness and action" (italics in original) "the practice of these actions involves changes in values, shifts in the focus of one's attention, re-inspection of one's past experience with people". We are, as he says, "messing with [people's] heads as well as their 'hands', as it were".[46]

Mastery, mystery, and muddling through

To conclude, Vaill describes a whole chapter in one of his books as, "a contribution to 'muddling through' in the world of permanent white water". "Why", he asks, "In the face of all this [rationalistic analysis, design and control of human systems] do those living in the midst of these systems, including managers, continue to find them mysterious, recalcitrant, intractable, unpredictable, paradoxical, absurd, and – unless it's your own ox getting gored – funny?" This is, he says, the "grand paradox of management".[47]

Stacey expresses similar frustration and incredulity in his response to the financial meltdown of 2008.[48] As he points out, the world's major financial institutions, commercial organizations and public policy bodies are peopled by scores of MBA graduates, advised by the world's foremost consultancies, and informed by millions of research papers, books and journals on business and organizational performance. Despite this, the global economy plunged into a crisis that nobody planned, few predicted and none of these 'highly tuned' organizations was able to control. How could this be? And, equally significantly, how is it that – at least until the COVID pandemic – most things continued largely 'as normal' in the face of these high-level failures? The fundamental question that he raises in response to this is to ask why we continue to talk, explain and prescribe on an intellectual basis which runs completely counter to our experience. Why indeed! Vaill further argues that leading and working with people in purposeful situations requires a greater sense of the interplay between each individual's "specialness and [their] commonness".[49] However, when we set out to weave the net of management orthodoxy, as I described it in Chapter 1, we default to this "commonness" dimension and tend to ignore or deny the specialness of human being.

In this regard, as Robert Louis Flood says in relation to complexity,[50]

> Balancing mystery with mastery means living somewhere between the hopelessness of the belief that we are unable to understand anything and, at the other extreme, the naivety of the belief that we can know everything. Human beings in this way know of and learn within the unknowable.

If we are to take complexity seriously, then, we need to recognize that muddling through is not a second-best option; devoid of the intentionality, insights and inspiration that 'proper management' and textbook leadership practice are supposed to bring to the fore. It is the *only* thing that we can do. And, pursued with purpose, courage, and skill, it is the *very best* that we can do. It is through the coming together of people's differing intentions, interpretations, interests, ideologies, identities, idiosyncrasies, and so on, that whatever happens, happens. In other words, through the playing out of the ordinary politics of everyday life, in which we are all, inextricably involved. Finding our way through this real-world wiggliness and unknowability – "balancing mystery with mastery", as Flood puts it – is what muddling through is all about. It's what we all do. And it's time we owned up to it!

Notes

1 American Professor of Politics and Economics Charles E. Lindblom used this term in his 1959 paper on approaches to public policy-making: *The Science of "Muddling Through"*. In it, he advocated what he described as an incremental approach of "Successive Limited Comparisons" in contrast to the "Rational-Comprehensive" perspective, which reflected the dominant view. There are some parallels between what Lindblom is saying and the thrust of the points I'm making here. However, I'm suggesting that "muddling through" is *what managers do anyway* – regardless of what they might set out to do, or what they think that they are doing when they adopt what Lindblom describes as the "rational-comprehensive" tools of conventional management practice. As argued in Chapter 3, I also see muddling through (and organizational dynamics in general) as a complex social process, rather than as a science of any kind.

2 Allenby, B. and Sarewitz, D. (2013: 110) *The Techno-Human Condition*. MIT Press.

3 Watts, D. (2012) *Everything is Obvious – Once You Know the Answer*. Atlantic Books.

4 Allenby, B. and Sarewitz, D. ibid: 92–93.

What I'm arguing here is that muddling through is what managers do in practice, even when the accompanying narrative suggests otherwise. That is to say, it is descriptive of what's actually going on – whether done well or badly. Allenby and Sarewitz talk about it instead as a prescription for managers to follow, if they are to deal effectively with the complexities arising from what they describe as the techno-human condition.

5 *New Scientist* magazine (28 June 2014).

6 Li, O (2009) *Keats and Negative Capability*. Continuum International Publishing Group.

7 Fortun, M. and Bernstein, H.J. *Muddling Through* (1998: x) Counterpoint.

8 Stacey, R.D. and Mowles, C. (2016: 155) *Strategic Management and Organisational Dynamics 7Ed*. Pearson.

9 Dannatt, R. (2011) *Leading from the Front*. Corgi.
10 Dannatt, R. ibid: 139.
11 Dannatt, R. ibid: 169.
12 Dannatt, R. ibid: 314.
13 US Marine Corps (1997; Ch.4: 11–12) *Warfighting*. Marine Corps Doctrinal Publication 1.
14 Fortun, M. and Bernstein, H.J. (ibid: xvi).
15 Kay, J. (2010) *Obliquity*. Profile Books.
16 Lindblom, C.F. (1979) Still Muddling, Not Yet Through. *Public Administration Review*, Nov–Dec 1979, pp. 517–526.
17 Hoeyer, K. and Anja M.B. Jensen (2011) Organ Donation and the Ethics of Muddling Through, *Crit Care*,15(109). https://doi.org/10.1186/cc9379
18 Griffin, D. (2010) *Speaking of Managers and Leaders being Ruthless: The Deepening Crisis of Everyday Ethics in Business* in Complexity and Management blog: https://complexityandmanagement.com/2010/04/15/speaking-of-managers-and-leaders-being-ruthless-the-ongoing-crisis-of-everyday-ethics-in-business-2/
19 Mechanic, D. (1997) Muddling Through Elegantly: Finding the Proper Balance in Rationing. *Health Affairs*, 16(5): 83–92.
20 Kuper, S. (2014) *'Muddling Through' is the New Politics*. FT Magazine.
21 Stokes, P. (2011: 15) *Critical Concepts in Management and Organization Studies*. Palgrave.
22 Cleaver, F. (2012: 44) *Development Through Bricolage*. Routledge.
23 Gabriel, Y. (2002) Essai: On Paragrammatic Uses of Organizational Theory – A Provocation. *Organization Studies*, 23(1), 133–151, p.139.
24 Barrett, F. (2012: 27) *Yes To The Mess*. HBR Press.
25 The term "wicked problem" was coined by professors Horst Rittel and Melvin Webber in 1973, in their paper *Dilemmas in a General Theory of Planning* (Policy Sciences 4, 1973: 155–169). At the time, their focus was on social planning and policy-making. They contrasted this with the notion of a "tame problem", which was amenable to scientific analysis and had a definite solution. This mirrors the distinction I made, in Chapter 1, between unknowable and knowable aspects of organization and management practice.
26 Grint, K. (2008) *Wicked Problems and Clumsy Solutions: the Role of Leadership* Clinical Leader, 1(2), December, BAMM Publications.

27 Weick, K.E. (2001) *Making Sense of the Organization*. Blackwell Business.
28 Stacey, R.D. (2009) *Complexity and Organizational Reality*. Routledge; Stacey, R.D. and Mowles, C. (2016) *Strategic Management and Organisational Dynamics, 7Ed.* Pearson Education. See also note 4 in Chapter 3.
29 De Bono, E. (1977) *The Happiness Purpose*. Penguin.
30 Gabriel, Y. (2002: 143–145).
31 Vaill, P.B. (1989: 35) *Managing as a Performing Art*. Jossey-Bass.
32 Clarke, J. *et al* (2015:9) *Making Policy Move*. Policy Press.
33 Clarke, J. *et al* ibid:15–16.
34 Stacey, R.D. and Mowles, C. (2016: 507).
35 Sachs, J. (2018) *Unsafe Thinking*. Random House Business.
36 Mowles, C. (2011: 140) *Rethinking Management*. Gower.
37 Board, D. and Warwick, R. (2012: 13) *The Social Development of Leadership and Knowledge*. Centre for Progressive Leadership.
38 Stacey, R.D. (2012) *Tools and Techniques of Leadership and Management*. Routledge.
39 Grint, K. (2007) *Learning to Lead: Can Aristotle Help Us Find the Road to Wisdom?* Sage. Leadership, Vol. 3, No. 2, May.
40 Flyvbjerg, B. *et al*, Eds. (2012) *Real Social Science: Applied Phronesis*. Cambridge University Press.
41 Scott (1998:328) *Seeing Like a State*. Yale University Press concludes, "A step-by-step 'muddling through' approach would seem to be the only prudent course in a field . . . where surprises are all but guaranteed". He makes specific reference to his research into the fields of erosion management and public policy implementation. But, as I'm arguing here, muddling through is *a description of what we are all doing all of the time*, rather than a prescription of what we might choose to do by design. Being consciously aware of this, and how we might muddle through more skillfully, is where Scott's observations (as well as those of Allenby and Sarewitiz, referred to in note 4) support this central theme.
42 Scott, J.C. ibid: 311.
43 The Greek word metis combines the qualities of wisdom and cunning.
44 Scott J.C. ibid: 329.
45 Griffin, D. (2010) *Speaking of managers and leaders being ruthless: The deepening crisis of everyday ethics in business*. From Complexity and Management Blog: https://complexityandmanagement.wordpress.com/

2010/04/15/speaking-of-managers-and-leaders-being-ruthless-the-ongoing-crisis-of-everyday-ethics-in-business-2/#more-71

46 Vaill, P.B. ibid: 47.

47 Vaill, P.B. ibid: 77–78.

48 Stacey, R.D. (2010).

49 Vaill, P.B. (ibid: 40) argues that having "a greater sense of this interplay [of one's specialness with one's commonness] and the capacity to perform it oneself . . . *is* what managing is".

50 Flood, R.L. (1999: 83) *Rethinking the Fifth Discipline*. Routledge.

5

THE SUFFOCATING GRIP OF MANAGEMENT ORTHODOXY

EXPOSING THE GENERALLY ACCEPTED 'TRUTHS' THAT LIMIT PROGRESS

For several years, I have run a bimonthly network meeting for senior organizational development practitioners and other managers in central London. At one such session, we were each invited to write a brief narrative on an experience that had struck us in some way, and which had left some residual feelings and/or recollections that might merit further exploration. We were then asked to reflect on this personal narrative, both ourselves (as we were reading it out loud to a couple of other participants) and those others who were listening to our recollection of the event from an 'external' perspective. In this small-group setting, we then talked about what we had heard during the retelling of our story, as part of a process that session leaders Douglas Board and Rob Warwick call "immersed reflexivity".[1]

My "striking moment" concerned a meeting that I had attended some weeks earlier, in support of another independent consultant. We had met with a group of senior managers in an organization in the UK public sector. Our aim had been to secure a contract to help them with a major change programme. Although the meeting itself was an awkward affair, with the client director exhibiting some behaviour which suggested that any resulting work would be somewhat of a challenge, the initial response was positive. By that I mean that we were asked to design and deliver the first event of a number that we had proposed for the project team, line managers, and the Board. However, as we left, we shared our concerns about what – despite the outcome – had been a very unsatisfactory affair. I felt in particular that the main client didn't 'get' what it was that we were proposing – and that she didn't appear particularly interested in exploring anything beyond the mechanics (timing, attendees, reporting back, etc.) of the initial workshop with the Board. Her matter-of-fact response to our proposals suggested a level of anxiety about how her Board colleagues might respond to what we were proposing. And, in turn, what implications that might have for her own role and relationships going forward. This is a perfectly natural – if not always helpful – reaction to something that we see as posing a threat to our personal frame of reference.[2] That is, to the ongoing process of social construction which enables us to find our way through the complexities and uncertainties of life in ways that preserve our feeling of personal meaning and self-worth. It also gives us our sense of identity, our perceived place in the world, and so on. Ironically, the intervention that we were proposing would have addressed the part that this dynamic plays in the change process.

In writing my brief narrative, I mentioned the fact that the director's PA had arranged for sandwiches to be provided for the lunchtime meeting, which remained unopened throughout. Although I'd seen this as somewhat of a throwaway remark in my telling of the story, it was seized upon by those listening as a significant inclusion. When we began to unpack this further (no pun intended), it seemed to me that the director's unwillingness to spare the time to unwrap the sandwiches – or to ask others to do so – provided a perfect metaphor for her unexpressed but patently obvious unwillingness to 'open up' anything that might require her and her colleagues on the Board to do things differently from the ways in which they were accustomed to think and act. In particular, the unwrapped sandwiches had come to symbolize my residual frustration that the view of leadership and organizational dynamics embodied in our proposal similarly remained 'unopened'. On further reflection, the fact that I'd chosen to include this seemingly trivial point in this short piece probably reflected my deeper frustration about the (metaphorical) sandwiches remaining unwrapped in relation to management and organizational dynamics more generally. Hence this book!

This failure to take seriously the complex social dynamics of organization also has important implications for the ways in which 'success' and 'failure' are judged and responded to. And it contributes significantly to many of the ills that currently plague commercial enterprises, public services, and political institutions. Within this, it also seriously distorts people's understanding of the actual nature of management and leadership practice, and the extent to which managers can determine the outcomes of their own and others' actions. So why is it so difficult to shift the prevailing view on how organization works and what this means for management and leadership practice? Especially so, given that this is so far removed from the practical reality of organizational life as people experience it.

The challenge

The first thing to say is that, somewhat ironically perhaps, this 'do it better and get it right' view of organization is itself an outcome of the complex social process of everyday human interaction! That is to say, this pattern of understanding has emerged in, and is sustained by, the widespread interplay of people's ongoing, local interactions. This includes those people most obviously involved, such as managers and other practitioners. But it also involves numerous others. People such as politicians; media commentators; regulators, professional bodies, members of the general public; and so on. Establishing, reinforcing (and potentially shifting) this characteristic pattern is therefore a social endeavour. It is not a solo practice. The notion of organization, and the related practices of management and leadership, are social objects, around which people co-create their understanding of what is going on and the part they play within them. As part of this, those themes that are central to the dominant interpretation (such as order, predictability, control and so on) organize the patterning of people's ongoing interactions in the public arena. In this way, the established narrative on the nature of organization and management practice tends to become further ingrained.

This was vividly illustrated a couple of years ago, when I was introducing the CEO of a large commercial enterprise and his senior team to a particular approach to strategic management and performance. As always, I'd prefaced my introduction to this by a discussion of the real-world wiggliness of organization. Towards the end of the session, the CEO asked how the success or otherwise of the approach in relation to overall business performance could be measured. I reminded him that we'd just explored the complex social dynamics of organization and the implications of these for management practice. His response neatly encapsulates the tight grip that the currently dominant view of organization and management has on people's thoughts and actions. He said,

> I know you can't. But how do you?

Thankfully, he had the courage to support the proposal and to go ahead 'without the use of a safety net'!

Generally accepted 'truths' of management orthodoxy

So, what is it that keeps managers, consultants, policy-makers, regulators, media representatives and others trapped in these ways of thinking and talking about organization and management practice? Why do these persist, despite the fact that they are at odds with people's everyday lived experience? Besides the impact that day-to-day sense-making has on the localized patterning of thought and action, the ways in which people think and act are also influenced by broader "metanarratives". These emerge and become institutionalized over time, through the same self-organizing, patterning process of conversational interaction that I have outlined earlier. However, in relevant contexts, these become more pervasive and enduring than those that relate solely to local themes. As such, they come to define what counts as truth within that context; further reinforcing the dominant way of seeing, thinking and acting. In this same way, a number of mutually reinforcing propositions have become established as generally accepted 'truths' about organization and management. These exert a suffocating grip on the way that we think about organization, making efforts to establish a more reality-congruent view of organization and management practice more challenging. This is not least because many are typically seeded, and subsequently buttressed, by powerful voices in academia, mainstream consultancies, regulatory bodies, professional institutions, management journals, and so on.

Importantly, the more that this narrative is taken up in people's ongoing, local interactions, the more taken-for-granted it becomes. Once again, this process is self-maximizing. That is to say, it becomes ever more natural for people to perceive and interpret actions and events in this way, as alternative ways of framing what's happening tend to be dismissed or disappear from conscious awareness altogether. Indeed, where a manager feels that their own experience is out of sync with what 'should' be happening, they might well interpret this as a failure on their own part, rather than recognizing it as fundamentally flawed thinking in the governing narrative. With this in mind, I've set out below a number of recurring themes that have come to shape people's understanding of the nature of organization; define what 'good' management is supposed to look like; and set their expectations of what those in formal management roles should be capable of achieving. Since these are continuously reinforced by everyday repetition, as well as through official endorsement in all of its forms, the nature and content of people's ongoing interactions tend to become entrained in this socially constructed patterning of thinking, feeling, and acting. In practice, the various themes that I've identified below are intimately intertwined – and, hence, mutually reinforcing. However, to aid sensemaking, I've set them out separately.

'Truth' #1 – We know what 'proper management' looks like

Over recent decades, the notion and ideology of "managerialism" has come to define what 'proper management' is supposed to look like. It is centred on the pursuit of order, predictability and control, achieved through the widespread application of supposed 'best practice' policies, systems and procedures. In *Making Policy Move*, John Clarke argues that managerialist language, and the related ways of thinking and acting, have come to be accepted as "necessary, normal and natural" and that, "in the process, other ways of thinking, acting, calculating and organising are displaced".[3] From this perspective, all that is needed is for people to do things 'better' and get them 'right', according to the latest prescription[4] – and for them to be managed well to achieve this. In this context, this is taken to mean managers ensuring that people comply with the specified requirements. It is rooted in the belief that it is possible to derive general principles of organization and management that can be applied universally.

However, *nothing at all* happens "in general". Everything that takes place does so at a *specific* time, within a *specific* context, between *specific* people, and so on. That is to say, general principles and generalized patterns of thought and action are always particularized in the moment of people's interactions. In making sense of the continuously emerging context, paying attention to the *particular* circumstances that pertain in the moments of decision and action is essential. It's not so much 'big data' that we need to *make sense* of a complex world but more data that is live, in-the-moment, situationally contingent, temporary and provisional, and as-experienced.

Whilst the general application of best practice to the techno-rational aspects of organization can frequently make sense and add value (for example, in dealing with the physical infrastructure and components of plant and technology), extending this notion to the social world is seriously flawed. To begin with, approaches that are deemed to represent best practice (such as structures, systems, procedures and so on) are themselves abstract representations of people's day-to-day practices in a particular context. By convention, these are then transferred and applied wholesale in other contexts. But those contexts are necessarily different, even though they might appear to be the same on the surface. We see this most visibly in public services, where an incident at one location sparks inquiry-based recommendations and policy changes that are imposed across the sector as a whole. The same applies, though, in industry and commerce, where ideas and practices are often imported indiscriminately from one setting to another. Equally importantly, newly introduced 'best-practice' methodologies are then taken up in a multitude of different ways by those on the receiving end. This renders meaningless the notion of universal applicability that is implicit in the concept. Instead, real learning requires the *translation* of what are judged to be successful practices from elsewhere. *Selectively* and *imaginatively* integrating these into the diverse local contexts which reflect the real-world complexity of human being and human doing.

Despite knowing from their own, practical experience that things don't happen in the neatly packaged and predictable ways that this view embraces, managers find themselves striving to live up to the expectations that it represents. To fit in, get on and avoid the fear of sanction, this means accounting for their actions in ways that are considered to be managerially correct and politically acceptable. This tends to distort their practice, as they strive to live up to the image that this creates. Its dominant role in the established discourse also makes it more difficult for them to openly acknowledge the complex social dynamics of organization in which they and everyone else are inextricably immersed. This further reinforces the expectations of order, predictability and control, and normalizes the rhetoric that reflects this. The modelling of this language and behaviour in public arenas also encourages others to mimic it in their own formal interactions. This then consigns the well-understood but hidden, messy and informal aspects of day-to-day practice to the shadow conversations. Overall, this idealized view of what 'real management' is supposed to look like creates unrealistic expectations of what managers can achieve independently of the actions, inactions and interactions of countless others. As such, managerialist thinking underpins the other generally accepted 'truths' that I've set out below.

'Truth' #2 – An organization is a tangible entity that can be designed and built to achieve the sought-after aims and objectives

Conventionally, "the organization" is thought of as existing in its own right. An integrated 'whole' that has the capacity to act independently of people's in-the-moment interactions. In this way, it is capable of being designed, built and continually developed to deliver the required performance objectives. This perception is reinforced by the notion of organization as a legal entity. From a societal viewpoint, this provides a way of regulating business practice by focusing the minds of those involved on the need to satisfy the legal requirements of commercial management and corporate governance. It also provides a route for sanction, if the sought-after standards are not achieved.

However, as discussed extensively in Chapter 2, this sits in stark contrast to the wiggly-world view, which emphasizes the temporal, processual and emergent nature of everything that's going on. There is no physical entity or system that exists independently of people's in-the-moment interactions. This means that, whilst the various formal trappings of organization can be 'ordered' by design, the ongoing process of organization, and the social object that we come to think of as "the organization", cannot be re-engineered, transformed or otherwise changed at will. As a final point here, the notion of organization as a legal entity extends back to ancient Rome, where the collective was referred to as "persona ficta" or fictional person. However, regardless of the legal niceties, organizations don't 'do' things. People do. Real people, that is, not fictional ones! Speaking about these imagined entities as if they do things, deflects attention away from the living reality of people's everyday, local interactions. And it is through the self-organizing interplay of these local exchanges that organization is continuously re-enacted; continuity and change emerge; and whatever happens, happens.

'Truth' #3 – Organization exists as an integrated system, comprising a nested set of separate 'levels'

Those who think of organizations as systemic 'wholes' exemplify the above position. Not only managers, academics, and consultants but also journalists, politicians, inquiry chairmen, and other commentators routinely refer to "the system", or "systemic failure" when pronouncing on events that hit the headlines. So, seeing organisations as nested systems and subsystems, each of which has the capacity to act in some way separately from the actions of the other 'levels', appears natural and straightforward. This extends to the idea that each of these systems is embedded within a wider supra-system.

A high-profile example of this is the public inquiry into "conditions of appalling care" that existed at the UK's Mid Staffordshire NHS Foundation Trust. This took place in the mid-2000s. In his initial covering letter to the Secretary of State for Health, which accompanied his original report, Inquiry Chairman Robert Francis QC mentioned the word "system" or "systemic" 15 times. Readers would have been left in no doubt as to his view that "the system" played a central role in what he saw as the abject failure of those involved to ensure high-quality patient care. As a result, the overwhelming focus of his recommendations remained on redesign of "the system". The emphasis was therefore on the introduction of yet more standards, rules, regulations, and mechanisms for controlling and scrutinising the actions of hospital staff. Clearly, this systems-based view of the world remained undiminished – and, most likely, unquestioned. Also, despite stating in the Executive Summary that the NHS is "a service staffed by thousands of dedicated and committed staff and managers", his response to the localized wrongdoings in Mid-Staffordshire was to recommend that his proposals should be applied universally across the NHS. This is a classic systems-based response.

From this perspective, and in popular discourse, the emergent patterning of day-to-day activities is thought of as being determined by "the system". But, as Ann Cunliffe points out,[5]

> it's a bit of a cop out when organizational members say they can't change things or deal with problems effectively because it's 'the system'. What is the system, who creates it, and who keeps it going? We talk and act 'systems' into being, and maintain their existence in our talk about them. This requires a shift in thinking, because it means seeing the world in social interactions and relationships rather than in structures and systems.

Blaming "the system" for perceived failures shifts attention away from these practical realities to the supposed behaviour of an imaginary – but nevertheless designable – 'whole'. The "conditions of appalling care" to which Francis refers arose, and became the norm, in the course of people's everyday, human-to-human interactions. And it's by encouraging, assisting and enabling those involved to pay attention to the ways in which they and others participate in these same interactions that the virtues of humanity are more likely to come to the fore. It is these virtues with which health-service practitioners would more readily identify – and on which most will undoubtedly set out to base their practice. Simply adding more third-party rules and regulations obscures the essential intimacy, nuance and personalization of their work; shifting the focus from care to compliance. This does not, of course, ignore the benefits that can arise from enabling individual and collective learning through people's day-to-day interactions. Nor encouraging, where appropriate, the codification of the techno-rational aspects of practice (e.g. using checklists to avoid mistakes in routine processes). But it places the emphasis on the in-the-moment reality of people's ongoing interactions rather than the supposed omnipotence of "the system".

It simplifies the language, of course, to talk about "the organization" (as well as "the culture", "the management", "the system" and so on). In our interactions with others and our self-talk, we generalize patterns of meaning from disparate experiences and name these as part of our individual and collective sense-making. This book is peppered with such usage. In addition, feeling that one belongs to, works for, or otherwise relates to, something that is tangible and felt real can provide psychological and emotional benefits. Nevertheless, in the context of organizational dynamics, "the organization" is an imaginary construct. We therefore need to become more sharply aware of the ways in which describing our practice (there's another example!) in abstract terms can distort our own and others' perceptions and understanding of what's actually going on; blind us to the part that we and everyone else are playing in co-creating whatever is emerging; and divert us from thinking and acting in the only place, and at the only time, that we can do so – that is, in the here and now of our in-the-moment interactions.

'Truth' #4 – Complexity and uncertainty are bad and need to be overcome

If we start from the viewpoint that the job of the manager is to achieve order, predictability and control, it naturally follows that complexity and uncertainty are unquestionably bad. From this perspective, it makes sense to seek to "overcome", "iron out", "defeat" or otherwise get rid of such complexity by judicious application of principles of organizational design and management practice. Prescriptions for realizing this are in plentiful supply. Most of which are presented as having been derived from rigorous research – even though each of these invariably identifies a different set of critical factors for managers to plan, organize and control.

Besides being based on a false prospectus, this search for perfect order and a 'no surprises' future distracts managers and other participants from paying proper attention to their own experience of what's actually going on. The complex social process of everyday human interaction – out of which whatever happens, happens – cannot be designed out. It does not relate to the complicatedness of structures, systems and procedures that might be in place. Instead, *whatever the context*, it refers to the *underlying dynamics of everyday human interaction*. It is through this process that organization is continuously re-enacted, and outcomes (including any perceived complications) emerge in practice. In short, *all situations in which people are involved are unavoidably complex an ultimately unknowable*.

'Truth' #5 – Power and politics are dysfunctional and avoidable aspects of organization that 'proper management' will cure

It is particularly revealing how many of the books and consultancy offerings that purport to provide insights into the dynamics of organization make no reference at all to power and politics. Or else relegate them to the margins. Presenting these as dysfunctional aspects of organization that 'proper management' will overcome. This positions power and politics, by design or omission, in the area of self-interested politicking. In contrast, I have set out earlier how organization (in all human contexts) is unavoidably power-related and political. Within this, *nothing* happens in any aspect of organizational life – or in life more generally – other than through the exercise of power. Power is relational and dynamic. It reflects the combination of personal and situational factors in play at any one time that both enable and constrain the ability of those involved in a particular relationship to influence the knowledge, attitudes and behaviours of other participants. All interactions, out of which organization is perpetually being constructed, reflect the power relations that exist between those involved, in the moment of those interactions. This is the case whether such power manifests itself in 'soft' or 'hard' terms, as well as whether it is perceived as being just or unjust.

In a similar vein, everyone engages in political behaviour. This is a natural dynamic of the everyday interactional process, in which people are continually playing out their differences and making choices as to how best to proceed. Tension and conflict are therefore ever-present, whether openly expressed or operating 'in the shadows'. Co-operating, competing, collaborating and colluding to deal with such differences is what politics is all about. This means that organizational outcomes that are judged to be successful arise not only in spite of political behaviour *but also because of it*. Coming to terms with the *unavoidably* power-laden and political nature of organization – indeed, of all human interaction – is fundamental to management practice. Rehabilitating power and politics, as universal dynamics of organization that require conscious attention, is therefore an important pre-condition of muddling through skilfully. Acting politically to mobilize coalitions of support behind one particular construction of reality rather than another.

'Truth' #6 – It's the big things that matter

As we make our way through life, and as we strive to make sense of the world in which we are immersed, we identify specific happenings that we see as being especially significant in a particular context (the "Big Dots"). We then connect these together to construct a coherent narrative about what went on. The aim of this is both to consolidate our understanding and to provide a basis for our own and others' continuing action. In doing so, though, we necessarily abstract from the complexity of our in-the-moment activity, to make sense of our experience. Doing so both alone and with others. However, unless we recognize this as an abstraction from (and simplification of) the complex reality, this can create a false sense of certainty as to how the present situation came about, and what this might mean going forwards.

Earlier (Chapter 3), I suggested that the desire to be seen to have behaved in ways that are managerially 'correct' (according to the established narrative) and politically acceptable within the specific setting, can lead managers to provide idealized accounts of their experiences. They do this by connecting the Big Dots in ways that provide a seemingly logical, cause-and-effect explanation of their actions and the results that materialized. However, this necessarily fails to account for the complex social realities of their actual lived experience – and the muddling-through nature of what they inevitably found themselves doing in practice. It also carries with it many dysfunctional effects that constrain and distort their own and others' ongoing practice. Most damagingly, these sanitized accounts of what went on reinforce the misleading view of what 'proper management' looks like ('Truth' #1). This adds further support for the idea that research based on managers' formally reported experience is evidence-based and appears to validate the linear, step-wise prescriptions that flow from them.

All in all, this normalizes the belief that it's the 'big things' (high-profile actions, incidents, events etc.) which determine what happens. From this perspective, it follows that it's these aspects of organization that managers need to focus upon. That is, the set-piece events and major incidents (the 'match highlights', so to speak) rather than the complex social dynamics of open play that are happening continuously 'in between' the Big Dots. In reality, what occurs in practice (*including those aspects that come to be identified as Big Dots*) is determined by the widespread interplay of people's moment-to-moment interactions. Any changes in these, however small, would *necessarily* result in the emergence of different 'patterns of play' and different outcomes – often dramatically so. This similarly highlights the significance of the specific point at which different individuals enter into the ongoing patterning of interactions in a particular instance. A minor shift in timing can have a substantial effect on their own and others' perceptions and interpretations of what's going on and on the possibilities that emerge from their coming together.

'Truth' #7 – The organizational world is linear and symmetrical

Consistent with the above, it tends to be taken for granted that perfect symmetry exists between the actual path that people take as they act forwards into the future and the linear, step-wise narrative that they construct 'backwards', to account for what happened. From this linear and symmetrical view of the world, it follows that the latter path could be enacted 'forwards', to bring about the same result in future. In actuality, as discussed in Chapter 2, the relationship between the muddling-through nature of what happens in practice and the step-wise rationalizations of how particular outcomes came about is *asymmetrical*. Although the explanations that are constructed to explain what has happened appear logical in hindsight, it would not have been possible to have arrived at that specific endpoint simply by using that same logic in advance. The actual paths that people find themselves following in practice are not accessible beforehand. Nor, therefore, can they expect to achieve the same outcome in the future by applying this rationalized view of what happened. Or correct perceived shortfalls by following an amended version of it.

This dynamic reflects the previously mentioned point made by Duncan Watts that everything is obvious once you know the answer.[6] It also underpins Edward de Bono's rationale for lateral thinking. Solutions arrived at using his various techniques always appear to be logical and rational in retrospect. To underline the point further, a similar dynamic applies to organizational changes that have been brought about by the skilful use of socio-political action (i.e. normal organizational behaviour!).[7] If outcomes are to be considered valid and praiseworthy within the established management discourse, then these (and the way that they have been achieved) need to be made sense of in acceptable terms. As a result, the stories that are told about them are retrospectively constructed to appear rationally coherent, goal-oriented and authoritative. This is especially so when people are required to account for their performance to others whose judgements are critical to the way in which their reputation and standing are constructed and/or their pay and future career path is determined.

However, ignoring or denying the unavoidably socio-political nature of what's going on maintains the illusion that organization is a rational, scientific endeavour, rather than a complex social process. That is, that it is logical, matter-of-fact and precisely designed, rather than being enacted through the political, emotional, and emergent dynamics of everyday human interaction. As a result, as discussed extensively earlier, the illusion is maintained that the power-and-politics-free stories constructed backwards can be used as prescriptions for acting forwards into the future. In this way, managers continue to be schooled in the belief that perfect order and 'the right answer' is within their grasp, provided that those involved follow the prescribed path. Failure then tends to be rationalized as poor implementation by others, rather than the result of thinking that is fundamentally flawed.

'Truth' #8 – Getting the implementation right is not rocket science!

So, what about the challenges of implementation? The phrase, "It's not rocket science!" is usually invoked to suggest that whatever is being contemplated is, by comparison with sending people into space, simple and straightforward. Its rhetorical use in the context of organization reflects the widely held view that dealing with the day-to-day challenges of management, and the implementation of plans and projects, ought to be relatively clear-cut. As such, these are seen as being amenable to the application of techno-rational thinking and project methodologies to organize and control what happens. Of course, people are capable of designing and developing technologies to facilitate their own human being and human doing – such as building a rocket and applying related capabilities in ways that enable astronauts to orbit the earth and land on the moon. But organization is not fundamentally an issue of science and technology. It is a social endeavour, with all of the complexities that that involves.

Unlike the technical challenges involved in sending people into space and returning them safely to earth, the dynamics and outcomes of human interaction are never fully knowable. They are not amenable to scientific analysis at all. Indeed, the practical realization of the technical certainties of rocket science, in relation to particular missions, ultimately depends on the behaviour of people – with all of their fallibility (e.g. the Challenger and Columbia space shuttle disasters) and ingenuity (e.g. Apollo 13). So, it is true that organizational management is not rocket science. It's not merely technically complicated, it's socially complex.

'Truth' #9 – It is possible to design and deliver "And they all lived happily ever after" futures

In the autumn 2015 edition of the UK Chartered Management Institute's journal, *Professional Manager*, Adrian Furnham wrote a great article entitled "Write a business bestseller".[8] In it he identifies 11 essential ingredients of what he describes as "a management blockbuster". Whilst setting out this recipe for success in the literary world, he neatly exposes the gaps between the simplistic view of organization that such books often present, and the complex reality that managers experience day in, day out. He does this so subtly, though, that some readers might eagerly follow his supposed advice.

At first glance, Furnham is proffering some guidance to budding authors. In actuality he is deriding the naive prescriptions that prevent meaningful engagement with the dynamics of organization and a more practical understanding of real-world management practice. More thoughtful practitioners will not be seduced by the simple messages, one-size-fits-all 'solutions' and "they all lived happily ever after" futures that Furnham exposes. Too often, though, they are offered a false prospectus, built on what are claimed to be fool-proof, step-by-step approaches to assured success. Supposedly freeing them from having to deal with the real-world challenges which are often more akin to walking in the fog. And, as Steph Lawler says, in her discussion of identity, "The idea that we can 'be whatever we want to be' relies on an illusory eclipsing of the social world".[9]

'Truth' #10 – Practice should be evidence-based

Over the past few years, led astray by the false promise of 'if you do this, you'll get that' certainties, there have been increasing calls for management practice, consulting interventions and public policy to be "evidence-based". From this perspective, the validity of a proposed new strategy, structure, business process or whatever is assumed to arise from objective evidence of its successful use in other settings (so-called "best practice") or from generalized principles derived from research conducted 'scientifically'. But, as Phil Rosenzweig argues,[10] there are many common flaws in the arguments put forward to support these claims. He also exposes the pseudo-scientific nature of much of the research on which they are based. This echoes the argument I make in Chapter 3, about the failure of conventional research practices to take seriously the complex social dynamics of organization and management practice.

Of course, whenever a new medicine or medical treatment is introduced, it is crucial to know that sufficient clinical trials have taken place to demonstrate evidence of their efficacy and safety. The same applies to the design and manufacture of aircraft or similar technology. In such cases, scientific methods and exhaustive testing can properly be deployed to provide the necessary assurances. However, we are not talking here about products and practices that can be tested meticulously in advance, and replicated precisely in design, development, manufacture and deployment. We are dealing with the complex social process of organization. And, whilst the *dynamics* of organization are the same in each case, the ways in which these play out in each particular situation are unique. These are also unpredictable in all but the most limited sense. This means that it is impossible to link specific interventions to organizational performance and practice – either before *or after* the event. Nor is it possible to carry out 'experiments' in limited settings and expect the repeatability and/or scalability of these to be unproblematic. The complex and uncertain dynamics of organizational life make the relationships between cause and effect untraceable. And these also place a premium on the unique history, contextual factors and interactional dynamics that are in play at any time.

Against this background, Table 5.1, below sets out some of the characteristics of so-called "evidence-based practice", as this is applied in an organizational context. And I've contrasted these with others that reflect the wiggly-world perspective. The latter calls for attention to be placed on the evidence that is arising in the midst of practice (i.e. "practice-based evidence").

Table 5.1 Relating evidence to practice in an organizational context

Evidence-based practice	Practice-based evidence
. . . is based on prescriptions derived from *generalized* representations of other people's past practices and third parties' observations, analyses and reports of these.	. . . is embodied in the specifics of people's own, present experience and practice. That is, on their perceptions, interpretations and evaluations of what's happening and what they find themselves doing – at that time, in that situation and within those relationships. It privileges the lived experience of people, and the generalized patterning of their being together.
. . . uses abstract, de-contextualized observations, analyses and conclusions to support the claimed universality of 'best practice' prescriptions. Rarely, if ever, exposes the 'warts and all' details of people's actual experience.	. . . uses context-rich experience that arises within - and at the same time informs – context-specific action, as people participate in ongoing, local interactions. Difference and intention are recognized as natural dynamics of everyday organizational life.
. . . plays to the established narrative, in which managers expect rational explanations, predictability of outcome and control of process ('levers to pull').	. . . recognizes the a-rational, interaction-based and political dynamics of real-world organization.
. . . prescribes formal and structured approaches for improving practice and performance, based on an idealized and rational model of organizational dynamics.	. . . facilitates 'improvised', 'in-the-moment' interventions, arising in the midst of local interaction.

(Continued)

Table 5.1 (Continued)

. . . often results in seductively simple 'recipes for success' - such as 'n-step' processes, 'best practice' guidelines, and prescriptive models and frameworks. Tends to be based on a superficial and/or sanitized understanding of past practice in other organizational contexts. Often confuses correlation with causation.	. . . avoids prescriptions and the promise of particular outcomes. Instead, sees people as acting with intention into the future, as this is emerging from their own and everyone else's participation. 'Frameworks', etc., if used at all, are seen as a means of facilitating ongoing sensemaking and provoking reflection on existing practice.
. . . maintains that skilled introduction of the formally agreed interventions will reliably and consistently deliver the intended outcomes. When shortfalls occur in practice, these are usually put down to the failure of individuals to implement the prescribed actions correctly.	. . . understands that formal interventions can only represent idealized statements of managers' intentions. These will be realized (or not) through local conversational interaction. And although managers and others might act with specific intentions in mind, what emerges will not be within their individual or collective ability to control.
. . . tends to provide 'managerialist' prescriptions – positive, structured and measurable – based on assumptions of technical rationality and managerial control.	. . . is indeterminate, reflexive and, complex. Any appeals to technical rationality and managerial control are heavily circumscribed by awareness of the complex social dynamics of human interaction.
. . . is presumed to be ethical because it requires practitioners to use knowledge that has been gathered and tested empirically, in what are claimed to be the most rigorous ways possible. It is thus assumed to provide 'objective' evidence of those actions most likely to achieve the desired results and to do so in ways that meet pre-defined standards of ethical behaviour.	. . . sees the ethics of practice as emerging in the specifics of people's ongoing interactions – as they seek to go on together in the midst of differing interests, ideologies, identities, and interpretations, etc.

The pursuit of supposedly scientific-based evidence in the context of organization is misguided. As set out in Chapter 3, the generalized prescriptions that result fail to reflect the complex dynamics and situatedness of human interaction. It can also leave managers blind to the visceral evidence that exists in the detail of their everyday practice. This is not to dismiss the value that the pragmatic application of relevant expertise can bring to their choice-making process. But this always needs to be framed by the sciences of uncertainty, not certainty. Using practice-based evidence as the basis for ongoing action, means managers and others taking seriously their own lived experience, rather than deferring to generalized prescriptions. This occurs between *specific* people, at *specific* times and in *specific* circumstances, whilst also recognizing the uniquely path-dependent nature of everything that happens. *At the same time*, in reflecting on their own practice, this exposes the broader social themes and generalized patterns of interaction within which these local practices are situated. And to which they are contributing.

'Truth' #11 – What gets measured gets done

The use of measurement as a central aspect of management practice is well-established. And, in the appropriate context, 'making the numbers' is vital. The ultimate measures of performance are likely to be stated and assessed in numerical terms of one form or another, whether in the public, private, or voluntary sectors. In relation to commercial performance, quality of service provision, compliance with legal and regulatory requirements, or other aspects of performance in a particular setting, numbers matter. At the same time, knowing these numbers gives us little clue as to how we might set about enabling performance on a continuing basis. And, whether outcomes turn out to be good, bad or indifferent, these emerge from the self-organizing interplay of vast swathes of local interactions, not simply those that are being monitored in relation to formal strategies, plans and programmes. In this regard, it is also important to recognize that high-quality performance can still result in unsuccessful outcomes and that positive results can sometimes be due more to luck than judgement. When we're talking about the complex social dynamics of organization, numbers don't cut it. To paraphrase Peter Drucker, only the notation is numerical, the decisions are entrepreneurial.[11] That is to say, managing performance, in any context, is about imaginatively using resources *today*, to deal with a continuously emerging and unknowable future.

Despite this, we remain locked-in to a view of organization and management practice that is based on extensive measurement, upward reporting and remote analysis. As far back as the 1950s, Drucker introduced what was intended to be an *enabling* philosophy of "management by objectives *and self-control*". This, though, was debased by its translation into the mechanistic, top-down system of MBO,[12] in which the pivotal element of self-control was absent. Ever since then, it has become the accepted wisdom to seek to direct business performance by establishing intricate networks of objectives and targets at each successive 'level' of organization (see Truth #3). This is usually accompanied by reliance on arms-length management, mediated by "traffic lights", "dashboards" and the like. The Balanced Scorecard (BSC), created by Robert Kaplan and David Norton in the mid-1990s,[13] is probably the most widely used of the many approaches that managers have taken up in their continuing quest to achieve "no surprise" outcomes. On the face of it, their efforts are aimed at complexifying the process, by shifting the emphasis away from the focus on a single measure – typically, financial performance – to embrace other aspects of organization. However, Kaplan and Norton identify linear, cause-and-effect links between the four elements of their scorecard. Maintaining that *organizational learning* improves those *internal processes* that deliver *value to customers*, and that this in turn leads to enhanced *financial performance*. This argument fits well with established wisdom and seems like common sense. But it is a version of common sense that still sees the business world as ordered, predictable and ultimately controllable, rather than wiggly and unknowable.

This overall stance is underpinned by the conviction that "what gets measured gets done". Given the inherent complexity, the temptation is for managers to focus their attention on what is easily measurable rather than what might be significantly meaningful. In addition, many procedures for assessing and reviewing performance are highly structured and formulaic, rather than encouraging and enabling open dialogue between those involved about what's actually going on. This limits flexibility and responsiveness, in a world of constantly shifting demands and priorities. Unsurprisingly, all of this is accompanied by a catalogue of high-profile stories about the 'gaming' of performance targets that such approaches inevitably spawn. With those affected channelling their creativity into 'making the numbers' rather than into the substance of whatever they are involved in. As Tim Harford says,[14] when we start counting and measuring things, we begin to change the world to fit with the ways in which we measure it.

'Truth' #12 – We need to be clear who is accountable – especially when things go wrong

Knowing who is accountable for particular elements of practice and performance is an important aspect of organizational design and management. Too often, though, the concept is misunderstood and misapplied. In particular, it is increasingly used as a label to hang around the necks of the supposed 'guilty' when things 'go wrong'. In everyday usage, accountability and blame tend to be used interchangeably. That is to say, the question, "Who is accountable" is usually read as, "Who is to blame?". The fear that this might happen, even where ill-founded, discourages openness, candour and learning. Instead, those involved seek – not unnaturally – to avoid being blamed for what has happened. This also neatly absolves others of any need to account for the contribution that their own actions and inactions might have made to the outcome, whether knowingly or otherwise. It is, though, based on the false premise that managers (and others) are able to control activities and outcomes in ways that guarantee particular results. But things don't happen in the straightforward ways that this implies. And the acts of managing, leading or participating more generally are much more nuanced and elusive practices than this line of argument presumes.

This is not to suggest that all of those called to account have nothing to answer for – although when, how and to whom is not so obvious. And, of course, some of those who have been involved in a particular issue might well have set out to engineer things solely to further their own self-interest, behaved dishonestly, or indeed been incompetent. But I'm inclined to agree with Yiannis Gabriel, when he argues that,[15]

> like the rest of us, managers are most of the time confused, erratic and irrational – they deserve neither exorbitant praise for success nor total vilification for failure. Their successes are more likely to be due to good fortune, adroit handling or good judgement rather than the application of quasi-scientific theories and propositions.

If we insist on seeing senior managers and others as all-seeing and all-conquering heroes when things are going well, then I guess that we're always likely to want to pin the blame on them when things go wrong – if only to preserve the anxiety-reducing myth that the rest of life is progressing in controllable and predictable ways. And, as a blame-seeking missile, this approach to accountability has been shown to work very well in 'locking onto' its intended target. Also, reprising an earlier point, criticism of people's actions is always made with the benefit of hindsight and armed with the knowledge of how the particular event being reviewed has been reacted to by the public, press and other commentators. However, given their own experience as inhabitants of the wiggly world, it is at best naive and at worst disingenuous for those doing the interrogating to pretend that life operates in the mechanistic way that this view of accountability implies.

A more reality-congruent perspective would recognize the complex interplay of factors and unique 'path to now' that account for whatever emerges. A starting point would be to take the word accountability literally. Seeing it as the ability of people to account (account-*ability*) for the Whys, Whats and Hows of their practice. This would mean everyone – whether manager or messenger – being able (*and enabled*) to give an authoritative account of those factors affecting the activities, capabilities and performance for which they are responsible (whether individually or collectively). Doing this in ways that enable them to:

- anticipate and respond appropriately to the issues and challenges that emerge in practice, without having constantly to seek permission or be excessively constrained by inflexible rules and regulations (i.e. facilitate their own response-*ability*);
- learn from their experience and improve their ongoing practice;
- be better informed in their relationships and transactions with third parties;
- explain the perceived contribution of their own decisions and actions to issues, events and outcomes that emerge in practice; and
- provide information that assists and enables other people's choices and (inter)actions.

Reframing the notion of accountability in this way still allows for deliberate malpractice in the context of a perceived failure to be exposed and dealt with. But it starts from a position of understanding and generosity. Coupled with a presumption of well-intended failure, rather than one that assumes deliberate malpractice and the need for someone to blame.

'Truth' #13 – Ever-advancing technology, Big Data and digitalization hold the keys to future success

To compound the over-reliance on measurement and data, the current drive is to "digitize" the above target-setting and performance-management procedures. This further reinforces the belief that the answer lies in the numbers, rather than in the actions and interactions of living and breathing human beings. However, it is misleading to believe that the collection and analysis of large quantities of data can represent, in any meaningful way, the inherent complexity, uncertainty and ambiguity of human interaction. Nevertheless, the temptation for this to happen has increased significantly with the emergence of Big Data and the algorithmic decision-making that sits at the core of Artificial Intelligence (AI). Worse still, the very sophistication implied by the accumulation and processing of masses of data imbues the resulting analyses with a 'false concreteness' that is far removed from the messiness and unknowability of what's actually going on. As a one-time engineer, I can fully appreciate the benefits that the imaginative and judicious use of technology can bring to the human condition. At the same time, it is important that the implications of integrating AI and other forms of advancing technology into organizational design and management practice are properly considered. My scepticism is not about the development of the technologies as such; although I do believe that use of the word "intelligence" in relation to technology and machines does risk degrading the nature of human being. The irony might be that we end up dumbing down the qualities of being human to match those of the machines, rather than succeed in achieving the impossible task of raising machine 'intelligence' to match that of humans.

One of the biggest barriers to the human-centred use of AI in relation to organizational dynamics is that proponents seem to take it for granted that all such developments are unquestionably good – invented by 'good' people, with the intention of doing 'good' things, for the 'good' of other individuals, and thereby enhancing the common 'good'. The real-world dynamics of human interaction are conveniently ignored, in favour of a utopian view in which there is universal wellbeing, co-operation and harmony, as well as near certainty in relation to the outcomes that will arise from these. This naivety undermines serious consideration of emerging technologies – both in terms of the genuine potential that these might have for improving the techno-human condition, organizational performance and societal wellbeing, as well as the risks involved in their misapplication and unforeseen consequences that might arise from their ill-thought-through deployment.

This is crucial, too, in relation to the challenge to management orthodoxy that is set out in this book. The more that human sense-making-cum-action-taking becomes dependent upon machine technologies, and governed by opaque algorithms, the more likely it is that we will become ever-more-firmly locked-in to currently established notions of organization and management practice. From a wiggly-world perspective, organization emerges in the complex interplay of people's moment-to-moment interactions. These take place between conscious, sentient and self-conscious individuals, whose understanding of what's going on is much more subtle and improvised than could ever be replicated by design. As Gary Smith points out, "computer programs do not possess anything resembling human wisdom and common sense. These programs do not have the general intelligence needed to deal with unfamiliar circumstances, ill-defined conditions, vague rules, and ambiguous, even contrary, goals".[16] That is, everyday life!

Technology can be put to good use, of course, in helping people to make better choices in appropriate circumstances. Provided that "better" is defined by human values and organizational/societal norms, as expressed in the moment of interaction. It can also facilitate delivery of the sought-after outcomes more efficiently than might otherwise be possible. What technology can't do is to overcome the inherent wiggliness of organization, out of which whatever happens, happens. Or make ethical choices. The infusion of technology into everyday (organizational) life is a matter of ethics. It also needs to be framed within a humbler and complexity-aware view of what is credible and what the implications might be of integrating it into people's day-to-day activities and relationships.

'Truth' #14 – Leadership is an elite practice

Intimately interwoven with the core managerialist narrative ('Truth' #1), is the way in which we have come to think and talk about management in general and leadership in particular. Often, leadership is positioned as an elite practice, confined to a few gifted individuals. In most cases, it is also spoken about as being separate from, and superior to, what is seen to be the more mundane practice of management. This positioning of leadership as a practice that is open only to a select few individuals is reinforced in many ways. These include the portrayal of high-profile business success stories as personally orchestrated achievements; the reward mechanisms that reflect this perspective; the investment in prestigious leadership development programmes for a select few; and so on. These and many other elements combine to institutionalize position-based leadership as the ultimate sign of achievement. A must have, for anyone who wants to be seen to be a success in business, politics, or society more broadly. This further reinforces the belief that such individuals have the ability to 'change the world'. And to do so independently of the choices and actions of everyone else. Consistent with this, Rosenzweig exposes what he calls "the halo effect", in which good performance outcomes are attributed, after the event, to good leadership by those 'at the top'.[17] Ironically, perhaps, this myth of the all-powerful individual is further strengthened by the occasional, high-profile resignation, dismissal, and/or vilification of a senior manager, following a corporate failure or other major incident that hits the headlines. As Rosenzweig again observes,[18]

> if we attribute great performance to a clear vision and brilliant leadership and a strong focus, it's natural to infer that poor performance is due to some error or mistake. Ex post facto, it's always easy to say that low performance was due to some blunder or to inept management.

In response, we need to recognize two things. First, that leadership is a natural dynamic of everyday interaction. It is enacted by many people in the course of the day-to-day exchanges. Secondly that, in the context of the *role* of management, leading and managing are complementary aspects of the same interactional process. Two sides of the same coin, as I described it earlier.

'Truth' #15 – As a manager, if you're not in control, you're not leading

Conventionally, we seek to deal with uncertainty and complexity by putting things in place that are intended to establish order and control. This typically includes the development, deployment and management of formal strategies, structures, systems and so on. All with the aim of 'catching the wiggliness in a net'. At one level, this reflects a natural human desire to be in control of one's life and, in certain roles (such as being a manager, say) of being seen to be in control. As regards the conduct of life more generally, it also makes sense to seek some formal ways of achieving greater integration and alignment. However, despite such efforts and desires, organization *as practised* is unavoidably fragmented, messy and self-organizing. As such, it is, at one and the same time, orderly and disorderly; co-operative and competitive; designed and emergent; and so on. And, despite the role expectations that flow from being formally in charge, managers are not in control of what arises in practice from people's myriad interactions.

By virtue of their position they can use disciplinary power (after Foucault[19]), such as coercion and/or calculative/contractual methods, to control the bodies and immediate actions of individuals and groups but they cannot control what emerges overall from their own and others' actions. As relatively powerful participants in the ongoing organizational process, those in formal management positions can have a significant influence on what happens. And, within the scope of their role, they often have 'first mover' advantage. But this widespread tendency to equate managing/leading with having the capacity to control what happens, provided that managers do their job 'right', places unrealistic expectations on them as individuals and distorts people's understanding of the dynamics of organization and society more broadly.

'Truth' #16 – Management orthodoxy sits at the core of professional practice

Besides regulatory regimes being rooted in the conventional view of organization and management, this pattern also extends to the certification of individual and collective practice in a range of related areas. Although efforts to professionalize the practice of directors, managers, specialists, consultants, coaches, and the like have merit, these still tend to be based on the same "do it better and get it right" assumptions and competency-based approaches concerning what constitutes excellence in these fields. Advocates see this as a commonsensical – and hence self-evidently(!) beneficial – approach. But is it?

My concern is that the natural tendency is for practices to be codified in ways that exclude any meaningful consideration of the inherent wiggliness of organization and the muddling-through nature or real-world management. Such approaches risk creating a 'tick box' or 'paint-by-numbers' approach that is the antithesis of professional practice. As such, it further reinforces the illusion that practitioners can ensure that things will turn out as planned – provided that they act in line with the formally approved recipe for success. For the most part, value-creating practice is less about project disciplines and more about personal dialogue; less about abstract prescriptions and more about active participation; less about procedural conformity and more about pattern-shifting creativity.

The pressure to conform

Taken together, the above perspectives preserve the myth that success or failure of the enterprise or institution is largely down to the characteristics, actions or omissions of those at the top. However, given the inherent complexity of organizational life, it is not credible to suggest that the behaviour of a small group of individuals accounts for organizational success or failure, regardless of how gifted or flawed they might be or the level of formal authority that they might command. Of course, with formal power relationships weighted in their favour, those in formal management positions contribute significantly to what happens overall. But none of this guarantees that things will turn out in the ways intended. Or that what are perceived to be successful outcomes can be isolated to the actions of particular individuals. This is the case however pivotal their contribution might appear to have been, when viewed with the benefit of hindsight. Especially where this is couched in terms that conform to the established narrative. At the other end of the performance spectrum, of course, a particularly toxic (or even illegal) way of doing business might be seeded or sanctioned at the top. But even then, this requires the active or passive collusion of many more people for it to take hold. Whilst the natural instinct might be to deny this dynamic, David Aaronovitch reminds us that human nature is such that we can never be sure that we would be the good guys.[20] Pointing to the ways in which some ordinary citizens behaved in countries that were occupied during The Second World War, he exposes as a myth this sense that individuals would never collude in the furtherance of things that, in the broader context, are indisputably bad. Despite this, the idea that an all-powerful elite exists, which can control outcomes at will, irrespective of the responses of other people, remains largely unchallenged. It provides the foundation for much of what people take for granted and 'know to be true' about organizational management – even though the reality is markedly different.

Vested interests

As a significant consequence of the institutionalization of the above factors, many powerful interests are served by maintaining the current discourse concerning the nature of organization and management. This makes it all the more challenging to achieve a shift in the way in which the manager's role is officially framed and put into practice. A fairer and more realistic view of the contribution made by those in formal management positions might not simply raise questions about the justification of the reward packages of those at the top of major corporations and public institutions. It would also call into question the roles and standing (that is to say, the identities) of those in the industries and institutions that have been created around the search and recruitment, development, accreditation, remuneration and idealization of individual managers. Others whose interests are currently served by the widespread acceptance of the established discourse include those practitioners who sell 'solutions' based on its highly appealing 'do this and you'll get that' promises and the supposed replicability of these across multiple contexts. Shifting this particular pattern is, therefore, one of the most challenging tasks for those whose goal it is to encourage, assist and enable people to take complexity seriously.

In the end . . .

The above discussion points to the existence of a wide gap between the currently dominant view of organization and management practice – as supposedly enacted by those in formal management positions – and the complex social dynamics of organizational life as managers and others actually experience it. Despite what might be suggested by the formal trappings of organization, decisions arising wholly from rational analysis of 'the facts', step-by-step decision-making by people whose agendas are fully aligned, and the seamless translation of those decisions into programmable action 'on the ground' are rare – if they exist at all. Most significantly, perhaps, whilst managers might be formally 'in charge', we have seen that they are not – indeed cannot be – in control of the outcomes that emerge from the complex interplay of the countless local interactions that constitute everyday organizational life. In practice, managers tend to make progress through informal interactions, ad hoc sense-making conversations, ongoing political accommodations, and the like. That is, they – like everyone else – muddle through.

This is not a matter of incompetence. Far from it. But it might be portrayed as such, were it not to be covered over by the superficial gloss of management speak and formal process rituals that maintain the illusion of rationality, predictability and control. Or if there was no post-hoc rationalization of actual outcomes that savvy political behaviour demands. Unfortunately, this veneer of goal-maximising objectivity reinforces the fantasy. This view of organization and management has become so ingrained that those who sense that 'it isn't really like that' can often find it difficult to acknowledge this openly. Or to shift their practice in public arenas to match their intuitive understanding. The continuing enactment of the process rituals and routines that flow from the mainstream leadership ideology then serve to strengthen it still further.

All of this might appear to be a damning indictment of individual managers, were it not for the natural dynamics of organizational interaction that are highlighted in earlier chapters. In my judgement, most of the managers with whom I have worked during my professional career – or that I've come across in other forums – have been trying to make a worthwhile difference in the complex, uncertain and ambiguous conditions in which they find themselves. The problem is that they are 'on a hiding to nothing' in their pursuit of leadership 'perfection', as this is prescribed by management orthodoxy, sustained by popular misconception and reinforced by current performance measurement and reward mechanisms. They find themselves enmeshed in a web of formally codified expectations; explicit 'best-practice' guidelines; and widely held assumptions relating to the nature and powerfulness of expert management practice. All of which suggests that they should be doing something much more sophisticated and 'manager-like' than the things that they actually find themselves doing every day.

Ultimately, it is in the give-and-take of everyday interaction that the capacity exists for new patterns to form and changes in perspective and practice to emerge. Whether or not such pattern-shifting occurs will depend on whether or not those managers who recognize the existing deficiencies and dysfunctionalities are willing and able to mobilize sufficient support for change.

Notes

1 Rob Warwick and Douglas Board introduce the notion of "immersed reflexivity" in their book, *The Social Development of Leadership and Knowledge* (Palgrave Macmillan, 2013).

2 Rodgers, C. (2007: 122–124) *Informal Coalitions*. Palgrave Macmillan.

3 Clarke, J. in Clarke *et al* (Eds). (2015: 97) *Making Policy Move* (Policy Press).

4 See *The Paradox of Control in Organizations* by Philip Streatfield (Routledge, 2001).

5 Cunliffe, A.L. (2009: 59) *A Very Short, Fairly Interesting and Reasonably Cheap Book about Management*. Sage.

6 Watts, D. (2012) *Everything is Obvious – Once You Know the Answer.* Atlantic Books.

7 Rodgers, C. (2007) *Informal Coalitions*. Palgrave.

8 Article by Adrian Furnham in the CMI's journal *Professional Manager* (Autumn 2015): Write a Business Bestseller.

9 Lawler, S. (2008: 144) *Identity: Sociological Perspectives*. Polity.

10 Rosenzweig, P. (2007) *The Halo Effect: How Managers Let Themselves Be Deceived*. The Free Press.

11 Drucker was actually talking about budgeting, when he said, "Only the notation is financial, the decisions are entrepreneurial" in Drucker, P.F. (1974: 118) *Management: Tasks, Responsibilities, Practices*. Heinemann.

12 Importantly, Peter Drucker spoke about the importance of management by objectives *and self-control* as the governing principle in *The Practice of Management* (first published in 1955). However, consistent with the main thrust of this chapter of the book, consultants commercialized the approach by dropping Drucker's reference to self-control and introducing

the acronym MBO. Drucker, P.F. (2007: 105 *et seq.*) *The Practice of Management.* Routledge.

13 Kaplan, R.S and Norton, D.P. (1996) *The Balanced Scorecard.* HBR Press.

14 Harford, T. (2016) *Messy.* Abacus.

15 Gabriel, Y. (1999: 288) *Organizations in Depth.* Sage.

16 Smith, G. (2018: 20) *The AI Delusion.* Oxford University Press.

17 Rosenzweig (ibid).

18 Rosenzweig (ibid: 91).

19 Michel Foucault maintains that "disciplinary power" can be exercised by those with more formal power (authority), to make others comply with their wishes. Also that the prevailing power relations can cause people to discipline themselves (and possibly others) to comply, to avoid the anticipated sanctions of not doing so. See, for example, Taylor, D. (Ed.) (2010) *Michel Foucault – Key Concepts.* Routledge.

20 Article by David Aaronovitch in *The Times* 1 January 2020: *We can never be sure we'd be the good guys.*

6

LEADING AND MANAGING IN A WIGGLY WORLD

MUDDLING THROUGH WITH PURPOSE, COURAGE AND SKILL

In Chapter 1, I began by exposing the basic flaws in the established view of how organization works and the implications of this for management practice. In its place, I described a view of the organizational world that is rooted in people's everyday lived experience. A world in which managers and other practitioners are invited to take complexity seriously. A wiggly world. Building on this more reality-congruent understanding of organization, Chapter 2 explains this wiggliness in terms of the complex social dynamics of everyday human interaction, in which we are all participating. This perspective offers a radical challenge to the assumptions about organization that underpin mainstream thinking on the nature of organization and what 'proper management' is supposed to look like.

In my closing words to the opening chapter, I said that it was time for managers and others to 'get real'. Foregrounding and embracing the real-world wiggliness of organization, which they and others experience every day, offers managers a way of escaping from what I called in Chapter 5 "the suffocating grip of management orthodoxy". That is, from a view of the world that misrepresents what those in formal management roles can sensibly achieve through their own endeavours. Striving to conform to this fantasized view of organization, serves only to reinforce the assumptions of scientific rationality, predictability, and control on which the established conception of organization and management is based (Chapter 3). Fuelled by this, and other dynamics that tend to maintain the established order, it can then be particularly challenging for managers to escape from the dominant management discourse. And so, the fantasy continues.

This is the world within which managers find themselves operating every day. And it's why I'm arguing that they need to draw – first and foremost – on their own experience in engaging with the specific challenges that emerge. That is, they need to take seriously the complex social dynamics of organization and the muddling-through nature of real-world management practice that is set out in Chapter 4. In particular, I'm arguing that muddling through with purpose, courage and skill is the *best* that they – indeed, any of us – can do, as they find their way through the multiplicity of roles and relationships in which they are engaged, and seek to address the many and various challenges that they encounter along the way. It's here, in the midst of our reciprocal muddling through, that we need to begin our quest to find out what this might mean *in practice* for those who are formally charged with managing others. As well as those who, in the course of their everyday interactions, find themselves taking the lead spontaneously.

So, what can managers *do*?

Given this real-world wiggliness, and the inability to predict and control outcomes, the obvious question for managers is "So, what can I do?". The first thing to say is that, like the rest of us, managers have no choice but to muddle through their multiplicity of roles and relationships. Acting forwards into the future, as it is emerging from the interplay of their own and others' actions. The more pressing question is how they might enhance the quality of their own participation in this process. That is to say, given the inherent complexity of organization, what can they do *in practical terms* to muddle through with *purpose*, *courage* and *skill?*

The question of purpose

As I touched upon in Chapter 4, I want to draw attention to four, complementary aspects of purpose that are central to the notion of muddling through 'well'. These are:

- Acting *with a sense of* purpose
- Acting *on* purpose
- Acting purpose*fully*
- Acting purpos*ively*.

These are explored more fully below.

Acting with a sense of purpose

Most obviously, the phrase "with purpose" conjures up the notion of a sense of direction and sought-after outcome. This is particularly important in relation to the idea of muddling through that I'm setting out here, to counter any idea that it might suggest a sense of helplessness and lack of meaningful engagement. At the same time, the ways in which purpose manifests itself from moment to moment is an emergent property of interaction. In the words of Pete Burden and Rob Warwick, it is best viewed as "temporary, contextual, relational and multi-headed".[1]

In the context of managing by muddling through, then, acting with purpose is about pursuing a general sense of direction rather than a fixed end-point. It is about perpetual wayfinding rather than navigating a charted course. The aim is not to produce detailed plans, programmes, or blueprints for a cast-in-concrete future. It is about people becoming so immersed in conversations about the Whys, Whats and Hows of their practice that, when the 'real world' happens (as a result of their own and everyone else's participation in it), they are better placed to deal with whatever emerges. And to do so in ways that are congruent with the demands of the current situation. This includes any formally stated intentions and the inevitably diverse interpretations and enactments of others as to what the purpose is and how best to fulfil it. It also means managers acknowledging that, despite their acting with purpose and intent, they still can't predict or control what will happen in practice. It's important, too, that others recognize and understand the implications of these dynamics; especially those who comment on managers' and others' practice, pass judgement on their performance, or seek to circumscribe their actions with an excess of rules and regulations. As Matthew Syed says, "It is easy for those on the outside, without pressure of time and without having to juggle contradictory demands, to offer marvellously manicured critiques".[2]

So far in the book, I have sought to raise awareness of what is going on *in all organizational contexts*. My focus has been on description rather than prescription. However, in considering the implications of these dynamics for managers' day-to-day practice, and what this means for the purpose of their role, differing and potentially competing ideologies are unavoidably brought into play. In other words, this is a political question, the answer to which is imbued with norms and values about the nature of human being and human doing. As mentioned earlier, managers can, by virtue of their position, use disciplinary power to control the bodies and immediate actions of particular individuals and groups. At least in formal settings. That is to say, they can use coercion and/or calculative methods (contractual conditions, incentives, etc.) in an effort to get people to comply with their wishes. Even then, though, they still can't control what emerges overall. Nor can they command people to apply their individual and collective talents in ways that would achieve more than baseline compliance. For example, whatever the formal power relationships might imply, those who are officially in charge cannot command people to respond in creative and innovative ways; to participate with commitment and enthusiasm; or to 'go the extra mile'.

So, if managing and leading are to mean anything in these circumstances, it seems to me that their purpose must be to encourage, assist and *enable* people to perform better than they might otherwise do. And to do so more often than not. Whatever the specific circumstances in which they might find themselves at any particular time. This is in stark contrast to tying them up in an excess of targets, rules and regulations, with which they are expected to comply. In other words, the aim is to enable ordinary people (which we all are!) to perform *extra*ordinarily well – whatever "well" might mean in a particular context.

This, then, is about managers seeking to encourage, assist and enable people to find their way through *their own* challenges. And to do so with greater purpose, courage and skill than they might otherwise have done.

Implicit in this is a belief in the general willingness and ability of people to perform, provided that they have the motive, means and opportunity to do so. Crucially, this is not about sidestepping the challenges of dealing with those who don't fit this pattern. Nor does it ignore the fact that the interdependent nature of human being, coupled with personal differences of character and in-the-moment circumstances, means that everyone falls short of this ideal on occasion. It does, though, signal a determination not to limit the creative potential of the many, by tying them up in controls designed to catch the few. From this perspective, addressing the dysfunctional behaviours of the limited number of people who persistently fall short of what is required is itself an act of enablement for the majority.

With this in mind, Table 6.1 identifies some of the main organizing themes that reflect an enabling approach to leading and managing. The proposition here is that those managers whose practice reflects these themes are more likely to engender a constructive and 'complexity-congruent' response to the real-world wiggliness than those who continue to pursue management orthodoxy. It should be clear from what has gone before, of course, that I'm not positioning this as the route to a guaranteed, 'and they all lived happily ever after' future. Taking complexity seriously demands a humbler and less pretentious view of the management/leadership role than that which is ordinarily presented. Managers can, though, act with the intention of fostering a more successful and personally meaningful way forward, even if they can't be sure that such a future will materialize or that some less attractive outcomes won't arise along the way.

Muddling through on purpose

This is about acting deliberately, with awareness and intent. That is to say, muddling through with purpose is not about proceeding aimlessly and oblivious to what's going on. Or leaving things to chance. It is the antithesis of this. The emphasis is on the word *through*. This means managers *consciously* finding their way through the exigencies of organizational life, as these emerge from their own and others' behaviour. As well as encouraging, assisting and enabling others to do so. It's about 'tuning-in' to the patterns of interaction and shadow conversational themes that are organizing people's participation, and setting out intentionally to pursue the sought-after purpose, *despite not knowing what will emerge overall.*

Table 6.1 Enabling individual and collective practice and performance

Organizing themes that reflect an enabling approach to leading and managing
Enabling people to perform means: • Paying attention to *what's actually going on in the business*, rather than relying on the supposed indicators of performance that find their way onto "scorecards", "dashboards", and the like. • Maintaining high expectations of people's willingness and ability to contribute. • Expecting surprises – helping people to anticipate and respond creatively to *what actually emerges*, rather than to those things that might have occurred if the real world had been kind enough to comply with the planning assumptions. • Providing vision – helping people to 'see better' (make 'better' sense) through everyday interactions – what is *meaningful* gets done. • Dealing directly with the few people who consistently under-perform, rather than tying everyone up in a web of catch-all rules and regulations – making sure that trust is spelled: T-R-U-S-T . . . not T-R-U-S-S-E-D! • Fostering personal response-*ability* – ensuring that people are able to respond to events without constantly having to seek permission. • Framing account-*ability* as the ability of people to account, in an informed an insightful way, for the Whys, Whats and Hows of their practice. • Enabling people to grow their contribution in line with their developing capabilities and emerging challenges – flexing roles to make the most of people's talents rather than shoehorning them into fixed boxes. • Using measurement to facilitate *movement in practice* rather than as a basis for passing judgement on people – ensuring that locally meaningful information is available to people to facilitate the *collaborative self-management* of their own and others' work practices and performance. • Making sure that scorekeepers and commentators aren't seen to be more important than the players. • Demonstrating and encouraging openness and candour, to expose policy issues, process weaknesses and poor practices, as a basis for ongoing learning and improvement. • Understanding that high-quality practice will often be accompanied by unsuccessful outcomes – and that some positive outcomes are likely to be due more to luck than judgement. • Seeing performance management as an *ongoing conversation*, punctuated by periodic structured events to frame issues, take stock, and unblock progress. • Taking with a pinch of salt all claims that a particular action or intervention can be proven to have led to a measurable improvement in overall business performance. • Remaining confident in the knowledge that the best that anyone can do is to muddle through the complex, uncertain, and ambiguous challenges that they face – while striving to do so with purpose, courage, and skill.

Muddling through purposefully

This is about acting forward with determination and resolve. Being resolute and determined to deal with whatever turns up. Stick-to-it-iveness is one way of putting it, which echoes the informality and improvisatory nature of muddling through. A corollary of this is the need for managers to remain resilient in the face of the inevitable setbacks and unintended consequences that arise along the way, as a result of the complex interrelationships between their own and others' actions, inactions and interactions.

Muddling through purposively

Finally, and most pertinently in the context of the inherent wiggliness of organization, is the need to act purpos*ively*. That is to say, participating in *contingently useful ways*, in the ongoing process through which organization is being continuously (re-)enacted and outcomes are emerging. This means doing whatever is necessary *at that time* and *in those circumstances*, rather than acting formulaically and in strict accordance with some preordained policy, plan or procedure. This carries with it, of course, the need to continue to act ethically in the moment and to collaborate with others who might be affected. But it places adaptiveness, imagination and creativity ahead of procedural rigidity, clichéd responses and identikit 'solutions'. "Good enough for now" and "work in progress" are the guiding principles.

Muddling through with courage

In relation to muddling through, the question of courage arises, first and foremost, from the unknowability of a future that is emerging continuously from the widespread interplay of people's moment-to-moment interactions. This requires managers to "act with confidence even as they are doubting, questioning, and probing their assumptions".[3]

Uncertainty, mystery and doubt

In Chapter 4, I referred to the words of the poet John Keats, who coined the phrase "Negative Capability" to describe "*being in uncertainties, mysteries, doubts, without any irritable reaching after fact and reason*". We all face uncertainties, mysteries and doubts, as we seek to find our way through the demands of day-to-day organizational life. As well as life more generally. It can, though, be particularly challenging for managers to acknowledge this openly, given that the deeply ingrained narrative on management/leadership practice sees this as being very much about "reaching after fact and reason". Not only that, but doing so in full expectancy of being able to achieve it! As such, uncertainty, mystery and doubt are not part of the mainstream vocabulary. Instead, these are viewed as signs of dysfunction and poor practice, rather than being accepted as natural and ever-present dynamics of organization This further reinforces an idealized and unrealistic representation of the management task that bears little relationship to managers' everyday lived reality.

This ever-present tension, between what is supposed to be happening and managers' real-world experience, is anxiety-inducing. As I characterized it in Chapter 5, the established mantra is, "if you're not in control, you're not leading". As such, accepting the state of not knowing appears to put at risk their sense of identity, as highly competent professionals. The natural response is for managers to seek to overcome the "uncertainties, mysteries and doubts", by colluding with the illusion of order, predictability and control that is reinforced by the formal structures, systems and controls. In Chapter 1, drawing on the metaphor used by philosopher Alan Watts, I described this as seeking to "catch the wiggliness in a net". This carries with it the felt need to account for one's practice in ways which are considered to be managerially 'correct' (i.e. which match the established narrative) and which are politically acceptable within the prevailing context. In reality, many of these formal trappings of organization act more as containers of anxiety than as ways of ensuring particular performance outcomes. As such, the requirements that these seek to impose on people's ongoing interactions, coupled with the need for managers to meet the control-based role expectations that flow from them, adds further to the wiggliness in which they are immersed and through which they are seeking to find their way.

The challenge for those in formal management roles then becomes one of how they might best participate in this ongoing process, so as to help people move forward in more useful ways. Besides doing so with *purpose*, this requires them to have the *courage* to take complexity seriously, confront unrealistic expectations when it makes sense to do so, and to work through their own and others' inevitable anxieties, despite having no certainty as to what will emerge. To paraphrase Ralph Stacey and Chris Mowles on this, management/leadership is having the courage to go on participating creatively *despite not knowing*.

Consistent with this, Peter Vaill observes that "so far, systems science has not rescued leaders and managers from needing the ability to 'Band-Aid', 'muddle through', 'learn as we go along', 'fly by the seat of our pants', and 'keep our fingers crossed'".[4] Given the complex interdependencies of human interaction, this is inevitable. More data does nothing to address the complex social dynamics out of which whatever happens, happens. Equally, more controls do little or nothing to calm what Vaill refers to as "permanent white water", which he describes as "surprising, novel, messy, costly, recurring, and unpreventable events".[5] Importantly, he goes on to stress that this term also refers to the *feelings* that people attach to their experience, such as "lack of direction, absence of coherence, and loss of meaning". These are all characteristics of the real-world wiggliness. In response, he speaks of "spiritual learning" as a way of being. That is, "learning of the ways that our courageous daily struggles in white water connect us to the ground of being and ensure our participation in it".[6]

The courage to talk

Since organization emerges in conversation, it makes sense for managers to engage *regularly, consciously and deliberately* in this process. Most of these conversations take place informally and spontaneously. And, for some, the thought of letting go of the structural trappings and arms-length formality of their role can be anxiety-inducing. It exposes them to unscripted questions and potential challenges to their own sensemaking and formal authority. So, 'getting out and about' might be an act of courage in its own right. It's important to remember, though, that this does not require a degree in conversational skills. It's simply about managers actively participating in everyday conversations, in ways that strengthen relationships; enable them to tune in to the themes that are organizing people's thoughts and actions; and help people make more useful sense of what's going on than they might otherwise do.

Taking this a stage further, James Traeger and Rob Warwick[7] suggest that managers might deliberately put themselves "in conversations and situations that might feel unsettling". They argue that those who act courageously in this way, "experience and sense the world differently". This is especially important for managers. It helps them to gain what David Ewing refers to as a "veridical perception" of what's going on.[8] As used here, this means the manager observing pertinent conditions directly, personally and immediately. It implies seeing, feeling, sensing, and being there, as opposed to judging on the basis of hearsay, wish, or data provided from afar by others. As Ewing goes on to say, because the manager sees, hears, feels, ponders the facts and feelings directly, and reacts emotionally, they develop a sense of commitment which is more deeply felt than it might otherwise be.

Challenging the generally accepted 'truths'

Muddling through with courage is also about being willing to expose the myths and misunderstandings that distort management practice and undermine organizational performance. As I mentioned earlier, these tend to result in unrealistic expectations of what managers can achieve. Confronting them takes courage, because it involves challenging much of the established thinking on the nature of organization and management, as well as the increasingly taken-for-granted ways of operating that flow from it. This is so much so that to question the validity of this line of thinking is likely to be greeted in some quarters with disbelief – and even derision. But it is the unquestioning acceptance of this approach that constrains the ways in which managers conceive of the organization's constantly shifting context; and which limit their imagination in dealing with the challenges and opportunities that arise from it.

Recognizing and confronting biases

Finally, here, it is important for managers to recognize that their own and others' assessments of what is going on, and how best to proceed, are necessarily incomplete and biased. As discussed in Chapter 2, this is a result of the self-organizing patterning of interaction that is a fundamental dynamic of everyday human behaviour. On the one hand, this enables people to go on together, without having to think afresh each time that they interact. As such, it is the essence of organization. By the same token, it is prejudiced – in the sense that it is based on 'pre-judgement'. That is to say, thought and action tend to be channelled imperceptibly along pre-established pathways.

You can't have organization (i.e. organizing), in any context, without the possibility of patterns emerging that are unjustifiably prejudicial to the interests of some of those who are directly or indirectly involved.

Although the potential always exists for new patterns to arise spontaneously from this process – as established ways of thinking, feeling and acting are reiterated in the moment – the tendency is for past patterns of thought and action to re-emerge spontaneously. Strengthening these still further. And so, although such bias does not naturally occur with malicious intent, it can be particularly problematic where it leads to the unjust treatment of particular individuals and groups. This tendency also risks excluding valuable knowledge, ideas and resources from the mix. So, becoming aware of the expression of their own and others' biases in their day-to-day exchanges, and being willing to challenge the assumptions that are serving to reinforce any unhelpful patterns, is an important aspect of managing and leading courageously.

Muddling through with skill

Against this background, what does muddling through *skilfully* mean in practice? What can managers actually *do* to enhance people's individual and collective performance? How can they take complexity seriously and, *at the same time*, act in ways that they judge to be both practical and organizationally beneficial?

The approach blends together four, complementary aspects of skilful practice. These are:

- An *orientation to practice*, which is tuned-in to the paradoxical, 'both-and at the same time' nature of organization.
- *Complexity-congruent capabilities*, honed through personal experience, that underpin the ability to act forward skilfully into the future as it is emerging.
- A *mode of operating* that is enabled by these capabilities, informed by relevant theory and applied pragmatically in the moment.
- The development and deployment of a personally resonant and lightly held *practice theory*, comprising practical rules of thumb.

These four aspects of muddling through skilfully are illustrated in Figure 6.1 and explored below.

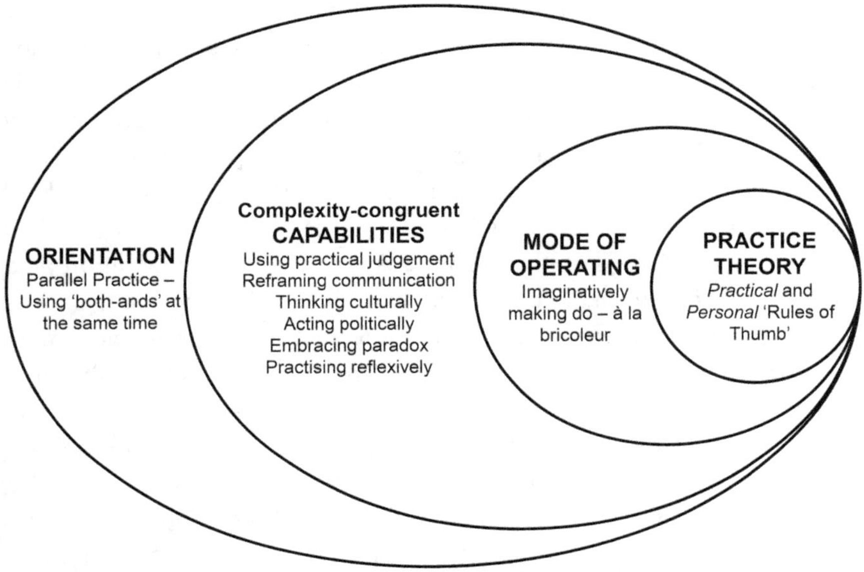

Figure 6.1 Muddling through skilfully

Reorienting the approach to managing/leading – the pursuit of parallel practice

Let's begin with the question of *orientation* to practice. Muddling through skilfully is about managers finding a way through the wiggly world of organization by paying attention to the multiple, and often conflicting, dynamics that are simultaneously in play in all organizational contexts. I call this "parallel practice". This emphasizes the intimately intertwined, 'both-and-at-the-same-time' nature of the response required. It rejects the arrogance and rigidity of one-size-fits-all 'solutions'; the simplistic nature of either-or thinking; the tendency to dismiss the shadow-side dynamics of organization (especially power relations and politics) as aberrations that 'proper management' will cure; and so on.

At its most basic, this is about managers skilfully engaging with the hidden, messy and informal aspects of everyday human interaction whilst, *at the same time* (i.e. 'in parallel'), paying attention to the formal, structured elements of organization, which both enable and constrain people's actions. Although I introduced and illustrated these separately in Chapter 1, to draw-out (literally) the differences, these designed and emergent elements occur simultaneously. They are fully interwoven aspects of the same interactional process: conceptually distinct but practically inseparable. Crucially, too, this inseparability recognizes that formal decisions to introduce the structural elements of organization *always originate in people's informal conversations*. As do the ways in which these are subsequently *designed, adopted, reinforced, adapted and potentially changed*. That is to say, decisions on the design of the formal aspects of organization, as well as how these are taken up in practice, are infused throughout with the underlying, shadow-side dynamics. *At the same time*, what we think of as the informal, 'under-the-table' aspects of everyday practice are affected by the formal roles and relationships that are in play in a particular situation. It is not possible to choose between the designed and emergent aspects of organization. Or for managers and others to engineer their way out of the inherent wiggliness. Nor can they ignore the formality and structure, which they and others are continuously co-creating through their ongoing participation in the process. Not only is it impossible to ignore the more formal aspects of organization, but to try to do so would also blind them to the specific effects that these are having on people's everyday practice and performance – for better and/or worse. Instead, their challenge is to find a way through these real-world dynamics, using whatever is available to make progress in meaningful ways. Recognizing that, at all times, they are both helped and hindered in everything they do by what everyone else happens to be doing and not doing.

In participating simultaneously in this process of design and emergence, managers engage in multiple, parallel roles, relationships, issues and tasks. These account for the excitement, achievement, and sense of belonging that they and others might experience in their lives, as well as for any disillusionment, disappointment, and feelings of exclusion. They are the source of co-operation and of conflict. Of apparent clarity and inherent ambiguity. Of opposition and support. Of stability and change. Muddling through with purpose, courage and skill is, fundamentally, an act of parallel practice.

Table 6.2 illustrates some of the 'macro' aspects of organization and management practice that are simultaneously present, whether acknowledged to be so or not. Muddling through skilfully requires managers to attend to these *in parallel*. Or, as I've characterized it here, to use 'both-ands' *at the same time*.

Table 6.2 Parallel practice

Muddling through skilfully needs to reflect the 'both-and at the same time' (i.e. paradoxical) nature of management/leadership practice. Some examples of this are set out below.

On the one hand . . .	**And, at the same time . . .**
… Managing – coping with the context as it is emerging, including the intended and unintended consequences of one's own contribution to it.	… Leading - making sense of the context in which you find yourself and articulating a next step that others recognize and support.
Based on Flinn (2018: 174)	
… seeking to 'wire up' the open, structured and formal aspects of organization, in line with officially adopted design parameters.	… 'tuning in' to the hidden, messy and informal (shadow-side) dynamics that are organizing people's actions, inactions and interactions 'on the ground'.
… managing the role expectations that arise from being officially in control (i.e. 'in charge').	… dealing with the reality of not being in control of what emerges from the multiplicity of interactions through which organization is being continuously (re)enacted.
… 'mission making' – actively sponsoring actions intended to realize officially adopted changes in purpose, ethos, strategic structure, operating practice, etc.	… 'meaning making' – helping people to make sense of, and deal with, *what actually happens in practice*, as this is emerging.
… pursuing success – identifying and introducing perceived enablers of performance.	… avoiding excess – guarding against having 'too much of a good thing'.
… being fully immersed in 'the game' as an involved participant.	… seeking to 'detach' oneself from it – consciously abstracting oneself from the intensity of what is emerging moment-to-moment, 'to make sense of what's going on and articulate a next step' – i.e. striving to adopt a position of detached involvement.
… seeking coherence, integration and collaboration (sameness).	… valuing challenge, diversity and competition (difference).
… striving to achieve a 'better' future, however defined (reach).	… keeping one's 'feet on the ground' as to the real-world dynamics of organization (realism).
And, at the core of all of this, *parallel practice* means:	

(Continued)

Table 6.2 (Continued)

… seeing the general relevance of particular activities ('generalizing')	… seeing the significance of the particular in the general ('particularizing').
Based on Stacey and Mowles's discussion of practical judgement or phronesis (2016: 500)	
… recognizing and embracing the paradoxical, 'both-and at the same time' nature of organization, for which there is no resolution and no simple, either/or 'solutions'.	… helping to make this paradox of simultaneous knowing and not knowing liveable for people.

Complexity-congruent capabilities

Muddling through with skill is fundamentally about managers and others applying their judgement in the specific conditions that they are experiencing – at that time, in that situation, and with those people. It's here, in the practical reality of people's ongoing interactions, that managers can strive to make a difference – using formal and informal interactions, joint sensemaking conversations, and political acumen in an effort to shift their own and others' practice in ways that they judge to be both beneficial and ethically sound. Before looking at some of the specific methods that managers might adopt and adapt, as they seek to find their way through the continuously emerging challenges of managing/leading in a wiggly world, there are a number of specific capabilities that are core to the practice of muddling through as I'm describing it here. These are: using practical judgement, reframing communication, thinking culturally, acting politically, embracing paradox and practising reflexively.

Using practical judgement

Practical judgement or, as some call it, "practical wisdom",[9] is the fundamental capability that managers need to exercise, if they are to participate skilfully in their management/leadership role, within the inherent uncertainties, complexities and ambiguities of organization. This is about applying their knowledge and skills contingently in each particular situation in which they find themselves. Its attention is on what is emerging within their own and others' ongoing interactions, and why and how that might be; the habitual and contingent themes that are organizing their conversations, and enabling and constraining their practice; how they are participating in the process; potential shifts in the current content and patterning of interaction that might be helpful; and so on. It is also here, in the specific local context, that managers can reflect on and develop their own and others' practice.

As introduced in Chapter 4, practical judgement draws on Aristotle's notion of phronesis. This (again using Aristotlean terminology) is in contrast to the usual focus of leadership development on episteme (universally applicable, context-free and scientifically derived knowledge) and techné (reflected in the tools and techniques of management practice). Phronesis is about pragmatically applying expert judgement in the *specific circumstances* one is facing, as *derived from practical experience.* As such, it is not generalizeable in the sense of being able to derive a universally applicable model of practice or definitive n-step process for bringing about change. It is context-specific. Being able to sense the nature and disposition of that context – both its most obvious features and its more peripheral aspects – and to respond appropriately, is what practical judgement is all about. At the same time, of course, the ability to do so itself draws on the capacity to derive generalized rules of thumb from those specifics and to hone these through practice.

The pragmatism, as Yiannis Gabriel suggests, "lies not in the recipe or the rule-of-thumb itself, but in the ability to identify when and how to invoke them".[10] Such timing is critical to muddling through skilfully. The precise point of intervention is never wholly within the gift of the manager to decide, of course, Here, as in all other aspects of organization, they are enabled and constrained by what everyone else is doing and not doing. Even though their formal position might allow them to take the initiative in a particular situation, they cannot control what has gone before. Or how what others happen to be doing around them might change conditions in the moment. Once again, the nature of their response rests solely on the practical judgement and creative insight that they – and anyone else they might call upon – apply at the time. Drawing again on de Bono, the precise point at which anyone 'enters into' an emerging (and historically situated) pattern of interaction affects what is perceived, what is possible, and what eventually emerges.

As Chris Mowles sums up this general position,[11]

> there is nothing more practical for a manager to be doing than to pay close attention to how they are working with others in everyday work

situations; to find time to reflect with colleagues on how they are working and thinking, and to have the courage to stay engaged with each other as they negotiate how to go on together.

Whilst practical judgement is the 'core capability' of muddling through skilfully, a number of others sit alongside this. These, which home-in on the conversational, socio-political, paradoxical and immersive-abstractive nature of organization, are set out below.

Reframing communication

Conventionally, those in charge in a particular context ("the management") are thought of as determining and transmitting the meaning of particular events, changes or policies *from* themselves *to* other employees. The emphasis is on how best to "get the message across". The success of this then tends to be judged in terms of the extent to which "the right facts are transmitted to the right people at the right time". This notion sits at the heart of mainstream thinking on the nature of leadership communication. In contrast, from a wiggly-world perspective, organization emerges in, and is enacted through, conversation. That is to say, outcomes emerge spontaneously from people's perceptions, interpretations and evaluations of issues and events, in the midst of their ongoing, one-to-one and small-group conversations. This includes the process through which formal statements issued by management, and the decisions that underpin them, originate in the first place. And it is how these are made sense of and acted upon by others.

For managers, then, *the conversations are the work*. The more conventional, structured elements of organizational communication provide a formal informational backcloth to this dynamic and ongoing process of joint sensemaking and power relating. But statements from on high *communicate* nothing. Instead, communication happens in the plethora of local conversations that flow from them. It is a relational practice. And, although paying attention to content and delivery is important, no amount of staging can create the conditions for this to take place. Whether this is through crafting the content, polishing the presentation or perfecting the performance. Instead, the manager's task becomes one of seeking to connect with people as they are participating in their own conversational networks. These 'touch points' provide important opportunities for them to influence the context, content and patterning of those myriad interactions through which organization is being continuously enacted. Their aim is to tune-in to the themes that are organizing people's understanding and action; identify and tap into the natural credibility paths[12] of interaction, through which perceptions and interpretations of emerging events tend to be honed; and to try to shift the patterning and quality of interaction in ways that they judge to be beneficial, doing so through the effectiveness of their own participation. Put simply, the task is one of joint sensemaking and relationship building rather than one-way message passing. For managers, then, 'talk' – in its broadest sense – is their primary *action* 'tool'.[13]

It is important to re-emphasize that the focus here is on the natural dynamics of everyday conversations. It is not about convening structured dialogue sessions or needing a degree in conversational skills. Instead, it is primarily about managers shifting the emphasis of their own approach to communication. Practising in ways that are based more on informal, unstructured interaction than formal, structured interventions. Table 6.3 gives a flavour of what this shift might mean in terms of the nature and content of leadership communication. This contrasts the joint sensemaking/relationship building nature of communication with the conventional approach based on 'getting the message across'.[14] It is the former mode of communication that is most relevant to the task of muddling through skilfully.

The main emphasis here is on paying attention to the 'open play' of everyday conversational interaction, rather than overly focusing on 'set-piece' events, such as team workshops, structured dialogue sessions and the like. Given the intuitive and improvisational dimensions of muddling through, doing so skilfully can also be thought of in terms of what Flemming Toft calls improvisational dialogue and which he describes as "a free flowing intuitive and responsive dialogue that surrenders to the present and the action".[15] At the same time, it can be helpful to be aware of some of the methodologies that have been developed specifically to improve the quality of conversation. These can provide managers with some useful insights into the underlying dynamics of conversation, when they reflect on their own practice and wider conversations, as well as offering some in-the-moment guidance for skilled practitioners.[16]

As a final point here, it is important to recognize that *the vast majority of conversations through which organization is enacted and outcomes emerge take place without the*

Table 6.3 Reframing communication

The table below illustrates some of the sought-after shifts in emphasis in the nature and content of leadership communication when muddling through skilfully.

ASPECT	FORMAL, STRUCTURED APPROACH *Getting the 'right facts' TO the 'right people' at the 'right time'*	INFORMAL, UNSTRUCTURED APPROACH *Joint sense-making and relationship building WITH people*
WHAT **does this form of communication contain?**	Carefully crafted *facts* about specific issues – e.g. the Whys, Whats, Hows, Whens and so on of the current state of play and/or forthcoming changes.	Feelings, reactions, understandings, anxieties, etc. that people have about what's going on and about formally delivered 'messages'. Efforts to understand and influence the ongoing patterning of interaction, to encourage and enable fluid conversation to take place more widely.
WHEN **does it take place?**	Routinely via scheduled briefings of ongoing activities. Before any formal change begins and at relevant points during the process – i.e. 'when the Plan says'.	Actually or potentially via every interaction – deliberately or as opportunity presents itself. Also, after each formal intervention, to understand how it 'landed', and whenever prompted by signs of communication blockages and repetitive patterns of conversation.
HOW **is it done?**	Formally and using a planned and contained approach – e.g. using a formal communication pack, agenda, set format, etc.	Informally. One-to-one and small-group interactions. Face-to-face wherever possible. Questioning and listening. *Joint* exploration and sense-making. Challenge and support.
WHERE **does it take place?**	In a formal setting. Away from the day-to-day workplace.	Anywhere that the opportunity presents itself. Not a special setting.
WHO **is responsible for it?**	Often prepared by a specialist group (e.g. internal comms/HR) and then typically cascaded mechanistically through successive management levels.	The manager themself. Encourage and enable others to initiate, too. Then listen!

ASPECT	FORMAL, STRUCTURED APPROACH *Getting the 'right facts' TO the 'right people' at the 'right time'*	INFORMAL, UNSTRUCTURED APPROACH *Joint sense-making and relationship building WITH people*
WHEN THINGS GO WRONG, what is the response?	'Gone wrong' means: failure to 'get the message across'. Assumption: *They* didn't get it. Response: Say it again – perhaps using a different format. Emphasis: Output and telling.	'Gone wrong' means: failure to connect. Lack of fluidity in conversation (stuck patterns) and unwillingness to explore what's going on. Mutual lack of trust, etc. Assumption: *We* need to work on this. Conversation is key. Listen. *I might need to change.* Emphasis: Input and listening.

relevant line manager being physically present. As such, it is unlikely that these will be governed by any understanding of such conversational niceties. The challenge for managers is how they might tap into, and help shape, the nature and content of this diverse and informal network of conversations, which are a critical dynamic of organizational practice and performance.

Thinking culturally

The call for managers to "think culturally" follows naturally from the fact that they can't *not* communicate. As soon as they become a manager, everything that they say and do – *including everything that they don't say and don't do* – 'sends messages' to people about such things as what matters and what doesn't; how they are viewed by the manager; whether or not the manager is interested in, and cares about, their opinions and feelings on matters that are important to them; whether or not what the manager says in public is consistent with how they are seen to act in practice; whether or not the manager can be trusted; and so on. No aspect of communication escapes this process. The problem from the manager's viewpoint is that it is not they who decide what their actions mean and what message is sent. It's the people who observe them in action, through the sharing of their observations and opinions with others. It is a sobering thought for managers that neither they nor others within the formal communication apparatus have a hand in crafting some of the most powerful 'messages' that others 'receive'. These emerge instead from, and become amplified by, the conversations that flow naturally from their observed behaviour. This is the case whether or not the manager perceives them to be accurate (assuming, that is, that they have any awareness at all of what's being communicated!).

Thinking culturally is therefore about the manager remaining aware of the possible effects that their own words and actions might be having on people's sense-making-cum-action-taking conversations – and taking responsibility for the symbolic impact of their own behaviour on the patterns of understanding and action that emerge. Coupled with this is an eagerness to explore any mismatch that becomes evident between their intentions and what is actually happening in practice. This can be a powerful source of information on their own practice and, through this, on broader aspects of organization. By definition, the way in which the manager sets out to explore this will itself 'send messages' about their willingness to listen, their openness to change and so on. As implied by the "reframing communication" capability, this is best pursued by adopting the broad stance to communication set out in column 3 of Figure 6.3. In *Informal Coalitions*, I referred to the manager's interactions with others as "moments of leadership truth". Where people's reactions run counter to the manager's expectations, this suggests the need for the manager to:

- inquire into the whys, whats and hows of others' perspectives;
- listen respectfully (if questioningly) to differing views, feelings, motivations, and concerns;
- in light of this, reflect seriously on what is going on;
- acknowledge and explore their own contribution, as a participant in – *and co-creator of* – the current context in which they find themselves; and
- accept that their own perspective – like everyone else's – can only ever be partial, in the sense of being both incomplete and one-sided.

Acting politically

As discussed extensively in earlier chapters, organization is a political process. That is to say, *everything* that happens in the context of organization does so as the result of political action.[17] This is not a choice open to managers. It arises naturally from the coming together of people who have differing interests that they wish to satisfy; differing interpretations of what's going on; differing intentions as to what they want to do next and the direction that they would wish to pursue; different ideologies (personal values, world views and norms, etc.) that are informing their judgements; differing identities (individual and group) to which they relate and that they wish to advance, preserve and protect; personal idiosyncrasies that will affect the ways in which they interact with others; and so on.

In seeking to further their interests, remain true to their ideological standpoint (or world view), and strengthen their sense of individual and collective identities, etc. people tend to coalesce informally around themes that resonate with them and which they judge will best serve their own needs and/or those of others who are important to them. As a result, shifting coalitions of diverse – and potentially competing – interest groups emerge informally, in pursuit of particular collective outcomes. At the same time, those involved are also seeking to satisfy their disparate personal needs and wants, through these same interactions. Because resources are limited, choices and trade-offs need to be made between competing demands and possible ways forward. This need for choices and trade-offs, coupled with the differing interests and perspectives of those doing the choosing, means that tension, confrontation and disagreement are inevitable. As are successful efforts to reconcile the differences and make progress from time to time – whether settled completely or, more likely, sufficiently enough for the next step to be taken.

Organizational politics is concerned with the ways in which these differences and conflicts are continuously being played out and choices made. As I said in *Informal Coalitions*, those organizations that succeed do so not only in spite of political behaviour but also because of it.[18] The differences that arise can never be wholly resolved through formal statements and processes, since these always have to be interpreted and enacted 'locally'. This means that there is always ample scope for these to be taken-up in interest-skewed ways (whether intentionally or otherwise). The scale and scope of these political dynamics will increase the greater the level of uncertainty that exists and the further away from agreement that people find themselves. However, politics will *always* be in play, regardless of how straightforward the situation appears to be. The natural tendency is for polarization to occur between contrasting points of view, different interests, diverse patterns of interaction, and the groups who identify with them. Different opinions and perspectives that exist *within* a particular grouping tend to be glossed over, actively discouraged or disappear through habit. At the same time, the differences that exist *between* this position and those advocated by others tend to be accentuated, with any similarity between the positions tending to be disregarded or ignored altogether. In this way, people's individual and collective experience is polarized into similarity within a particular category and difference between them. This natural pattern-maximizing dynamic of interaction, favouring sameness, consistency and continuity over difference and novelty, is at the root of groupthink and related dysfunctional aspects of organization that we discussed in Chapter 2.

The above dynamics intensify the need for savvy political behaviour, in which the manager participates skilfully in the ongoing politics of everyday organizational life. Or, as I'm referring to it here, muddles through skilfully by *acting politically*. Fundamentally, this is about their seeking to integrate difference whilst, at the same time, doing so without losing the potential benefits that difference, differentiation and diversity bring. This requires them to exercise their power to influence what happens, by dealing proactively and imaginatively with the differences that emerge. And doing so with conscious awareness. It is about acting ethically in the moment, in an effort to shift the nature and patterning of their own and/or others' interactions, in ways that they judge to be beneficial.

Overall, the task is one of encouraging, enabling and participating in conversations that tend to be free-flowing, rather than stuck in fixed patterns and clichéd responses. Conversations which are simultaneously co-operative and competitive; and which mobilize collective action in support of organizationally enhancing themes and practices. This process is never-ending. Whatever actions might result, unintended consequences will always arise. This inevitably creates further difference and contention; adding to the ongoing political challenge.

Embracing paradox

I've earlier spoken extensively about the paradoxical nature of organization. Most particularly in Chapter 2. That is, the simultaneous presence of mutually contradictory conditions, neither of which can be eliminated. Muddling through skilfully requires managers to embrace this dynamic, in the sense of acknowledging and working creatively with the tensions and conflicts that this brings. Rather than seeking to resolve these through the futile search for a supposedly clear and decisive position. This dynamic sits at the core of the need for, and exercise of, parallel practice.

In the previous section, I described the natural tendency for polarization to occur between different viewpoints, choices and the like. This often results in positions being taken that favour one attribute over the other (either-or); that adopt a 'sometimes this and sometimes that' compromise, according to circumstance (both-and); or that seek to avoid the conflict altogether, in a 'lowest common denominator' sort of way (neither-nor). In all such cases, though, the rejected or subordinated aspects will continue to affect what happens, through the embodiment of these in many of the shadow-side themes and practices. In contrast, embracing paradox means being receptive to the *unavoidable* 'both-and, at the same time' nature of organizational dynamics and seeking to respond imaginatively to the challenges and opportunities that this brings.

So, what does this mean in practical terms? First and foremost, it is about raising awareness of the inherent contradictions and recognizing that there are no simple, either-or choices that can be made. The challenge then becomes one of helping people to live and work *dynamically* and *creatively* with the inevitable tensions and conflicts that this brings in its wake. There is no formulaic response to this challenge that will lead inexorably to the 'right answer'. Instead, it requires a willingness for people (including managers themselves) to:

- normalize the contradictions that arise, as natural aspects of everyday organizational practice;
- engage *constructively* in their interactions with others, in ways that seek to draw out what they judge to be the positive attributes of seemingly contradictory positions whilst, at the same time seeking to limit the potential downsides;
- resist the tendency to view aspects of organization one-dimensionally – seeing things as wholly good (e.g. "leadership") or wholly bad (e.g. "resistance to change") – but rather to recognize and deal with both the positive and negative attributes that exist in all contexts; and
- be aware that success can readily turn into failure, if apparently successful characteristics are taken to excess and become unquestioned (or, worse still, unquestionable) ways of working.

Practising reflexively

Practising reflexively is about taking experience seriously. It calls on managers to reflect *in the midst of their practice.* This means their paying deliberate attention to the details of the particular situation in which they are participating, *as well as to their own process of making sense and responding to them.* It is central to the idea of muddling through skilfully and is intimately associated with a manager's capacity to apply practical judgement. It is about their remaining alert to the specific context in which they are immersed, and to how this is shifting over time, as a result of their own and others' interactions. Paying attention to the movement of their joint sensemaking and action-taking with others. Identifying and exploring dominant themes; noticing cues and signs; checking-out hunches and making on-the-spot adjustments. Noticing differences – as well as connections and complementarities. Observing clichéd patterns in their own and others' thoughts and actions. Spotting contradictions between the stated intentions, what they find themselves doing in practice, and what is emerging overall.

In essence, it means managers thinking on their feet and adjusting their practice accordingly. The focus is on the specific needs of the situation, ahead of generalized principles. All as this is being played out in the "living present"[19] of people's in-the-moment interactions. And, as a *reflexive* practice, it means recognizing that the very act of reflecting on what is emerging in the midst of their participation in a particular context calls out different responses and changes that context. This is at the core of participating from a complex social process perspective. But none of this takes place in any way 'outside' those interactions.

The theories and responses that emerge in this way are situation-specific. They integrate knowledge drawn from past experience in similar situations, relevant empirical research, and the particularities of the circumstances that pertain there and then. In addition, as noted by Gary Rolfe,[20] skilful reflexive practice also involves knowing how these sources of knowledge might best be combined to arrive at a plausible theory and facilitate practical actions in the moment. Also, as pointed out by Christopher Johns,[21] "Reflexivity acknowledges that 'an experience' is not an isolated moment but part of a continuous flow of experience over time. As such, 'an experience' is always a reflection of past experience that anticipates future experience. Indeed, this is the fundamental learning process, of making sense of the present in terms of the past, with a view towards the future". This accords with the notion of "the living present", as discussed in Chapter 2.

Finally, it is worth noting that this fits well with my earlier (Chapter 5) reframing of accountability as the ability to account for one's practice (account-*ability*), as well as with the notion of practice-based evidence that I also introduced in Chapter 5 and shall refer to again later. By virtue of their ongoing learning and research, coupled with the in-the-moment adaptation of their practice to suit the specific needs of the moment, the reflexive practitioner is better positioned to account for the Whys, Whats and Hows of their actions.

Mode of Operating

Against this background, muddling through skilfully requires a general way of operating that is enabled by the above capabilities, informed by relevant theory and applied pragmatically in the moment. As trailed in Chapter 4, this calls on managers to adopt the mode of operation of the bricoleur, both alone and in concert with others. It is about their anticipating and responding flexibly to the complex, uncertain, paradoxical and constantly shifting nature of whatever emerges. Creatively applying their individual and collective capabilities to the challenges that they face. In essence, it means managers *imaginatively making do* with whatever knowledge, ideas and resources they can pull together in the moment. In this sense, the term "resource" refers to any factor, actual or potential, tangible or intangible, through which benefit can be derived.

At times, based on their experience and practical judgement, they might draw on aspects of highly structured, procedurally straightforward, and scientifically rational approaches to particular issues, problems or situations. In the context of muddling through, though, the approach would not simply be to apply these in their complexity-free purity. Instead, as mentioned by Gabriel (Chapter 4), it would be to elaborate upon and adapt them as appropriate; using these as improvisational 'props', rather than procedural straitjackets. And so, other than seeking to act ethically in the moment, the responses that they might make would not be limited by any sense of the 'right way' to approach a particular issue. They would just be looking to identify and deploy whatever appeared to be useful and plausible ways forward, given the specific circumstances. The important criteria to bear in mind in this are congruence, contingency, creativity and, most importantly, conversation. That is, adopting approaches that:

- are congruent with the complex social dynamics (i.e. wiggliness) of real-word organization;
- offer contingently useful ways forward, given the particular circumstances 'in play' there and then;
- make creative use of whatever resources happen to be available at the time; and
- use conversation as the primary means of arriving at 'the next step' and coping with whatever emerges from it.

Practice theory

To complete the picture, the final element of muddling through skilfully takes us into the realm of what would conventionally be thought of as concepts, tools and techniques. This is a controversial theme in the context of the complex social dynamics of organization as set out here. It risks managers being drawn into the seductive but ill-conceived 'if you do this, you'll get that' logic that ordinarily dominates in this area. It is also highly susceptible to fads and fashions. As a result, those who take complexity seriously often challenge the suggestion that tools and techniques have any meaningful part to play in managing/leading from a complexity viewpoint. In turn, this inevitably begs the question from practising managers, "So what can I *do*?". The response then, quite rightly, becomes one of advocating their more skilful participation in the everyday politics of organizational life. That is, using their practical judgement to make progress, whilst acknowledging the fact that, despite acting with deliberate intent, they cannot know with certainty what will emerge in practice.

For my own part, whilst fully endorsing the validity of this position, I also recognize that most managers have a felt need for some underlying schema that, by implication at least, validates their actions. As I've argued extensively here, there are no step-by-step recipes for success or related, 'plug and play' tools and techniques. There are no models that can be applied universally to produce guaranteed outcomes. No one-size-fits-all theories that provide the necessary sureties. At the same time, it *is* possible (and I believe helpfully so) for managers to develop and deploy various rules of thumb and other pragmatic approaches to support their practice. These can serve as *provocations* and *stepping stones*, to stimulate and enable novel and practical ways of engaging with the challenges that emerge. They include what Gabriel describes as "flexible routines", which invite "improvisation and elaboration rather than copying and imitation" (Chapter 4). In some instances, these can serve a similar purpose to what de Bono refers to as "random stimulation" in relation to lateral thinking. That is, something being added in to the sensemaking-cum-action-taking process, the value of which might only become apparent after the event.

As set out above, it is important for managers to *develop their own* practice theories based on their own context, history and lived experience. Theories that they have found to be both practical and beneficial in finding their way through the complexities of organizational life, and which resonate with them personally. However, by way of illustration, I've set out below some examples of things that I have found useful as a practising manager and, latterly, consultant. These form part of my own "practice theory", as Peter Vaill describes it (Chapter 4). The list is not exhaustive. And there are inevitably overlaps between the items listed. As such, these are only meant to be indicative of the sort of rules of thumb and pragmatic approaches that managers might draw-out from their own experience and practice-based research.

As always, what matter most are the real-world conversations that flow from the use of such approaches, and the ideas and responses that these evoke.

Creatively cutting and pasting – using what 'works'

This captures the essence of Gabriel's argument in support of using theories, models, techniques and so on "paragrammatically" (Chapter 4). That is, using them – or aspects of them – to the extent that they provide useful ways forward but not treating them as cast-in-concrete statements of fact or definitive prescriptions for action. It also sits four-square with the "imaginatively making do" spirit of bricolage. Typical questions might be:

- Does a particular approach – or elements if it – look and feel 'right enough' in the current circumstances?
- Does it offer a different perspective around which the manager and others can improvise and adapt?

- Does it help to unblock thinking and stimulate new ideas?
- Is it likely to be useful as a way of helping to identify and shape potential next steps(s)?

Whatever theory or approach might be drawn upon, the nature, content and patterning of conversations will change. And so, therefore, will the outcome. It will only become apparent after the event, though, whether or not the ideas and actions that emerge from this repositioning of people's contribution help or hinder progress. The important thing is to 'cut and paste' with a light touch – using what proves to be helpful and not worrying too much about what doesn't.

This 'creatively cut and paste' approach might usefully be applied to the examples that follow.

Hosting conversations – creating opportunities for shared meaning making and relationship building

I first came across the idea of relating managing/leading to the role of hosting several years ago. This provided a central element in a book by Richard Lester and Michael Piore, entitled *Innovation: The Missing Dimension.*[22] The particular "missing dimension" to which they refer is the failure of conventional management to take account of the role that interpretation plays in the innovation process. Their case is that an interpretive perspective is needed to counter-balance the problem-solving approach that dominates the established discourse on the nature of management thinking and practice.

In advancing their argument, they draw an analogy between the role of a host (or, as they position it, hostess) at a cocktail party and the leader's need to stimulate and help sustain ongoing, interpretive conversations around emerging issues and possibilities. This reaffirms the critical dynamic as one of conversation. And, although Lester and Piore's focus is on conversations relating to innovation, this dynamic is fundamental to all aspects of organization and management practice. Within the context of muddling through, hosting is primarily concerned with the interactional dynamics of the *process*, rather than describing someone who adopts a particular style of practice. It is here that existing patterns of understanding and action are established and reinforced whilst, at the same time, retaining the potential for new meaning and novel practices to emerge.

As discussed in detail earlier, acts of leadership emerge, and are recognized as such, in the continuous process of people's day-to-day interactions. Stimulating and participating in meaning-making conversations, and seeking to articulate and mobilize the actions of others around important emerging themes, is the essence of this practice. Drawing analogies from the widely understood process of 'hosting' (and being hosted) helps managers to recognize this as a fundamental part of their everyday practice. And it might also help with the task of chipping away some of the false mystique that surrounds leadership as it is ordinarily constructed. Making the most of the concept of hosting will depend – in this case as in all others – on the ways in which managers perceive, interpret, evaluate and make use of it in the context of their own, local interactions. This is as much about joining-in the conversations, as an active participant, as it is about joining-up other people. It includes such things as:

- identifying, enriching, and/or establishing from scratch, interaction-friendly spaces;
- encouraging participation and stimulating interest;
- linking people around important ideas and themes;
- actively participating in the sensemaking-cum-action-taking process, both to offer their own perspective and to surface other, shadow-side themes that are organizing people's day-to-day practice;
- refreshing the interactions, as appropriate, with new people and/or organizing themes; and
- seeking to channel the everyday politics of human interaction – in which difference and contention are recognized as normal and valued – in directions that serve to stimulate people's creativity and collaborative action.

Framing the conversations - facilitating joint sensemaking

Whilst it is impossible to *model* the complex social dynamics of organization, in ways that offer definitive ways forward, there can be merit in making sensible use of non-prescriptive frameworks to stimulate and frame the conversations around particular novel and/or repeating issues. I have developed – and regularly help managers deploy – a number of such sense-making frameworks during my own consulting practice. In all cases, though, the value lies in the conversations that emerge from their use, not in the frameworks themselves. Use of the latter can help with the challenge that I mentioned earlier about starting from where people are, rather than from where we might prefer them to be. In an organizational context, people are familiar with using frameworks of one sort or another to support their practice. So, using these as pragmatic aids to joint sensemaking, rather than as definitive 'if you do this, you'll get that' prescriptions, can be helpful in shifting the patterns of understanding and action.

In this regard, although I have reservations about some aspects of it, Dave Snowden's Cynefin Framework fits into this broad category of 'aids to sensemaking and action-taking'. I don't advocate its use myself, but many people do use it. As I mentioned in note 9 in Chapter 1, there are similarities here with the so-called "Stacey Diagram" and at least two other formulations. Ralph Stacey no longer advocates the use of his mid-1990s diagram to understand and address the dynamics in play, although it is still regularly referenced.[23] His argument against its use provides an important cautionary note in the deployment of any frameworks of this kind. In particular, people can become seduced into viewing these as prescriptions of what they should be doing, rather than as coarse-grained representations of the dynamics within which they are immersed. This highlights the risk of stepping over the line from using these as pragmatic stimulants to sensemaking conversations – *in which the conversations remain the primary focus* – to seeing them instead as offering definitive statements of how things are.

It is always important, of course, to guard against the risk of reifying frameworks. However, I believe that it's possible both to remain true to the idea that it is the in-the-moment conversational exchanges that matter most and, at the same time, to recognize that the occasional use of an appropriate framework can provide new insights and help conversations to become unstuck. As stated earlier, de Bono's notion of proto-truths introduces the idea of temporary or contingent truths.[24] He suggests that with a proto-truth there is a constant readiness for change but, at the same time, a willingness to use it *as if* it were absolute. In this way, sense-making frameworks can be thought of as proto-truths – offering help with the sensemaking process but cautioning users against becoming trapped by them. The important question when using any such framework then becomes "Is it useful in this situation and at this time?", rather than "Is it right?".

Providing vision, support and challenge – helping people to 'see better'

The first point to make here is that providing vision is about managers helping people to 'see better' *through their everyday interactions.*[25] It has nothing to do with providing *a Vision*, with a capital 'V'. 'Seeing better' is about people (including managers themselves) making better sense of emerging events than they might otherwise have done. Ambition and intention still have important parts to play in providing vision in the ways described here. However, the emphasis is much more on sharing experiences and offering new perspectives around the everyday events, situations and activities that are happening in the here and now. In other words, it is much more about insight than supposed far sight.

It has become well established to argue the need for managers to ensure that their everyday actions are consistent with their words. This is often characterized as "walking the talk". Using a similar formulation, what I'm talking about here can be thought of as "talking the walk". That is, helping people to make sense of what's going on; and how they and others are responding to emerging events. Crucially too, it is about doing so primarily in the midst of their day-to-day interactions, rather than in set-piece meetings and presentations.

Interwoven with this in-the-moment, interactional process of providing vision are the paradoxical notions of support and challenge.[26] Supporting people in their efforts to shift their understanding and practice; and challenging constructively, to explore differences of perspective, uncover assumptions, expose flawed thinking, and so on.

Building coalitions – mobilizing collective action and integrating difference

Coalitional activity is a fundamental dynamic of effective management practice. It is how changes are brought about in a social context, where political dynamics driven by difference are always in play. It is also, therefore, how things are prevented from happening. Or how things end up being diverted from the path that they were originally intended to follow. People coalesce informally around particular themes and actions, as they seek to support, modify or oppose changes that are being proposed by others, or to initiate shifts in practice and performance that run counter to the formally established position. This goes on with or without a manager's involvement. So, tapping into the themes around which people are coalescing is a critical aspect of muddling through skilfully. As are practices aimed at mobilizing the collective action of people in support of what the manager judges to be worthwhile changes. It is through such coalition building that differences can be integrated in pursuit of broader goals. Seeking to achieve a coherent approach to the issues that emerge, without losing the individual and collective benefits that difference can bring.

Crucially, when people coalesce around a particular theme or desired outcome, they do not have to agree on everything or subscribe to an identical set of values to make progress. Although some underpinning values and beliefs might be shared by those involved, often they won't be. In many cases, people will differ greatly in their worldviews and personal values. Indeed, different people may hold opposing views across a range of issues. Despite this, in relation to the particular theme or sought-after objective, they set aside their differences temporarily and contingently – at least in the public arena.

In terms of management practice, the basic 'rule of thumb' here is to push at half-open doors. This means working at first with those who show enthusiasm for – or, at least, interest in – what is being proposed, before working outwards from, and through, them to mobilize others. This runs counter to the usual practice of 'rolling out' messages in a highly regimented, precisely scripted way – either layer-by-layer or simultaneously.

Using 'both-ands' at the same time – making paradox liveable for people

Implicit in the notion of parallel practice, and explicit in the core capability of embracing paradox, is recognition of the ambiguous and paradoxical nature of organization. This presents a particular challenge, because it runs counter to many of the ingrained assumptions about effective organization and management practice. With the latter, the emphasis is on clarity and precision, order and knowability, finding the one best way with which everyone can agree, and so on. In contrast, paradox brings with it *unavoidable* tensions and conflicts, messiness and uncertainty.

As well as the simultaneous presence of characteristics that sit uncomfortably together from a conventional standpoint. Making this reality liveable for people is therefore an important aspect of muddling through skilfully. Given this, I have found it helpful on occasions to make pragmatic use of a number of frameworks that make explicit the paradoxical nature of organization. Amongst other things, these can help to:

- normalize the inherent tensions, conflicts and contradictions;
- seek to counter the polarizing tendencies that are inherent in the natural, 'pattern-maximizing' dynamics of interaction and groupthink;
- expose the fact that there are potential downsides to even the most overtly positive of positions, as well as positive attributes associated with less-favoured aspects;
- as a corollary of this, show how a particular attribute can be expressed in both positive and negative terms – encouraging pursuit of the former and seeking to limit the effects of the latter;
- show that *any attribute* taken to excess can become negative and debilitating;
- surface the different perspectives that people hold in relation to particular topics, as well as the sources both of strong advocacy and staunch resistance to a proposed shift in organizational strategy and/or practice;
- map what's going on, as a basis for self-reflection and constructive action-taking.

In *Informal Coalitions*, I mentioned three such frameworks, in which I continue to find value. These are *Johnson's Polarity Map; Fletcher and Olwyler's Paradoxical Thinking*; and the *Strategic Dimensions* element of my own *Business Performance Framework*.[27]

In the spirit of "creatively cutting and pasting", with which I opened this section, such frameworks should be held lightly; applying them to the extent that they help to move the conversations on, but not treating them as rigid methodologies to be applied mechanistically.

Enhancing people's response-ability *and account*-ability *– taking experience seriously*

To underscore the fundamentally conversational nature of organization, the purpose of this is to enable people to become so immersed in conversations about the Whys, Whats and Hows of their practice that they are:

- better placed to deal with whatever emerges 'when the real world happens', without having to ask permission or being excessively constrained by inflexible rules and regulations (i.e. they have response-*ability*);
- able to provide a meaningful and authoritative account of those factors affecting the activities, capabilities and performance for which they are responsible, both individually and collectively (i.e. they have account-*ability*);
- able to explain the perceived contribution of their own decisions and actions to issues, events and outcomes that emerge in practice;
- better informed in their relationships and transactions with third parties;
- able to learn from their experience and improve their ongoing practice; and
- able to provide information and commentary that assists and enables other people in their choices and (inter)actions.

As mentioned earlier, viewing accountability in this way still allows for deliberate malpractice or gross negligence in the context of a perceived failure to be exposed and dealt with. But it begins with the presumption of well-intended failure and recognition of the complex interdependencies involved, rather than looking immediately for someone to blame.

Keep chipping away – pursuing sought-after change incrementally, contingently and opportunistically

This rule of thumb is rooted in an apocryphal story of Michaelangelo's approach to his sculpting of the statue of David, which currently sits in the Accademia Gallery in Florence. According to the legend, he was asked how he had managed to sculpt the statue from a large block of marble. "It's easy", he replied, "You just chip away the bits that don't look like David".

True or not, this serves as a helpful nudge in the direction of, metaphorically, 'chipping away the bits that don't look like David' whenever one judges that some things are getting in the way of the broad intentions being pursued. Such as, progressively chipping away at those trappings of organization that run counter to the expressed intention of *enabling* people to perform (as in Table 6.1). Or making use of "teachable moments", which are discussed further in Chapter 7.

Avoiding 'paint-by-numbers' approaches – valuing emergent practice ahead of procedural rigidity and 'best practice' prescriptions

In essence, the rule of thumb is to avoid being seduced by the idea that expert practice, in the socially complex context of organization and management, can be reduced to a list of step-wise procedures, uniform methodologies and related competencies. It can't. To use Eddie Obeng's phrase, for much of the time, managers are "walking in the fog".[28]

A few years ago, as I was facilitating a workshop with a management team in Germany, I challenged the idea that the transfer of so-called best practice from one organizational context to another was a credible way of improving performance. In the discussion that followed, I suggested that one of the main problems with this seemingly common-sense approach is that it typically ignores the critical factors of organizational context and the path dependency of whatever happens. In particular, it takes no account of the unique ways in which the complex social dynamics of organization play out in each specific context.

One of the other participants then described this phenomenon beautifully in terms of the "logic" and the "magic" of organizational practice. The conventional notion of best practice transfer focuses exclusively on the logic – the formal, structured and visible aspects of what is assumed to be the source of the superior performance. This should be no surprise. It ticks all of the boxes that are supposed to be ticked, in terms of its focus on the rational aspects of organization – the tangible, the programmable, the measurable and so on. However, it's the magic that makes the difference. It's the magic that brings the presumed logic to life. The idealized designs, that others studiously copy, are only made real through the ways in which people enact them via their local interactions. And it is from these wiggly dynamics of everyday organizational life that the outcomes viewed as "best practice" emerge. These local exchanges take place continuously – between specific people, at specific times and in specific situations. And it's in the unknowable interplay of these interactions that the magic of 'best practice' lies.

This magic can't be "captured" and then transplanted, grafted on, or otherwise transferred. People must make their own, through their everyday conversations and interactions with others. The more opportunity that they get to make these connections, within and beyond their immediate relationships, the more likely it is that magic will happen – including the translation of what appear to be the successful practices of others into their own context.

Using self – recognizing oneself as an involved participant and 'walking case study'

As I mentioned at the outset, readers can engage most effectively with the perspective set out here if they view themselves as "walking case studies" of these dynamics in action. For managers, adopting this stance can be very useful in orientating themselves to what's actually going on and in validating the shifts in perspective and practice set out in the book. Challenging others in their team and beyond to recognize this can also be helpful in gaining traction for the ideas and the implications of these for day-to-day practice. That is to say, managers (and others) *already know* that things happen in the ways that I've set out here. It's simply that this intuitive understanding has been suppressed for years by a narrative of organization and management which is rooted in the notions of order, predictability and control. Even though this bears little relationship to their everyday lived reality, power relations and vested interests are such that special and persistent effort is required to achieve the necessary shift.

The second element of "Using Self" is for managers to recognize that they are involved participants in the process of organization, not objective observers of other people's actions. As such, they are subject to the same effects as everyone else. This includes both the general (albeit fragmented) patterning of behaviour, which emerges from and helps to shape the self-organizing dynamics of everyday interaction, and the immediacy of their in-the-moment interactions.

As regards the former, they can glean clues about the general (cultural) patterning of interaction by observing, questioning and reflecting on what appears to be happening in their own exchanges. That is, unpicking moments that strike them as potentially significant in a broader sense. These might include, for example, a habitual response that might have become stuck in an unhelpful pattern. Or a novel response that, if it could be regularized, might enable more effective ways of working going forwards. In relation to the immediate and more 'local' significance of particular in-the-moment experiences, the manager needs to remain alert to the mood and feel of their everyday interactions which might merit more in-depth inquiry and exploration.

Exploring logic bubbles, cliché units and the developing 'rules of the game' – understanding and shifting the patterns that are shaping one's own and others' participation

When faced with people who think or act differently, a manager might regard them as ill-informed or disruptive and try to impose their own interpretation and will on events. Alternatively, they could think of them as acting in an intelligent manner (even if they can't immediately make sense of it themselves) but doing so from within what de Bono calls a different "logic bubble".[29] It is too easy (and simplistic) to adopt the former position. The change of perspective shifts the emphasis away from advocacy of one position over another towards joint inquiry. It involves exploration of the differences, how these have arisen, and what this might mean as regards the best way to move forward.

Another concept that de Bono introduced in his early writing is the notion of "cliché units".[30] As the term suggests, these are taken-for-granted ways of thinking and acting that have become so ingrained in people's day-to-day practice (including, perhaps, the manager's own ways of working) that they are used unthinkingly and block consideration of alternatives. In a similar way, how people are participating together in the organizational 'game', including the 'rules' by which they are playing it, the power relations that prevail and so on, can also become clichéd.

Exploring the characteristic patterning of people's ways of thinking and acting can open up potential ways of shifting individual and collective practice and performance to something more useful. In doing so, though, it is important to recognize that this is not a scientific, matter-of-fact exercise. It is unavoidably power-related and political, with all of the psychosocial and emotional effects that this brings into play.

Provoking movement – offering potential stepping-stones towards a different future

Closely related to the pattern-shifting associated with challenging logic bubbles, cliché units and the like are efforts to achieve movement in people's practice by using provocation (in its lateral thinking sense) as a deliberate way of generating new insights and innovative ways of moving forward. Unsurprisingly, given the parallels that I have drawn between de Bono's wide-ranging commentary on the self-organizing, patterning nature of the brain and the analogous dynamics of human interaction, I would primarily turn to the various techniques of lateral thinking. There are, though, many ways of provoking sought-after shifts in practice, in the process of what Frank J. Barrett calls "pragmatic experimentation".[31] This includes,

> questioning assumptions, exploring tangential ideas, and creating metaphors that stimulate thinking. [Where] actions are experimental, and knowledge is applied, pragmatic, and ongoing rather than stable, objective, and predictive.

Focusing on contribution – avoiding the activity trap

When thinking about roles and relationships, it can be useful to frame these in terms of my notion of Contribution Statements. These define roles in ways that help individuals and groups to create greater meaning and purpose in their work, through their everyday interactions with others in the business. The focus on outputs (sought-after contribution and results) rather than inputs (resource usage and activities carried out) is an invitation to escape from the "activity trap"[32] of rigid job descriptions and procedural straight-jackets that too often limit perspective, practice and performance. Instead, they encourage, assist and enable people to contribute their time and talents to the full, in pursuit both of high-quality performance and

Table 6.4 Contribution statements

The table below illustrates the difference between rigid job descriptions, and flexible and responsive contribution statements.

Contribution Statements ...	Job Descriptions ...
• focus on **outward contribution** • relate to **purpose** and **value** • are **positive** and **challenging** • encourage a **pro-active approach** • increase the scope for **initiative** • encourage **continuous adaptation** in line with emerging possibilities • stimulate **personal growth** and **development** beyond the role • seek to **enable** performance	• focus on **internal activities** • relate to **tasks** and **resources used** • are **neutral** and **matter-of-fact** • accept a **passive approach** • seek **conformity** and **compliance** • look for performance **within defined boundaries** • discourage **personal growth** and **development** beyond the role • inevitably **constrain** performance

personal growth. The main differences between Contribution Statements and job descriptions are summarized in Table 6.4.

Defining roles in terms of fixed activities rather than outward contribution is another example of attempting to "catch the wiggliness in a net". In such cases, job descriptions are seen as being at the core of organization design, as well as providing the basis for job analysis, grading and remuneration schemes. However, given the real-world complexities, these contribute little to organizational practice and performance, beyond the procedural rigidities of administrative accounting, disciplinary management and industrial relations disputes.

Cultivating marginality – sharpening the edge

Brian Wallace and Christopher Ridgeway argue:[33]

> ['Marginal men' (sic) have] . . . in an ambiguous environment . . . the capability to spot differences, to determine the patterns in unconnected data, and thus to perceive the factors that are relevant. . . . They spot ideas that others do not and then they make public the ideas that others might not understand or appreciate. . . .

Seeking to cultivate the characteristics of, and gain insights from, those 'at the margins' is an important aspect of muddling through skilfully. It recognizes that the patterning of human interaction, whilst enabling people to go on together, inhibits potentially beneficial shifts in thought and action arising from the contrary experiences and perspectives of those on the fringes. Shifts that, as Wallace and Ridgeway point out, may not be understood, appreciated – or even seen – by others.

In seeking to develop this capacity as part of their own practice, the trick for the manager is to strive to embrace some of the attributes and perspectives of the 'marginal man' without becoming a 'nowhere man' – sitting in his nowhere land, making all his nowhere plans for nobody, as Lennon and McCartney so eloquently put it. This remains a challenge in a world in which leadership still tends to be viewed (and rewarded) as the elite practice of a few gifted and formally appointed individuals, rather than as an emergent property of the ongoing social process of everyday human interaction.

Exposing and challenging 'Big Dot thinking' – taking complexity seriously

On several occasions I've mentioned how we tend to deploy what I call "Big Dot thinking", to make sense of our experiences and to explain them to others. This arises naturally from the way in which we highlight and join-up specific happenings (Big Dots) post-event, to construct an explanatory narrative of what went on, why and how it happened, our part in it, and so on. This is a useful and necessary part of the sensemaking process. It also enables people to relate their own experiences to those of others, as they strive to go on together.

At the same time, though, it results in a sanitized abstraction from the wiggly reality. And this can cause problems when these simplified constructions are treated as accurate representations of what's going on; whether as the basis for research (Chapter 3) or as part of everyday discourse. As we saw in Chapter 5, a plausible explanation of what happened can always be drawn up after the event, by working backwards from the outcome to the supposed starting point. However, it does not follow from this that the same outcome could have been arrived at by following that (imaginary) path forwards, in a logical step-by-step fashion, from that same, notional starting position. Calling out the limits of Big Dot thinking, so that the complexities can be acknowledged and explored, is an important aspect of muddling through skilfully.

Drawing on practice-based evidence – towards more informed participation

As discussed extensively in Chapter 5, deciding whether or not a particular action is worthy of pursuit is a subjective and interpretive task. It is not possible to derive universally applicable, so-called "evidence-based" prescriptions in relation to the complex social dynamics of organization. Instead, evidence of the worthwhileness or otherwise of any changed way of working only emerges in the midst of its practice. It is context-dependent.

I'm not arguing here for an 'anything goes' approach. On the contrary, drawing on valid evidence is an important aspect of muddling through skilfully. What counts most, though, is the evidence that is embodied in current practice. That is, what managers and others perceive to be happening in the 'here and now' and how they interpret what is going on. This relies on joint-sense-making conversations and critical thinking around current and prospective practice, based on situationally specific observations and explorations, rather than generalized principles. It values the lived experience, practical judgement and reflexivity of those who work in and around the specific situation. As well as seeking to raise awareness of the taken-for-granted assumptions that imperceptibly pattern their being together.

The focus, then, is on what habitual and contingent themes are organizing the conversations through which the future is perpetually being constructed in the present. As well as how the manager is participating in this process. As noted earlier, it's within this specific local context, that managers can inquire into and enhance their own and others' practice in the currency of their present interactions. Identifying the main contextual factors, organizing themes, patterns of behaviour and governing assumptions:

- that are structuring people's interactions, and enabling and constraining their practice;
- out of which local and more extensive outcomes are emerging; and
- which point to potentially beneficial shifts that might be made in their current sensemaking-cum-action-taking conversations – both locally and more widely.

This recognizes that all anyone can ever do is to act into the future as it is emerging – facilitated by a reflective and reflexive approach to their own individual and collective practice. The success (or otherwise) of such interventions will only become evident, of course, as 'outcomes' emerge and come to be recognized as such. And, even then, what constitutes "success" or "failure" will be a matter of interpretation and social construction.

Viewing organization and management as work in progress – keeping it 'live'

As a closing rule of thumb, everything in the context of organization is best viewed as work in progress. Tentative and provisional rather than fixed and final. Built on proto-truth rather than absolute truth. Flexibly rigid. Unintended consequences will inevitably arise. New priorities will emerge. Perspectives will change. And so on. Thinking of muddling through skilfully as a continuing process of conversational interaction – punctuated by specific and emergent acts of leadership – keeps issues 'live' and people 'open to learning'. This is also why paying attention to purpose, in the ways set out earlier, is crucial. And why muddling through skilfully in this way requires, in Stacey and Mowles's words again, "the courage to go on participating creatively, despite not knowing".

Pulling it all together – Muddling through skilfully

Table 6.5 summarizes the elements of muddling through skilfully as set out in the preceding paragraphs.

Table 6.5 The elements of muddling through skilfully

The table below summarizes the four elements of muddling through skilfully, in ways that take complexity seriously.

Muddling through skilfully
ORIENTATION *An orientation to practice, which is tuned-in to the paradoxical, 'both-and at the same time' nature of organization.*
Parallel Practice
COMPLEXITY-CONGRUENT CAPABILITIES *Capabilities, honed through personal experience, that underpin the ability to act forwards skilfully into the future, as this is emerging continuously from their own and others' participation.*

<table>
<tr><td>Using practical judgement
Reframing communication
Thinking culturally
Acting politically
Embracing paradox
Practising reflexively</td></tr>
<tr><td>MODE OF OPERATING
A mode of operating that is enabled by these capabilities, informed by relevant theory and applied pragmatically in the moment.</td></tr>
<tr><td>Imaginatively making do (i.e. adopting the stance of the bricoleur).</td></tr>
<tr><td>PERSONAL PRACTICE THEORY (PRACTICAL 'RULES OF THUMB')
The sensible and selective use of personally resonant, individually adapted and lightly held 'rules of thumb'.</td></tr>
<tr><td>For example (indicative only):
• Creatively cutting and pasting – using what 'works'.
• Hosting conversations – creating opportunities for shared meaning-making and relationship building.
• Framing the conversations – facilitating sense-making.
• Providing vision, support and challenge – helping people to 'see better'.
• Building coalitions – mobilizing collective action and integrating difference.
• Using 'both-ands' at the same time – making paradox liveable for people.
• Enhancing people's response-ability and account-ability – taking experience seriously.
• Keep chipping away – pursuing sought-after change incrementally and contingently.
• Avoiding 'paint-by-numbers' approaches – valuing emergent practice ahead of procedural rigidity.
• Using self – recognizing oneself as an involved participant and 'walking case study'.
• Exploring logic bubbles, cliché units and the developing 'rules of the game' – seeking to understand and shift the patterns that are shaping people's participation.
• Provoking movement – laying stepping-stones towards a different future.
• Focusing on contribution – avoiding the activity trap.
• Cultivating marginality – sharpening the edge.
• Exposing and challenging 'Big Dot thinking' – taking complexity seriously.
• Drawing on practice-based evidence – towards more informed participation.
• Viewing organization and management as work in progress – keeping it 'live'. . . .

. . . Doing all of this without any certainty as to what will emerge in practice – but paying attention to the future, as it is emerging in people's present interactions.</td></tr>
</table>

Muddling through with purpose, courage and skill . . . and with awareness

As a final point, I would suggest that one of the most important advances that managers can make is to become *consciously aware of what they already know instinctively*. That is, that the seemingly disjointed and fragmentary nature of their

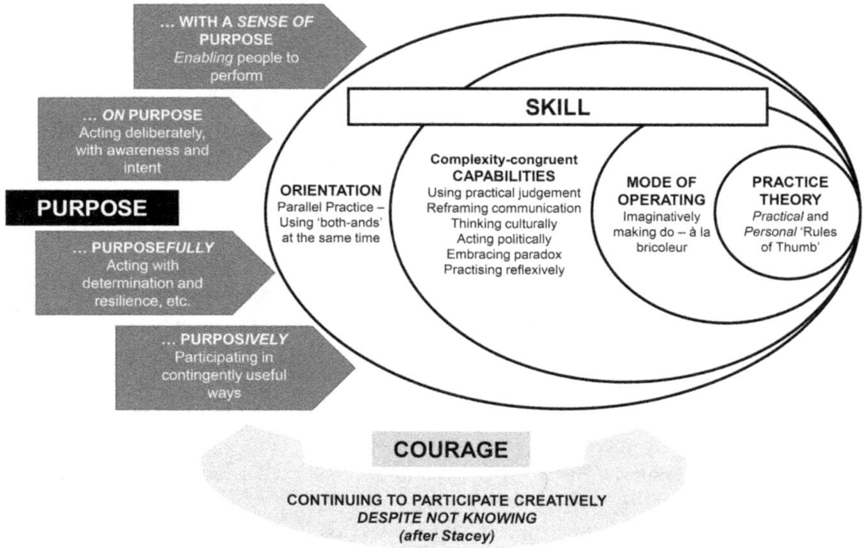

Figure 6.2 Muddling through with purpose, courage and skill

day-to-day inter(actions) – what I'm calling here "muddling through" – is not a sign of dysfunction or substandard performance. On the contrary, it is the very essence of their role. And that doing this with purpose, courage and skill is the very best that they – or anyone else – can do. This is illustrated in Figure 6.2.

Notes

1 Burden, P. and Warwick, R. (2015: 113) *Leading Mindfully*. Self-published.
2 Matthew Syed, commenting in the *Sunday Times* of 29 March 2020 on the leadership challenge presented by the coronavirus crisis: *Coronavirus: an unimaginable challenge for our leaders, but what great lessons they will be learning.*
3 Barrett, F.J. (2012: 151) *Yes to the Mess*. HBR Press.
4 Vaill, P.B. (1996: 10) *Learning as a Way of Being*. Jossey-Bass.
5 Vaill, P.B. ibid: 16.
6 Vaill, P.B. ibid: 183.

7 Traeger, J. and Warwick, R. (2018: 11) *Organisation Development*. Libri Publishing.
8 Ewing, D. (1968) *The Practice of Planning*. Harper and Row.
9 Ralph Stacey (2012) calls this "practical judgement". Others (such as Keith Grint (2007) and Bent Flyvbjerg *et al* (2012) for instance) call it "practical wisdom".
10 Gabriel, Y. (2002: 146) Essai: On Paragrammatic Uses of Organizational Theory – A Provocation. Article published in *Organizational Studies*, January 2002.
11 Mowles, C. (2011: 265) *Rethinking Management*. Gower.
12 The "credibility paths" are the prevailing influence networks.
13 See extensive discussion of this in Rodgers, C. (2007) *Informal Coalitions*. Palgrave Macmillan.
14 In *Informal Coalitions*, I introduced the *Leadership Communication Grid* as a means of extending managers' understanding of their communication task. This expands the scope beyond the formal, structured message passing that conventionally governs set-piece meetings, presentations and the like, towards more informal and unstructured ways of jointly making sense of emerging issues and events.
15 Toft, F. (2014) Unpublished paper. See also https://www.emerging.dk/
16 David Kantor's discussion of the relationship between inquiry and advocacy is regularly referred to in this regard. Also, my friend and fellow consultant, Rowena Davis, is a skilled practitioner and trainer in the use of the SAVI® Grid. This provides a visual map of communication used to understand and seek to improve the quality of people's interactions. You can find out more about the SAVI® Grid at http://www.savicommunications.com/savi.html.
17 Political action is one of the most fundamental dynamics of organization. And yet the vast majority of books and consulting methodologies that purport to describe how organization works, and provide guidance on management/leadership practice, either make no reference at all to power and politics or else argue that these are dysfunctional aspects of organization that proper management will overcome. As discussed in Chapter 2, they aren't and it won't!
18 Rodgers, C. (2007: 118) ibid.
19 See Chapter 2, for a description of the living present.

20 Rolfe, G. (1998: 29) Beyond Expertise: Reflective and Reflexive Nursing Practice in Johns, C. and Freshwater, D. (Eds.) *Transforming Nursing through Reflective Practice*. Blackwell.

21 Johns, C. (1998: 7) Opening the Doors of Perception in Johns, C. and Freshwater, D. (Eds.) *Transforming Nursing through Reflective Practice*. Blackwell.

22 The primary reference here is Lester, R.K. and Piore, M.J. (2006) *Innovation: The Missing Dimension*. Harvard University Press. In their 2014 book, *Host*, Mark McKergow and Helen Bailey compare and contrast "host leadership" with the established forms of heroic leadership and servant leadership. In it, they identify what they describe as "six roles of engagement".

23 In broad terms, Stacey argues that the diagram perpetuates the view that there are distinct categories of human (inter)action between which people can choose – ranging from Close to Certainty/Close to Agreement (Clear, say, in Cynefin terms) to Far from Certainty/Far from Agreement (Chaotic). As part of his response to a blog post (on a site that no longer exists), he wrote:

> life is complex all the time in the sense that stability and instability are so intertwined that they constitute a pattern of movement through time which is stable and unstable at the same time and the two cannot be separated. Even in what seems to be the most mundane predictable situation some tiny unexpected change could occur and escalate up into a situation which is totally unexpected . . . there are no levels of complexity, indeed no levels in human action.

He argues that use of the diagram inhibits attempts to challenge the established way of thinking about organization.

24 De Bono, E. (1977) *The Happiness Purpose*. Penguin.

25 See Chapter 8 of *Informal Coalitions* – Rodgers, C. (2007) ibid: 226 *et seq*.

26 Daloz, L.A. (1986) *Effective Teaching and Mentoring*. Jossey-Bass.

27 The first two of the frameworks mentioned are described in the following publications: Johnson, B. (2014) *Polarity Management 2Ed*. HRD Press; and Fletcher, J. and Olwyler, K. (1997) *Paradoxical Thinking*. Berrett-Koehler. The 'kit-e' diagram is referred to in the *Embracing Paradox* chapter of *Informal Coalitions*. At that time, what I now call the Business Performance Framework was referred to as the Performance Management Framework.

28 See Note 9 in Chapter 1. Obeng, E. (1995) *Putting Strategy to Work*. FT Management.
29 De Bono, E. (1979) *Future Positive*. Penguin.
30 De Bono introduces the notion of cliché units in *Lateral Thinking – A Textbook of Creativity* (Penguin Life, 2016).
31 Barrett, F.J. (2012: 138) *Yes to the Mess*. HBR Press.
32 Odiorne, G. (1974) *Management and the Activity Trap*. Heinemann.
33 Wallace, B. and Ridgeway, C. (1996) *Leadership for Strategic Change*. CiPD.

7

IMPLICATIONS FOR ORGANIZATIONAL CONSULTING

INFLUENCING PEOPLE'S PERSPECTIVES, PRACTICES AND PERFORMANCE

In the previous chapter, we looked in detail at the implications of the wiggly world for those who are formally charged with managing and leading various aspects of organizational practice and performance. Here, I want to look at what these dynamics mean for those who set out to help managers to achieve this task more successfully. This includes the work of consultants, coaches, mentors, facilitators, developers and so on. In what follows, to simplify the language, I've mainly used the terms "consultant" or "specialist" to refer to any and all of these various contributors.

Although this chapter is primarily directed at such specialists, it also sets out further ideas and perspectives that managers might find helpful and relevant to their own work. Especially if, as suggested in Chapter 6, they recognize the need to shift the emphasis of their practice towards *enabling* people to perform. If they do so, they will often find themselves operating in a consultant- or coach-like manner with members of their own teams.

Understanding the context

In any assignment, the context within which the work is being carried out is a central consideration for consultants, client managers and others in deciding how best to position their respective contributions. By context, I mean the specific circumstances surrounding the work. In common management and consulting practice, these are likely to be spoken of in terms of the 'external' environment, within which the work is set, as well as the relevant 'internal' conditions and capabilities that are enabling and constraining the ability to respond. I'll refer to this engagement-specific and content-based aspect in more detail later. There are, though, some characteristics of the work context, relating to the wiggly-world dynamics of organization, that are always in play. So, I want to begin with those.

Acting into ongoing situations

Specialist practitioners must begin by recognizing that they – like everyone else – are *always acting into ongoing situations*. People don't wait for consultants to give meaning and direction to their work before moving forward. They continually make sense of what's going on, and act into the world as they see it. Doing so both habitually and with conscious intent. Change does not start and stop with consulting interventions. It emerges continuously in people's moment-to-moment interactions. At the same time, these conversational exchanges tend to reinforce existing patterns of thought and action. The tension that exists between change and continuity, and the paradoxical dynamics that underpin it, helps define the 'possibility space' within which consultants can act. At any particular time, the current situation is both contextually specific and historically situated within people's individual and collective experiences. Those involved in this continuous flow of interactions include not only people who are immediately present but also myriad others. Individuals and groups – some long gone – whose past (inter)actions have left imprints on the ways in which organization is currently being played out.

Immersed in the game

Another important consideration for consultants to consider is that they, too, are immersed in the 'game' of everyday human interaction. As with everybody else's contribution, their inputs form part of the complex social process through which organization is being continuously (re-)enacted and outcomes are emerging. This affects everything that they do, both in terms of their relationships with clients and in the conduct of their work and lives more generally. They cannot stand apart from the action; commentating and making recommendations from a position of supposed objectivity. They are involved in – and contributing to – the wiggliness, at the same time as they are attempting to help others to deal with it more successfully.

This also means that they are actively participating in the everyday politics of organization. *And necessarily so.* It is not credible for consultants to claim that they steer clear of the politics of the situations in which they are engaged. Consultants' work is subject to the same interactional dynamics that we have discussed at length in earlier chapters. That is to say, the nature of their interactions with others, and what emerges from them, will always be affected by their own and others' interests, intentions, interpretations, ideologies, identities, personal idiosyncrasies and so on. It is what being human is all about. As is seeking to cope with the differences that emerge from this.

Power relations

As suggested above, the role of the consultant shares many aspects with that of the manager, which is discussed extensively in Chapter 6. A crucial difference, though, is that consultants don't have formal authority to 'command' the actions of others. That is to say, they are *neither* in control *nor* in charge. Nevertheless, the power relations that are at play in a particular client-consultant situation will often 'tilt the playing field' in their favour. Whether this helps or hinders their efforts to achieve their specific functional objectives (such as by opening up or closing down the conversations) depends on the circumstances at the time. Importantly, too, the role also has the capacity for acts of leadership to emerge, in the way that I have described this in earlier chapters. Indeed, it demands it. And, like managers, specialists will have their own informal support networks and spheres of influence, which don't rely on formally allocated roles and relationships for their existence and potency. Gaining and applying knowledge and insight into the dynamics of power and influence ("acting politically", as I referred to it in relation to the manager's task) is therefore a crucial aspect of the consulting craft.

Muddling through together

Given the nature of the situations in which they are immersed, and the diverse and constantly shifting demands that they find themselves facing along the way, consultants (like their clients) have no option but to muddle through the everyday politics of organizational life. They, too, are acting forwards into a continuously emerging future that is never fully knowable. They are doing so, of course, with the aim of helping people to make sense of what's going on and influencing what happens in organizationally beneficial ways. At the same time, they will be seeking to proceed in ways that are beneficial to their own practice. Pursuing these challenges with purpose, courage and skill is therefore equally relevant to their own muddling through as it is to that of client managers and others. This means, in particular, using conversation as their primary action 'tool'. Doing so in ways that enable those involved (including themselves) to make better sense of what's going on and continually enhance their practice. The remainder of this chapter considers what those three touchstones of effective muddling through – purpose, courage and skill – mean in relation to consultancy and related specialisms.

The question of purpose

To begin with, what can we say about purpose in relation to the work of consultants and other organizational specialists? As with the practice of leading and managing, muddling through with *purpose* calls for consultants to pay attention to four aspects of their practice. These are:

- acting *with a sense of purpose*, and not simply meandering along or leaving things to chance;
- doing so with deliberate and renewed intent on each occasion, rather than habitually (i.e. *on purpose*);
- pursuing the task with determination and perseverance, in pursuit of beneficial shifts in capability and/or performance (i.e. *purposefully*); and, most importantly given the unavoidable wiggliness;

- anticipating and responding with a willingness and ability to adapt what they do to match the contingent needs of the situation, rather than sticking rigidly to the detail of particular methodologies and one-size-fits-all 'solutions' (i.e. anticipating and responding *purposively*).

Whatever experience, insights and skills a consultant might bring, the need to operate with a *sense of purpose* underlines the importance of contributing in ways that are of practical value to clients *in the midst of their own muddling through*. Clients, that is, who are continually making choices and acting forwards into the future, as this is emerging from the interplay of their own and everyone else's involvement. This positions the specialist's role as one of helping them, individually and collectively, to bring about beneficial changes in their activities, capabilities and performance *that otherwise would not occur*. Seeking to achieve this both in those with whom they are interacting directly and, through them, others in the wider client population. This is the case whether they are operating as a consultant, coach, mentor, facilitator, developer or whatever. And whether they are employed in-house or via an external contract.

In relation to the wiggly-world dynamics of organization, this means rehabilitating talk, power and politics as fundamental aspects of organization and management practice. Also, as with the manager's role, this requires the various specialists to offer vision, challenge and support to clients, through their ongoing interactions. That is, seeking to help those involved to 'see better', through their day-to-day interactions (providing vision); provoking shifts in the patterning of their clients' thinking and acting, to open up potential new pathways and overcome blockages (challenge); and helping them to deal with the physical, intellectual, emotional and psychological, etc. ups and downs of organizational practice (support). The mix of vision, challenge and support that is appropriate in any instance is context-dependent and situationally contingent. There is no simple formula for determining this. Like everything else in the wiggly world of organization, it is a matter of practical judgement. Underpinning all of this is the need for consultants to help those involved to recognize and cope with the challenges of living and working in a world that does not operate in neat straight lines. A world in which "muddling through" best describes the way in which people cope with, contribute to and thereby co-create the future that is continuously emerging from their own and others' participation in it.

Consulting with courage

As with the acts of leading and managing, consulting from a wiggly-world perspective (in its myriad forms) similarly requires "the courage to go on participating creatively despite not knowing". Conventionally, though, there is great pressure on consultants to use language and approaches that reflect a world which is knowable. An idealized world. A world in which outcomes can be assured, provided that people do things better and get them right, according to the prescriptions that they happen to be offering. This pressure applies both to the ways in which they position their own work and when they are speaking about organizational dynamics more broadly. Given the dominant narrative about the nature of organization and management practice, and the commercial and professional structures that buttress it, there is a powerful incentive for consultants to adopt this stance. Where they do so, of course, they reinforce the expectations of order, predictability and control. And so, the pattern continues.

Neither consultants nor their clients can escape from this reality by seeking to perpetuate the myth that order and control are within a manager's grasp. As one of my clients said, "Very linear approaches to management feel like playing chess when your opponent's pieces are glued to the table".[1] Instead, the consulting challenge is to tolerate the uncomfortable sensation of not knowing. Feeling it. Understanding it. And moving through it. Having the courage to confront the felt need to be in control of what is happening – and helping the client to do the same, without leaving them feeling helpless – is a central aspect of consulting from a position that takes complexity seriously. It is also one of the most important contributions that a consultant can make. Organization is wiggly. Ignoring this, or suggesting that the wiggliness can be reduced or eliminated by using the latest technique, is neither helpful nor ethically sound. It can't be wished away. It just is.

At the same time, accepting this reality can be anxiety-inducing for clients and consultants alike. In this regard, the established trappings of consultancy practice (such as organizational models, surveys, n-step methodologies and so on) provide a degree of comfort, and promise a felt sense of control, that can be seductive to both parties. As I've suggested earlier, and as I shall discuss further below, it can be beneficial to use aspects of these approaches sparingly, selectively and with a light touch (Gabriel's "paragrammatically"[2]), as routes-in to more meaningful, and potentially pattern-shifting, conversations. This, again, calls for courage on the part of the consultant and, through them, the client. Courage, that is, to continue to participate meaningfully in the everyday conversations through which the future is being perpetually constructed by everyone involved. And, in the process, to imaginatively make do with whatever resources happen to be at hand, rather than seeking to follow a fixed 'recipe for success' – of which there are none!

A final consideration as regards consulting with courage is that each engagement brings into focus the consultant's own sense of identity, reputation and self-worth. As well as the hopes and anxieties that these can evoke. In this regard, it's important for them to recognize that their own identity is being continually reconstructed in the same conversational process in which they are engaging with clients around the work itself. As Patricia Shaw puts it,[3]

> We make a difference *and become different* in a patterning process we can never control. (My emphasis.)

By showing courage in dealing with these challenges, a consultant provides a role model of the sought-after response from their clients. Hopefully, evoking similarly courageous responses from them. And, by embracing their own vulnerability in this regard, they open-up the possibility that a more empathic client-consultant relationship might emerge. This means their being fully present in the moment of the relationship; open, receptive and connected.[4] As well as operating explicitly from a position of not knowing – and normalizing this as a universal dynamic of organization. Failing to do so, of course, might be interpreted by clients as offering tacit endorsement of management orthodoxy and make movement in their own practice less likely.

Participating skilfully

If consultants and other specialist practitioners are to participate skilfully in ways that take seriously the real-world wiggliness of organization, they might usefully pay particular attention to three broad aspects of their craft. First, it is important for them to *frame their involvement* – and any specific approaches that they might adopt – in ways that make explicit the wiggly-world dynamics of organization and the implications of these for everyday organizational practice. This includes the fact that there can be no guarantee as to what will emerge overall from the dynamic interplay of people's involvement. Secondly, they need to direct their attention to the specific issue(s) that they have been engaged to deal with, in ways that make a beneficial difference to the client's situation. Thirdly, underpinning both of these, is the need for consultants to pay attention to the quality of their own participation. This includes ensuring that their own practice takes full account of the real-world complexity and the fact that they, too, have no option but to muddle through the challenges that this brings. These three aspects of consulting skilfully are illustrated in Table 7.1 and discussed in detail below.

Table 7.1 Participating skilfully

<table>
<tr><th>Framing their involvement with the client
Taking complexity seriously</th><th>Shifting the patterning of interaction
Striving to bring about changes in practice and performance that otherwise would not occur</th></tr>
<tr><td>• Foregrounding the wiggly-world dynamics of organization.
• Highlighting the implications of these for everyday management practice: muddling through with purpose, courage and skill.</td><td>• Jointly making sense of the specific context and path to now within which help is being sought.
• Helping to shift the patterning of interaction in organizationally beneficial and personally meaningful ways – i.e. influencing people's perspectives, practices and performance.</td></tr>
<tr><td colspan="2">Paying attention to the quality of their own participation
Muddling through with purpose, courage and skill</td></tr>
<tr><td colspan="2">• Modelling the way by continuing to participate creatively despite not knowing:
- Adopting a 'both-and at the same time' orientation to practice – "parallel practice"
- Developing and deploying complexity-congruent capabilities: using practical judgement; reframing communication; thinking culturally; acting politically; embracing paradox; providing vision; and practising reflexively.
- Applying a mode of operating that is enabled by these capabilities, informed by relevant theory and applied pragmatically in the moment, i.e. imaginatively making do, in the mode of the bricoleur.
• Cultivating a personally resonant, individually adapted and lightly held set of 'concepts, tools and techniques' (practice theory), that they can apply pragmatically in the situations that emerge.</td></tr>
</table>

Framing the consultant's involvement

Framing their work with clients in ways that foreground a complexity-aware view of organization, and its implications for management practice, is the foundation block for consulting from a wiggly-world perspective.[5]

The requirement is twofold. First, there is a need to raise clients' understanding of the underlying, complex social dynamics of organization and, secondly, to explore what this means for their own and others' day-to-day practice. Failure to make these 'up front' investments would mean that any specific interventions would most likely be taken up in ways that reflected, and hence reinforced, conventional thinking and practice. How this understanding is best achieved is, of course, a matter of practical judgement. As well as reflecting the specific circumstances of the proposed intervention; the expressed needs and preferences of the client; and the consultant's personal style.

In some instances, identifying and exploring these dynamics might best be positioned as a specific 'leadership development' task, centred around structured input and participants' reflection on their own experience as 'walking case studies' of these dynamics in action. In other situations, it might make sense to place more emphasis on drawing-out the main themes and implications progressively. Doing this, for example, during a 'live project' and/or as a deliberate part of day-to-day exchanges. Another course might be to stimulate and support clients' self-discovery of the important insights and implications. Yet again, some elements of the above might be combined pragmatically to suit the situation. In any event, it is essential for consultants to work to ensure that an understanding of these dynamics underpins any issue- or task-related intervention that they make and the means that they use to carry it out. Some of the possible ways that might be adopted to pursue these aims are set out below. Regardless of the 'headline' approach, the main currency to be spent on raising awareness, understanding and insight is conversation. With those in formal management roles (from CEO to the front line) being particularly powerful participants in this process.

Structured input and participant reflection

Chapters 1, 6 and 8 set out the core material for approaching this task through a mixture of structured input and participants' exploration of the core themes. These provide the basis for designing and delivering a formal development programme or a specific input at the start of an engagement. I believe that it is important for consultants who are using this approach to understand the subject in greater depth than they would routinely share at the outset with their clients. The contents of Chapters 2 to 5 provide the means of achieving this enhanced level of understanding. As well as offering further scope for more in-depth exploration with clients over time.

Coaching and critical reflection, during a 'live' project

This approach seeks to highlight and explore aspects of the wiggly-world dynamics, and the implications of these for management/leadership practice, during the course of a live project or programme of work in which the consultant is involved. The aim is to achieve this progressively. Relevant inputs can be loosely structured around the elements of the planned programme or introduced as opportunities arise for reflection and learning during its practical implementation. In the latter case, the consultant aims to remain alert to, and make timely use of, situations that arise spontaneously and which provide what have been called "teachable moments". In this case, such occasions offer the chance of homing-in on incidents, experiences or comments that highlight particular aspects of the wiggly-world dynamics and/or the muddling-through nature of what people find themselves doing in practice.

Collective self-discovery

As an example of the self-discovery approach, I was once invited to lead a two-hour discussion on the topic of informal coalitions as part of an internal consultant conference. At the time, I was in the final throes of writing my book on the subject. In preparation for the event, I had circulated a brief paper, which outlined the dynamics of informal coalitions and identified some of the implications of these for leadership practice. On the day, participants were seated at a number of tables around the room. Ahead of my session, I had fixed a few posters to the walls, which outlined one or two of the sense-making frameworks that subsequently found their way into the book. I began by saying that I wanted to keep the last half-hour of the discussion free, to take stock of where we'd got to and to deal with any outstanding queries. I also pointed out that a couple of people in the room had already been exposed to the thinking in some depth. I then acknowledged that, although many others in the room would have read the summary paper, there would no doubt be some who had not yet had chance to do so. "By the end of the session", I said, "I want each one of you to have reached a much better understanding of the dynamics of informal coalitions than you might have at present". I added that I would also like participants to identify ways in which they might integrate this into their own consulting practice.

Having set the scene, I then gestured as if I was about to move into the expected set-piece presentation. Instead, I sat down and said nothing. Only one other person present, a member of the client's support staff, knew what I was going to do. The director in charge of the event, and his Board colleagues, didn't. There was a brief – and somewhat uncomfortable – period before anyone spoke at all. Then, a few murmurs began, and noise levels rose as people started to discuss the topic in hand – or anything else for that matter! Two people sitting on adjacent tables re-ignited their half-finished conversation about some upcoming coaching event that they were both involved in, before joining-in their relevant table discussions. As the minutes passed, the in-table conversations became quite animated and, for the most part, people seemed to be engaging thoroughly in the conversations. Only one or two of those who had been relying on a formal input from me, rather than reading the summary paper, appeared ill at ease in these early stages. I, though, was still a little anxious that the table-group discussions were isolated from each other and that there was no movement between tables. Just as my anxiety was about to get the better of me, the members of one of the groups stood up and moved to other tables, to continue their conversations. At that point, other people began to move around the room to further their understanding. And small groups gathered around the various posters that I had placed on the walls, deep in conversation about what these meant. By that stage, discussions were in full flow and the allotted time passed very quickly.

As we moved into the "So where have we got to?" phase, there was a healthy buzz in the room. One of the participants said that the process had raised her understanding of informal coalitions significantly; and she asked if others felt the same. Thankfully, many hands were raised in agreement. When I was asked how it had been for me, I shared my initial anxiety but then said that I had actually done very little, so I didn't really have much to say on that front. At that point, the woman who had asked the earlier, "Did we learn through this process?", question intervened again. Insightfully, she pointed out that I hadn't actually "done nothing". In fact, I'd done a number of things. For example, I had:

- stimulated people's curiosity, through the pre-conference briefing;
- set out a meaningful objective for the session;
- pointed out that there were a number of resources in the room that participants could draw upon (a few people who had already integrated the notion of informal coalitions into their consultancy practice and the wall posters); and
- created space for the necessary sense-making conversations to take place.

She was right, of course. And, having done that, the natural dynamics of informal coalitions took hold. Self-organizing conversations ensued, and new learning emerged. People's natural anxiety at having their understanding challenged, coupled with the possibility of gaining new insights at the edge of their current knowledge, was held in a good-enough state by the quality of their own and others' active involvement. These are the same dynamics that are at play in all organizational settings and, most significantly, in informal interactions. People continually share their perceptions and interpretations of emerging events, make sense of what's going on (in diverse ways) and make choices as to how they will respond – with conscious intent and/or through habit. Having pointed the group in the desired direction and sought to raise their confidence by highlighting some of the resources that were already available to them in the room, I 'lit the blue touch paper and retired immediately', so to speak. This helped to create a conducive environment within which the conversations could take their natural course (in that context and at that time) and for outcomes to emerge that many people felt were helpful to their understanding and practice. The ongoing management and leadership challenge – which the consultant is seeking to highlight and facilitate through this process – then becomes one of actively engaging in these conversational networks; seeking to stimulate and enable shifts in practice and performance; and coping with the context as it is emerging.

Hybrid approach

An approach that blends together a number of the above strands involves participants in co-facilitating elements of a workshop or other event on the topic. In preparation, separate groups of participants might typically be presented with a 'core brief', background notes and reflective questions on one central theme of (in this case) the wiggly world and muddling-through dynamics of organization. Participants are asked to explore their particular brief ahead of the event, and internalize their understanding, so that they can stimulate the ensuing conversations and contribute knowledgeably to them. The existence of prior and diverse knowledge of certain concepts, coupled with the natural co-operative-competitive dynamics of everyday human interaction, adds richness to the exchanges and encourages those involved to immerse themselves fully in the subject. Its use is particularly apposite in relation to the dynamics of the wiggly world and the practice of muddling through, given the focus of these on the notion of organization as conversation.

The consultant's role is one of *active participant* in this emergent process, with a particular focus on:

- drawing attention to specific aspects of the underlying dynamics of organization and management practice, as these are reflected in the themes that emerge from the conversations;
- encouraging other participants to share what they are experiencing 'in the moment', as a further stimulus to learning about the dynamics of organization – and to do so themselves;
- spurring joint exploration of some of the ideas and practices that emerge through this mixture of formal/informal and structured/unstructured interactions;
- encouraging and enabling personal reflection by participants – individually and collectively – on their developing understanding of the wiggly world; and
- challenging and supporting them, as they seek to make sense of this radically different understanding of organizational dynamics and relate it to their own, diverse experience of organization and management practice – as well as to life more generally.

In one instance, colleagues and I used this general approach to structure a development programme aimed at enhancing the capabilities and practice of internal consultants from diverse backgrounds. Over a series of workshops, we (as consultants) moved progressively from a position in which we orchestrated the initial event in its entirety to one in which the final module was wholly participant-led, from design through to execution. At that stage, we intervened solely on an *ad hoc* basis, to help to draw-out important themes and constructively challenge participants' thinking.

Shifting the patterning of interactions

The second aspect of the *Participating Skilfully* agenda (above) relates to the consultant's application of the wiggly-world insights to the particular situation being addressed. That is, working with the client to make sense of the *specific* context and seeking to shift the patterning and content of people's interactions in ways that are judged to be beneficial. Within this, it is important not to view the sense-making and action-taking elements of this process as separate and sequential. Given the complex social dynamics that I've described in detail earlier, these aspects are intimately interwoven. As such, new interactions, insights and incidents will inevitably emerge throughout the process, prompting minor course corrections, major rethinks and other shifts along the way. As I've stressed on several occasions earlier, the primary focus of muddling through skilfully (regardless of who might be involved) is on noticing and adjusting to what is actually going on. It is not about following blindly what is supposed to be happening according to the planning assumptions and/or accepted wisdom.

Against this background, I've set out below some specific aspects of engaging with the client that arise from the wiggly-world dynamics. Whether dealt with well or badly, these have a marked effect on the ways in which consultants and other specialist practitioners (coaches, mentors, developers, etc.) are able to act, as they seek to influence the perspectives, practices and performance of those with whom they are working. As I suggested above, although I've included these in this chapter on the work of consultants and other specialists, they are also relevant to the work of managers; both as regards their own practice and the nature of their relationship with these specialist contributors.

Recognizing the ever-present dynamics of change and continuity

Regardless of the specific challenge that is presented to a consultant at the outset, change is always involved. The manager's act of engaging them, coupled with the nature of their response, changes the status quo. As do the (inter)actions that flow from any later involvement. Indeed, at whatever point the consultant first meets with the client, they enter into (and at the same time contribute to) an ongoing process of conversational interaction that is historically situated and in constant flux. The dynamics of *change* are therefore ever-present. *At the same time*, there is a general tendency for this sense-making-cum-action-taking process to follow, without conscious awareness, the characteristic patterning of interaction that has become established over time. This patterned nature of people's response is what Pierre Bourdieu refers to as habitus[6] and which, in common terms, we think of as organizational culture. In continuing to affect the way in which today's interactions play out, this further 'deepens' the established sense-making 'channels', making similar responses more likely still. This means that the dynamics of *continuity* are also always in play. It is this self-organizing, patterning process which enables people to go on together with a sense of everyday predictability, whilst retaining within it the capacity for shifts to occur spontaneously and novelty to arise.

This paradoxical change-with-continuity dynamic highlights two important themes in relation to consultancy practice. First, as regards work that relates overtly to planned organizational change, it is essential to recognize that all activities that form part of the formal programme will be taken up (or not!) by people whose responses are affected by these same dynamics. Given this, it is important for client managers not to be seduced into seeing organizational change as occurring solely in the form of periodic, structured interventions that will be enacted in line with their strategic intent. That is, as periods of planned change within an otherwise stable state. Nor should they be led to believe that the oft-quoted failure of things to turn out as planned can simply be put down to poor implementation. It is especially important for consultants themselves not to perpetuate this flawed line of thinking. Or to offer interventions based on linear, stepwise methodologies that promise certainty of outcome. The second theme relates to the natural tendency for client managers to make sense of consultancy proposals in ways that are channelled imperceptibly along well-established pathways of thought and action. As such, it is likely that they will frame consultant offerings in ways that fit a familiar pattern. For example, a common response is for whatever is proposed to be seen as part of a centrally orchestrated, project-management approach to the change overall, even where the thrust of the intervention might be based on a more diffuse and less structured approach.

As a brief stimulant to reflection on the assumptions concerning organizational change, Table 7.2 contrasts some aspects of the classic view with others which recognize the complex social dynamics that are continuously in play.

Table 7.2 Assumptions about organizational change

Conventional View	Informal Coalitions/ Wiggly World View
• Change only happens when managers say that it should.	• Change is happening continuously, through people's ongoing interactions.
• Change is a formal, rational and structured process.	• Change is messy and complex.
• Managers can plan, organize and control the change process and the outcomes that arise from it.	• Managers are both 'in control' (i.e. in charge) and, *at the same time*, 'not in control'.
• If we do things better and get them right, outcomes will happen in line with official policies, plans and programmes.	• Outcomes depend on the sense that people make 'locally' of these policies and plans (i.e. in small-group and one-to-one conversations) – and on the actions that flow from these 'on the ground'.
• There is a best way to lead change – a specific methodology that can be applied universally on the back of success elsewhere.	• Context is critical to what works and what doesn't work.
• The 'big things' – strategies, structures, processes, etc. – are most critical.	• The 'little things' – what's actually happening, day-in-day-out, that is helping or hindering change – are most critical.
• Change and continuity are mutually exclusive contradictions.	• Change and continuity are inextricably interwoven aspects of past, current and future happenings – all expressed in the currency of today's interactions.
• Resistance to change, needs to be rooted out and decisively overcome, if the sought-after changes are to be realized.	• Perceptions of "resistance to change" emerge from the natural expression of "multi-directed energy" (below), which is always in play.
• Change leadership is an arms-length intellectual exercise.	• Change leadership is a 'contact sport'!
• Being decisive and acting with clear intent is key to successful outcomes.	• Managers can act with intent but can have no certainty as to the outcomes that will emerge. Here, as everywhere, they have no option but to muddle through – whilst striving to do so with purpose, courage, and skill.

Reframing "resistance to change" as a case of multi-directed energy

Conventionally, what we think of as resistance to change is seen as bad. Something that gets in the way of management's expressed intentions and slows down the process of planned improvements. By contrast, we might more usefully think of this as a natural human reaction to the individual and collective impact of changes imposed by others. That is, as a normal aspect of the wiggliness of organization. It is not, in itself, a sign of poor attitude, lack of team spirit or other negative characteristics. Amongst other things, it can often be an attempt by people to protect their sense of identity and self-worth. Or to preserve wider relationships that could be affected by the changes. Importantly, too, it might also highlight potential flaws in the existing proposals or scope for improvement that has been overlooked. Most significantly, it reveals energy that can be worked with constructively, rather than being dealt with confrontationally. In this last regard, it particularly doesn't help to resort to classifications that describe those who are most actively opposed to what is going on as "terrorists", "blockers", saboteurs" or the like. Or to generalize from the specifics of the situation to view such people negatively in other contexts This fails to reflect the complex social dynamics that are constantly in play. Dynamics which naturally affect people's individual and collective responses to what is proposed in a particular instance.

As I've pointed out earlier, the coalescing of people informally around particular themes is the main way that change happens, whether those in the coalition are seeking to initiate, modify, bring to fruition or frustrate a particular outcome. This is the case whether such sought-after outcomes are formally endorsed or being pursued covertly. And it is a practice that is engaged in by people at all 'levels' of the organizational hierarchy. A key dynamic in coalition formation – whether in support of, or contrary to, a proposed change – is that people 'sign-up' because they want to. Those involved don't have to agree on everything. They just share a desire to achieve a certain end-result. This carries with it the recognition that some people won't necessarily want to support the official line, as this is constructed and articulated at any particular time. That is to say, their energies will be directed towards achieving different ends. With this in mind, Edwin Nevis argues that referring to such a response as "resistance to change" is unhelpful and misrepresentative of what's going on. It presents a one-sided view of the factors that are in play. Instead, he argues that this should be reframed as "multi-directed energy":[7]

> This term conveys the notion of multiple forces or desires, not all of which support each other, and many of which pull in different directions. It represents more accurately than does the concept of resistance the experience of both individuals and groups in reacting to the initiation of change.

Whilst, as Nevis goes on to say, it might still not be easy to change the response, this does call for active engagement in a process of mutual exploration and potential flexibility, rather than approaching it as an 'I am right, you are wrong' confrontation. As regards consulting in a wiggly world, then, these multi-directed energies provide something to be worked with, rather than routinely suppressed and overcome. Where the proposed outcome is 'non-negotiable', it still makes sense to understand, explore and seek to accommodate aspects of contrasting points of view. In doing so, besides potentially improving the quality of the sought-after shifts in practice and performance, it would also facilitate individuals' movement through the Holding On, Letting Go and Engaging 'phases' of the transition process. The notion of multi-directed energy carries with it a range of other 'e-factors' that might be motivating many of those who would otherwise be perceived as resistors. Factors such as emotional engagement, enthusiasm, expertise and endeavour, for example, that are energizing the alternative positions that they are taking on the matter in hand.

Actively listening to people's ideas and concerns is likely to help them to begin the process of 'letting go' of the present familiarities and turning to face a future that will be different in many respects (as well as being much the same in many others). The space that opens up between their letting go of the past and beginning to engage with the future also offers the chance of surfacing, and drawing on, ideas, perspectives and resources that might otherwise be framed as representing acts of resistance. William Bridges calls this the "Neutral Zone" or, more evocatively, "the nowhere between two somewheres".[8] Although this is a natural state of ambiguity, and disorientation, it also opens up the possibility of generating more imaginative responses. A liminal space, in which seeking to engage with people's multi-directed energies might yield new insights, improve the overall outcome and facilitate the personal growth of those involved.

Finally, here, the idea of multi-directed energy also has particular resonance for the initiation and development of the client-consultant relationship. As I emphasized in introducing the previous section, the dynamics of change are in play from the moment of the consultant's first interaction with the client. Here again, Nevis highlights a number of contradictory conditions that are likely to be present at that initial stage and throughout any subsequent engagement.[9] Ordinarily unspoken, these reflect my own experience, both as an in-house manager and practising consultant. On the one hand, there is the client's genuine desire for the work to be carried out thoroughly and professionally, and for meaningful improvements to be made. On the other, the client is equally concerned to ensure that nothing is done which might cause irritation or embarrassment to themselves or significant others; that proposals can be implemented quickly, regardless of the recognized complexities; that any proposed new ways of working don't include anything that 'we know won't work here'; that it is they themselves who will determine if, and to what extent, any proposals will be implemented, even if that means doing so in ways that the consultant sees as dysfunctional; and so on.

Embracing paradox – making parallel practice explicit

Many years ago, in advocating a strategic-choice approach to managerial decision-making, Allen Hickling[10] identified what he called four trade-offs relating to the way in which 'technical' factors and 'political' considerations are brought to bear on the process. Viewed from the perspective of organization as a complex social process, the notion of planned outcomes arising from strategic choice would be seen as an unrealizable ideal. Nevertheless, we can agree that, in all but the most simple of situations, the perceived technical soundness of people's decisions and actions is always counterposed by considerations of political expediency. The four counteracting forces that Hickling identifies are: a desire for simplification and the recognition of complexity; urgency to decide/act and the lack of information to do so 'scientifically'; the need for commitment to action and flexibility to keep one's options open; and the incrementality of decision-making and the felt need for comprehensiveness.

Anyone who has worked as a manager or consultant will recognize such tensions. These, and an endless stream of other, seemingly contradictory requirements, define everyday organizational life. One that sits at the core of management practice, which we've looked at extensively earlier, is that managers are *in charge* of what happens whilst, at the same time, not being *in control* of the effects of people's actions, inactions and interactions on what emerges in practice. However, rather than viewing these tensions as trade-offs and choices to be made between contradictory factors, in a display of either-or decisiveness, they are best seen as further examples of the paradoxical nature of organizational dynamics. As such, this demands a more thoughtful (and inevitably more demanding) approach, in which *the simultaneous presence of what appear to be polar opposites* is openly embraced and worked with. Striving to pursue, *and explicitly advocate*, a stance of what I'm calling "parallel practice" offers a way of framing such polar opposites as desirable and undesirable aspects of organization in equal measure. Besides not being amenable to either-or decision-making, these cannot be separated out in ways that allow them to operate in different timeslots or other forms of differentiation. In all cases, the dynamic is not simply one in which both A and B apply but at different times and/or places. Instead, it is a matter of *both* A *and* B occurring *at the same time and in the 'same place', i.e. simultaneously.* As Ralph Stacey and Chris Mowles put it,[11] "Paradox means the presence together, at the same time, of self-contradictory, mutually constituting, essentially conflicting ideas, neither of which can be eliminated or resolved".

In relation to organizational consulting, adopting the 'paradoxical thinking' orientation of parallel practice opens up the possibility that new perspectives, practices and possibilities might emerge. Whilst privileging one or other of the polarities appears to 'tick the box' of clarity and decisiveness, this masks the complex reality. It covers over the inherent contradictions and fails to engage with the "multi-directed energies" that this generates, as mentioned above. Where each of the polarities tends to be identified with a particular constituency of people, such as individual business units (decentralized) and corporate functions (centralized) for example, the normal dynamics tend towards 'us and them' polarization. This fails to tap into the diverse range of insights and perspectives that might emerge from an approach to practice that is based on the paradoxical notion of collaborative self-management, say.

Participating in open play – understanding the limits of set-piece interventions and Big-Dot thinking

As mentioned in Chapter 6, most of the conversations through which organization is enacted and outcomes emerge take place without managers being present. This is even more the case with those operating in a consulting capacity. The scheduled (if not always pre-designed) conversations that consultants have with clients only represent a very small fraction of those that will be taking place every day. This is the issue faced by all consultants. Their work with clients is necessarily limited in time and space. Overtly at least, it often consists of a series of set-piece events, as part of a wider programme of activity. And the story of their contribution is often reduced to the connecting together of these Big Dots, when their real contribution might have extended – and hopefully did extend – to include a much more nuanced and improvised series of interactions.

Where these set-piece events and related interactions stimulate further conversations within the wider population, broader effects might be triggered, of course. Nevertheless, regardless of how participative such set-piece events might be, these cannot substitute for the impact of the widespread interplay of people's everyday conversations. It is through this self-organizing process of conversational interaction that whatever happens, happens. With this in mind, Patricia Shaw argues in favour of engaging 'live' with this ongoing conversational process. Several years ago, shortly after the publication of her book,[12] I had the pleasure of participating in a workshop that she ran at the University of Hertfordshire. At the end of a highly interactive session, she reiterated what she saw as some of the important points about working from the participative perspective that she, Ralph Stacey, Doug Griffin and some of their doctoral students were seeking to articulate. Set out below are some of the guidelines to practice that I took from the event.

- *On change . . .*
  - Work from the process outwards.
  - Change the conversation and then draw attention to it – does it make sense?
  - Work with energy and intent; but it happens in the moment, through the conversation.

  - There is no beginning of change – How did it come about? . . . And how did that? . . .
  - No start, just emergence – so work from here.
  - Understanding comes with insight; and faith and trust come with understanding.
  - Engage with people who have the motivation, interest and sense of urgency – invite them to take up the invitation to make sense of what's happening.
  - Beware of the reification of models.

- *On the mode of enquiry engaged through conversation . . .*

  - What have you made of this conversation?
  - How do we account for what we are doing, day-in-day-out?
  - What kind of causality do we employ to make sense of our decisions and actions?
  - How do we believe both change and continuity arise in human affairs – "enabling constraints"?
  - How do we recognize leadership?

- *On paying attention to the movement of sense-making . . .*

  - What parts are we coming to play as we account for our continuing presence in the conversation?
  - What are we finding ourselves talking about?
  - How are our endeavours evolving as the conversation progresses?
  - How are we reconfiguring constructs?
  - How are power relations shifting?
  - How are 'rules of the game' changing as we play?
  - How is the meaning of our actions developing as we act?
  - How are we opening up where we can go from here, as we rearticulate how we came to here?

- *On the attributes of 'good' conversation . . .*

  - Free flowing.
  - Sensitivity to emerging themes.
  - Alertness to rhetorical ploys.
  - Introducing themes from other communities.

  - Awareness of shifts in anxiety/spontaneity.
  - Holding ambiguity to allow the novel to emerge. Alertness to conscious processes which trap us.

- **My afterthoughts and comments . . .**
  - As a practising consultant, and subscribing to the general tenor and philosophy of Shaw's approach, I found the above observations extremely useful. Her comments on the nature and dynamics of change sit well with those set down in this book. At the same time, I would take issue with her comment about the potential danger in using models. Or, at least, qualify it. I've addressed this aspect of consulting practice below.

Making pragmatic use of sense-making frameworks

As I mentioned earlier, as part of my own consulting practice, I make pragmatic use of a number of sense-making frameworks that I have developed over the past several years. I see this as consistent with a mode of operating which draws on the approach of the bricoleur, and with Yiannis Gabriel's notion of using models and frameworks paragrammatically (as described in Chapter 4). The judicious use of appropriate *sense-making* frameworks can sometimes facilitate the collective task of muddling through with purpose, courage and skill. By starting from where people typically 'are' (i.e. being used to some sense of structure) it can also provide the mental 'scaffolding' that might be needed to enable people to step away from the established norms of management practice. Easing them towards a more complexity-aware view of organization and its practical implications. As an example of this, my Business Performance Framework offers a structured *process* for facilitating sense-making conversations in relation to a wide range of performance-related matters. Use of this encourages and enables meaningful conversations to take place on the Whys, Whats and Hows of people's individual and collective practice, to supplement and draw upon the myriad informal and unstructured interactions through which organization is being continually (re-)enacted. As always, it is the conversations that are important, not the framework as such. At the same time, the discipline involved in following the process can overcome anxiety, encourage candour, surface some of the hidden scripts that are organizing people's participation, identify creative ways forward, and expose potential conflicts and contradictions, etc.

Shaw's comment on the "reification" of management models reflects her justifiable concern that these can come to dominate the thinking of those who take them up and detract from what is happening in the "living present".[13] This can certainly be the case where these are seen as blueprints for achieving an 'And they all lived happily ever after' future. Or where they are offered as supposedly comprehensive models of organizational practice and performance. I'm less worried, though, where frameworks are seen as facilitative rather than prescriptive. And where they are recognized as being abstractions from the complex reality; incomplete and provisional, rather than all-encompassing and definitive. In my experience, it is possible both to remain true to the idea that it is the in-the-moment conversational exchanges that matter most and, at the same time, to recognize that appropriate use of a framework (or other similar 'excursion' from the immediacy of the moment[14]) can be helpful in stimulating those conversations. Thoughtfully applied, these can provoke new insights and help conversations to become unstuck. If Shaw's warning to "beware of reifying models" is seen as an advisory 'Give Way' sign rather than a mandatory 'Stop', I have no problems with it.

In Chapter 6, I mentioned Edward de Bono's idea of proto-truths. These are temporary or contingent truths, which are used *as* if they are absolute but which can readily and willingly be changed, if and when something better emerges. As suggested earlier, sense-making frameworks can also usefully be treated as proto-truths – facilitating the meaning-making and action-taking processes but without being applied mechanistically and uncritically. What is important is the helpfulness of these in each particular situation, rather than their "rightness" overall.

Keeping it 'live' – as ongoing work in progress

The above point about using frameworks thoughtfully and with a light touch was underscored by comments made by Larry Hirschhorn, during a workshop that I attended at the Tavistock Institute many years ago. The basis of his approach was to "get people to 'tell their story' and engage with it". Although he acknowledged that, in this case, he keeps a model of the psychodynamic process in mind, his basic message was to "stick with the data".

Referring to my notes from the time, many of the recommendations he made about the nature of consulting and coaching practice echo the points set out above in relation to Patricia Shaw's approach. For example:

- Focus on the work/task rather than adopting a therapeutic stance.
- Seek out concrete examples (such as critical incidents), which can be 'unpacked'.
- Listen for the cues – especially those that evoke emotions.
- Look for the key dilemma(s) with which the client is struggling.
- Identify what is "figure" and what is "ground".
- Explore the boundaries within which the problem is set.
- Reflect on what your own feelings might be telling you about organizational matters – use these as data.
- Listen to what's not being said as well as what is.
- Test hypotheses with the client.

His final piece of advice was also important, given the point I made earlier that consultants are always entering into an ongoing process, which has no beginning and no end. That is:

- Use working notes (rather than finished reports) to keep issues 'live'.

I continue to argue that the formally adopted 'outcomes' of conversations (such as choices made, strategies developed or whatever) should *always* be viewed as work in progress. This applies both to those involving consultants and the vast majority that do not. This is the case even where – especially where! – these have been facilitated by the use of a particular structured technique, which might be taken to imply that an endpoint has been reached.

Applying participative approaches with full awareness of the wiggly-world dynamics

The use of participative approaches and structured methodologies, to facilitate sense-making and action-taking in a particular setting, is widely seen as an important dimension of progressive consultancy. And of management practice more generally. Within this, there are a plethora of structured dialogical techniques and participatory methods, which seek to engage people in this way. These are often referred to collectively as "large group", "whole system" or "open space" methodologies, with Holman *et al*'s book, *The Change Handbook*,[15] probably providing one of the most comprehensive compilations of these. Over the years, besides applying my own frameworks (above), I have used a number of these approaches – or, more accurately, variations of them – to facilitate various aspects of group work. I have generally deployed them in an *ad hoc* way, as part of a broader approach to client engagement. I tend to think of these as occasional adjuncts to my core consulting practice, rather than as central elements of it. Using such resources as, when and how appropriate, is another example of "imaginatively making do" (à la Bricoleur).

Over recent years, interest has grown in approaches aimed at structuring the organizing process itself around more participative and co-operative ways of working. Sociocracy, and its more recent 'cousin', Holacracy, are probably the most prominent examples of this; each with their own methodologies, based on participative decision-making of one form or another. A central focus of Sociocracy is the pursuit of a decision-making approach that promotes inclusion, and which seeks to arrive at decisions to which everyone involved is prepared to give their consent. Holacracy is a trademarked concept, with all of the rules, regulations and licensing which that entails. At the time of writing, it is promoted as providing "a concrete framework for encoding autonomy, agility, and purpose-alignment into your organization's DNA".[16] Anyone who has read the book to this point, might – quite rightly – anticipate my having some problems with the notion of 'an' organization having DNA; the championing of autonomy in an interdependent world, in which everyone is necessarily enabled and constrained by the actions, inactions and interactions of everybody else; and the offering of a "concrete framework" as a means of enabling people to muddle through the fluid complexities of organizational life. Nevertheless, from an ideological standpoint, I do believe in the potential value of more distributed decision-making in appropriate contexts. As such, I have always been a keen advocate of what I've referred to earlier "collaborative self-management" as an organizing philosophy – albeit without this necessarily involving radical changes in organizational form. Or without seeing a structured means of participation as the primary way of creating an enabling space for the productive exchange of knowledge, ideas and resources.

Crucially, the aim of creating increased opportunities for people to participate more overtly in the decision-making process is not to make them "feel better", although that may well be a positive side-effect. Its purpose is to tap into their creative potential, to produce *better decisions*; to enable them to *give voice to their thoughts and feelings*; to build the relationships that are essential for *real communication*; and to encourage them, individually and collectively, to *embrace* the choices that emerge.[17] So, given what seem to be unquestionable benefits arising from these structured forms of participation, are there any further insights or cautionary notes that we might draw from a wiggly-world perspective of organizational dynamics?

To begin with, since organization is continuously (re-)emerging in the currency of people's everyday interactions, it's important to recognize that *everyone is always participating*. This is the case regardless of their formal status in a particular setting or the level of their physical, intellectual and emotional engagement with what's going on. In a similar way, although the notion of co-creation is regularly used to describe the dynamics involved in structured approaches to participation, this is not something that is limited to such set-piece events. It, too, is a natural dynamic of everyday interaction. As I set out in Chapter 2, *every conversation is a co-creation forum*. Given this, the nature and quality of everyone's day-to-day participation is critical to what emerges in practice. This is the case both in the immediacy of their in-the-moment interactions (including in any set-piece events) and, over time, through the widespread interplay of their own and others' formal and informal conversations. This applies equally, of course, to all aspects of the client-consultant relationship.

Secondly, as emphasized throughout the book and reiterated above, *all interactions* are partial, power-related and political. They are also historically situated within the patterning of past interactions and the imprints of those conversations (in the form of structures, strategies, systems, procedures, language, folklore, rituals, routines, and so on) that are still being taken up in today's exchanges. These socio-political dynamics do not disappear as a result of the introduction of structured participation-based methodologies. They continue to shape people's involvement in the formal structures and protocols that each approach entails. This is the case whether we are talking about the selective use of workshop-based interventions or the adoption of more co-operative ways of working as the core of the overall organizational design. The problem is that an over-socialized view of the process often prevails. This can seduce consultants, managers and others into thinking that people will naturally and inevitably come to behave in ways that ensure alignment of intent, commonality of interest, shared identity, co-operative endeavour, and so on. Rules of engagement are often negotiated or imposed at the outset, to reinforce this desired sense of non-confrontational 'oneness'. In reality, it is important for consultants and client managers to recognize that whatever emerges in practice will be affected by the hidden, messy and informal dynamics that characterize real-world human interaction. As will the ways in which any decisions are enacted going forwards. In the context of participative group processes, this means people engaging in shadow-side practices that reflect the underlying competitive-co-operative dynamics, such as:

- contributing in ways that enable them to become or remain included within particular social or professional groupings and to avoid the attendant fear of being excluded;
- modifying their behaviour in recognition of the formal and/or informal power relations that are currently at play, both in the immediate setting and more widely;
- tending to interact, without conscious awareness, in ways that preserve the established patterns of behaviour and hence reinforce the interests of those who are best served by current practices;
- subordinating independent, critical thinking to the dynamics of groupthink;[18]
- sticking to the 'rules of the game' rather than saying what they really think and feel;
- self-censoring to avoid overt conflict and competitiveness – contributing, by default, to a false sense of agreement; and
- deferring to the facilitator, where one is involved.

It is important for consultants (and client managers) to recognize that these dynamics will inevitably colour the process and outcome of any participative endeavour. Also, for them to pay attention to any shifts in the patterning of power relationships and political activity arising from their own involvement. Surfacing and addressing relevant aspects of the above practices during an ongoing engagement, or as part of people's membership of one or other of the 'dynamic governance' regimes (e.g. Sociocracy), can enhance people's self-awareness, enrich their participation and increase their understanding of the wiggly-world dynamics.

Tuning-in to the striking moments in people's ongoing interactions

As reiterated above, a wiggly-world view of organization recognizes that people are *always* participating; *always* interdependent; and *always* co-creating the future together through their everyday interactions. Whilst consultants and managers might seek to promote and facilitate the more frequent coming together of people for collective decision-making, and/or the use of more structured approaches to individual and collective inquiry and development, the quality of their participation in these *active processes of social construction* is pivotal. Drawing on the work of John Shotter and others, Roger Lowe points out the importance of using these in "more creative, improvisational and 'living' ways"[19] He argues that the ineffective use of structured methods, in which these are applied in "dead, mechanical, calculational" ways, can result in "conversational routines that have lost their capacity to engage or move participants". Conversations that, in my terms, have become stuck in ritualistic patterns of managerially 'correct' and politically acceptable responses. Lowe argues that any such models and methodologies should instead be used in a more "responsive, embodied, participatory" fashion. Consistent with what we have said earlier about the nature of people's engagement more generally, this means paying attention and being responsive to the in-the-moment movement of the conversation: "remain[ing] attuned to the conversation's striking moments and continually changing requirements".

Any structured methodology, with its own Big Dots of steps, stages and set-piece routines, is an abstraction from the everyday complex reality. Rather than seeing these as rigorously applied sequences of steps directed towards a defined end-point, therefore, Lowe argues that these should be viewed as "paths of inquiry", along which the clients are invited to journey together in line with certain organizing themes. This shifts attention towards whatever is emerging during people's in-the-moment exchanges. That is, on the continuously emerging process in which they (and the consultant) are perpetually constructing the future together. Without losing sight of the overall purpose, it pays particular attention to things that become focal at various points during people's lived experience of the exchanges. That is, through their individual and collective muddling through. Importantly, too, Lowe makes the point that this brings to the fore internally generated, relational and bodily knowledge (sensory feelings, emotional reactions, intuitive responses, and so on), to sit alongside the derivation and use of intellectual knowledge.

Evaluating interventions by using practical judgement

It is natural for client managers to want to understand the contribution made by a consultant to a particular piece of work, or to organizational practice and performance more generally. In many respects, this mirrors the attraction – and therefore the pursuit – of so-called evidence-based practice. Both are seeking the security offered by a world that is knowable. A world in which we can provide a definitive answer to the question "Has it worked?" (evaluation) or "Will it work?" (evidence). In the techno-rational aspects of the world that we spoke about in Chapter 1, where outcomes are clear and precise (that is, knowable), achieving this level of understanding is doable. Obtaining measurable data in response to either of these questions makes perfect sense. It links inputs to outputs in a linear, matter-of-fact way. However, the dynamics of the *complex social process* of organization are fundamentally different. Such linearity doesn't exist. It's wiggly. Consultants and clients alike are always acting forwards, moment-to-moment, into a continuously emerging and unknowable future. As such, it is not possible to relate a particular intervention to an observed outcome in the cause-and-effect way that this implies.

A crucial point here is that I am not arguing, in an instrumental way, that it is too difficult to measure ROI or otherwise to tie specific interventions precisely to particular outcomes. Nor am I suggesting that this means that consultants (and/or others) need to find ways of collecting and analysing ever-more data to establish the link between cause and effect. Given the complex social dynamics of organization, such *relationships simply do not exist*. Even though Big Data is being mined in a growing multitude of contexts, this does not change the fact that the 'answer' is nowhere to be found. In a world that is never fully knowable, attempting to use 'because we did this, we got that' logic is, at best, misleading. The central dynamic is not one of linear causation but the *self-organizing* patterning of people's everyday, local interactions (i.e. small-group and one-to-one exchanges). And it is through the boundaryless interplay of these that organization is enacted and outcomes emerge. Within a particular context, this creates expectancy that things will tend to happen in ways that reflect past precedent. At the same time, it allows for the possibility that novelty (i.e. pattern-shifting) will occur spontaneously. It is therefore impossible to say whether or not a specific organizational intervention has resulted in improved organizational performance, much less whether or not it was the 'best' thing that could have been done. There is no way of 'unpicking' the intricate patterns of deliberate interactions and chance encounters through which outcomes emerge. That is, we cannot isolate the effects of a particular intervention from those of all of the other factors – formal and informal, structured and spontaneous, overt and hidden – that are simultaneously in play. Nor can we rewind and say what would have happened if a different course had been taken at a particular point in time. As I said in relation to the work of managers, it is important to recognize that high-quality practice will often be accompanied by unsuccessful results, and that some positive outcomes are likely to be due more to luck than judgement. This applies just as surely to the work of consultants as it does to that of everyone else involved.

So what, if anything, can we say in relation to the evaluation of consulting interventions? As in all things wiggly, applying practical judgement and reflexivity in the light of what is actually going on offers the best way forward. Within this, the most constructive approach to adopt is one of mutual learning, both in terms of the progress of the work itself and the quality of the relationship(s) involved. Also, given the emergent nature of the process, evaluation should be seen as a natural part of the ongoing conversations through which the work is being enacted. This process is one of joint sense-making. Its primary aim is one of learning from any differences that emerge along the way between actual outcomes and what was supposed to happen. It means seeking to address any problems that come to light; exploit any unexpected gains; make any necessary course corrections along the way; attend to any relationship issues; and improve individual and collective understanding and practice. Any claim to be able to evaluate the overall outcome in a matter-or-fact, return-on-investment sort of way is pure fantasy. Too often, evaluation processes begin with the interventions themselves and work backwards, in an attempt to prove the business benefit. In contrast, the first need is to understand the context within which the specific actions are taking place. It is the context that validates the intervention, not the other way around. And all social contexts are unique and wiggly. Validating and evaluating development and improvement activities is therefore always a matter of practical judgement, not one of supposed mathematical precision.

Paying attention to the quality of their own participation

The consultant's framing of their overall involvement and the nature of their specific work with the client are both underpinned by the quality of their own participation. Central to this is the need for them to ensure that they participate in ways that are congruent with the complex social dynamics of organization and which role-model the practical implications of these for day-to-day practice. Also, that they adapt their approach to suit the specific context and relationships within which they are working, rather than deploying a supposedly one-size-fits-all intervention regardless of context.

There are three broad aspects to this: (1) *translating* the elements of complexity-aware management practice (as detailed in Chapter 6) to inform their *own participation as a consultant* in the organizing process; (2) *working with the client(s)* to make sense of the *specific context* and *'path to now'* within which help is being sought, including surfacing the *shadow-side dynamics* that are influencing people's participation; and (3) helping to shift the *patterning and content of people's day-to-day interactions*, in ways that are judged to be beneficial.

Central to this is the consultant's ability to place these dynamics at the core of their practice, in ways that achieve credibility with their clients.

Translating the elements of complexity-aware management practice into the consulting arena

Participating skilfully in relation to organizational consulting requires practitioners, first of all, to participate in ways that reflect the approach set out in detail in Chapter 6, in relation to the role of managers. That is to say, they need to:

- adopt an **orientation to practice**, which is tuned-in to the paradoxical, 'both-and at the same time' nature of organization – what I've earlier called, "parallel practice";
- develop and apply **complexity-congruent capabilities** that underpin their ability to act forwards skilfully into the future, as this is emerging from their own and others' ongoing participation – that is using practical judgement, reframing communication, thinking culturally, acting politically, embracing paradox and practising reflexively;
- apply a **mode of operating** that is enabled by these capabilities, informed by relevant theory and applied pragmatically in the moment – that is, one of adopting and the stance of the bricoleur,[20] in imaginatively making do with whatever felt-useful resources, etc. happen to be available at that time, in those circumstances and in the context of that relationship.

In support of this, it also means consultants developing a set of 'concepts, tools and techniques' that *resonate with them personally*; which they have *adapted* in the light of their own and others' experience; and which they *hold lightly* in their engagements with clients. The aim is that they can confidently apply these to the situations that they face and adapt them as the situation requires. This includes practical 'rules of thumb' that might infuse and inform their everyday interactions, as well as these and other approaches that might form the explicit basis of their work with clients. It is especially important to reiterate here that these are intended to be used as provocations or stepping-stones to new conversations, within the specifics of the situation. If introduced openly at all, these should not be seen as definitive, 'if you do this you'll get that' prescriptions. The aim instead is to use these to stimulate and facilitate movement towards new and practical ways of engaging with the challenges and possibilities that are emerging. It is not to apply them formulaically. Or to force-fit the self-organizing patterning of people's interactions into predetermined and abstract models, definitive categories, or rigid methodologies.[21] As both a consultant and former in-house manager, the examples set out in Chapter 6 (and summarized in Table 6.4) have informed my own practice over the years in both contexts. However, as I stressed earlier, it is important for each consultant (as with each manager) to cultivate their *own set* of empirical guidelines, resources, rules of thumb, and so on – or "**practice theory**" as Peter Vaill calls them (see Chapter 4) – based on their personal experience of using these in practical settings.

Consultant credibility and "idiosyncrasy credits"

A final point in relation to consulting skilfully concerns the perceived credibility of the consultant, and/or wider consultancy, within the client organization. This is a factor in all consulting situations, of course. But it is especially the case where the approach being proposed runs counter to the established wisdom. This is clearly so in relation to a wiggly-world explanation of organizational dynamics and a view which sees expert practice as one of muddling through with purpose, courage and skill. Despite my contention that these are fully in accord with people's everyday lived experience, there are substantial pressures on managers to adopt (and thereby reinforce) a normative view of organization and management practice. A view, that is, which ignores the real-world messiness in favour of a more neatly packaged – and formally endorsed - understanding of what's going on and how they *should* respond. And so, even though it opens up the possibility of operating in ways that are more congruent with the complex reality, escaping from this pressure to conform itself requires an act of courage.

Against this background, if consultants are to be able to influence the perspectives, practices and performance of client managers and others, demonstrating credibility and establishing mutual trust is an essential aspect of the client-consultant relationship. This will rest on such things as the consultant's known or perceived competence in relevant areas; their track record in delivering perceived value to the client; their foregrounding of the client's issues and objectives, ahead of pre-packaged, methodologies and their own self-interests; their ability to tune-in to the client's unexpressed needs and to articulate these in ways that resonate strongly with them; and the perceived risk to the client of the approach being offered. In this last regard, the idea of idiosyncrasy credits[22] is particularly relevant. This is a concept from social psychology, which (in this context) refers to the ability of the consultant to deviate from the established expectations of those they are seeking to influence. The more 'credits' that they have earned, by living up to people's past expectations, the more scope they have to introduce innovative perspectives and practices that run counter to those expectations and to what is currently accepted as the norm. That is to say, the more idiosyncratic their actions can be.

The consulting dilemma – to challenge or collude?

As discussed extensively earlier, the task of the manager is conventionally associated with efforts to achieve order, predictability and control. Consistent with this, the roles of consultants and other specialists tend to be framed by expectations of rationally structured approaches, optimal decision-making and the delivery of universally positive outcomes. The presumption is that value arises from the consultant standing apart from the day-to-day demands and routines of the client's day-to-day practice. From this perspective, their job is seen as one of analysing what is going on and prescribing the best way forward from a position of detachment and objectivity, supposedly applying well-defined methodologies to bring about measurable improvements in individual and/or organizational capability and performance. These same conditions are assumed to apply in the case of those operating as internal consultants, coaches and the like. However, all such specialists are 'on the pitch, playing'. They are involved participants, not detached observers. As such, they are affected by – *as well as contributors to* – the real-world wiggliness of organization, out of which whatever happens, happens.

As we've seen, this means that they are no more able to predict, control or measure the effects of their contribution on organizational capability and performance than can managers in relation to their own work. This doesn't sit well, of course, with the approaches that managers are typically called upon to adopt in assessing the benefits of using specialist support. It adds to the pressure on consultants and others to frame their offerings in ways that fit with the generally accepted 'truths' of management orthodoxy, as set out in Chapter 5. If they do so, they risk strengthening these still further, making it yet more difficult to escape from the effects that these have on people's ongoing practice. If this pattern is to be broken, therefore, it is essential for consultants to recast their role and approach in ways that are much more congruent with the wiggly reality.

So, if and when the call for help comes, how will the consultant respond? Faced with their own need to win business and earn fees to survive, or to maintain credibility and influence as an internal consultant, will they collude with those who are wedded to the established view of organization and management practice? Or will they challenge it? Are they prepared to take the risk of rowing against the stream? Can they afford to? Can they – *and those they set out to help* – afford not to?

Notes

1 The quotation is by Kevin Nix, who was then head of the generation business at a UK power company. It was included in an article by Carly Chynoweth, in *The Sunday Times* of 7 September 2014, entitled *Management by Muddling Through*. The article sprang from the *Five Acts of Management* graphic (see Chapter 3) and centres on my argument that we need to recognize the muddling-through nature of real-world management practice. A copy of the article can be found here: https://www.thetimes.co.uk/article/management-by-muddling-through-gfh2d9vwv8s.

2 See Chapter 4 for an explanation of this concept.

3 Shaw, P. (2002: 122) *Changing Conversations in Organizations*. Routledge.

4 World-leading voice coach, Patsy Rodenburg, talks of this in terms of "second-circle energy". See, for example, Rodenburg, P. (2009) *Presence.* Penguin.

5 As background to this, the essence of the wiggly world of organization (Point 1) is set out in Chapter 1. This is supported, in Chapter 2, by a more in-depth explanation of the complex social dynamics that determine what happens in all organizational contexts. The implications of these dynamics for management and leadership practice (Point 2) are then discussed extensively in Chapter 6, with the underpinning theory relating to muddling through detailed in Chapter 4.

6 Bourdieu, P. (1992) *The Logic of Practice*. Polity Press.

7 Nevis, E.C. (1987: 147) *Organizational Consulting*. Gestalt Press.

8 Bridges, W. and Bridges, S. (2017) *Managing Transitions*. Nicholas Brealey.

9 Nevis, E.C. (ibid: 148).

10 Hickling, A. (1974) *Managing Decisions: The Strategic Choice Approach.* Mantec Publications.

11 Stacey R.D. and Mowles, C. (2016: 39) *Strategic Management and Organisational Dynamics 7Ed.* FT Prentice Hall.

12 Shaw, P. (2002) ibid.

13 See discussion on the notion of "the living present" in Chapter 2.

14 Patricia Shaw herself advocates the skilful use of forum theatre as a metaphor for the complex dynamics of organization. Various forms of random stimulation can also provoke conversations that help to surface and shift 'stuck' patterns and expose other factors that are limiting movement.

15 Holman, P. *et al* (2007) *The Change Handbook 2Ed.* Berrett-Koehler.

16 https://www.holacracy.org, accessed on 28 February 2020.

17 An article by Raymond E. Miles, in the July 1965 issue of *Harvard Business Review*, "Human Relations or Human Resources", pointed to these two models of participation. In it, Miles suggested that, in the Human Relations model, the basic objective is to make "organizational members *feel* a useful and important part of the overall effort". In contrast, the Human Resources model, the purpose is to improve the quality of decision-making and overall performance, by including those directly involved in and affected by the issues". In a study carried out at the time, into managers' views on participation, the general pattern of responses suggested that managers took a view on the participation of team members that was predominantly in line with the Human Relations model. In contrast, as regards the case for their own participation in higher-level decision-making, this was most often argued on the basis of the Human Resources model!

18 See discussion of Groupthink in Chapter 2.

19 This draws on Roger Lowe's paper, *Structured Methods and Striking Moments: Using Question Sequences in 'Living' Ways* which was published in *Family Process* in 2005 [44(1): 65–75]. Lowe's focus is on the use of various forms of social constructionist theory in a therapeutic context, in which he contrasts – and seeks to draw together – various structured forms of engagement with a more conversational approach. This resonates strongly with the essence of my argument here, which seeks to use structured approaches to consulting and related practices.

20 Patricia Shaw (2002: 71) speaks of this general approach as "ensemble improvisation", to emphasize that this is a collaborative effort, not solely limited to the contribution of the consultant.

21 As I said in relation to the practice of managers (Chapter 6), these are what Gabriel describes as "flexible routines", which invite "improvisation and elaboration rather than copying and imitation" (Chapter 4). In essence,

this involves practitioners making pragmatic use of theories and other practices, that resonate strongly with them; that they have personalized or otherwise adapted in the light of their own experience; and which they can deploy selectively in different contexts, as they seek to find their way through the challenges and possibilities that emerge.

22 The term "idiosyncrasy credit" was coined by Edwin Hollander in his 1958 article "Conformity, Status, and Idiosyncrasy Credit" that was published in in *Psychological Review*, 65(2): 117–127.

8

SHIFTING THE PATTERNS

A MANIFESTO FOR MUDDLING THROUGH

A few years ago, whilst working with my friend and then client, Hans Haringa, in The Hague, we were joined by Dan Sarewitz. He is co-author of the book, *The Techno-Human Condition*,[1] which explores what it means to be human in a world that is increasingly affected by what he and his colleague, Braden Allenby, describe as "incomprehensible technological complexity and change". In a conversation over lunch, we spoke in passing about our shared interest in the notion of muddling through. This had been central to my own view of the dynamics of organization and management practice for a number of years; and they speak of this in their book as "the best that we can do". Dan referred briefly to our exchange as an argument for creating a sort of "manifesto for muddling". Our conversation then quickly moved on to other things. However, with this in mind, I've set out below some of the patterns of talk and action that might become evident, if the currently dominant view of organization was to shift towards one which more closely reflected our everyday lived reality. This is, in effect, my *manifesto for muddling through*. It is addressed to managers, other organizational practitioners, policy-makers . . . and anyone and everyone else whose actions, inactions and interactions are constantly co-creating the organizational world and our understanding of it. Its aim, again drawing on the writing of Alan Watts, is to expose "our tacit conspiracy to ignore who, or what, we really are"[2] and to suggest some of the ways in which that might change, if we were to pay proper attention to our own lived experience.

Manifesto for muddling through

Acting forwards, moment to moment, into a continuously emerging and unknowable future. Seeking to do so with purpose, courage and skill.

In previous chapters, I've set out why the process of organization is wiggly and why "muddling through" most accurately describes what managers – and everyone else – actually find themselves doing in practice. So, what patterns of talk and action might become evident, if the currently dominant view of organization was to be replaced by one which more closely reflected these complex social dynamics of everyday human interaction? And if those involved sought to muddle through the challenges they faced with purpose, courage and skill.

Below are a number of short statements that attempt to answer that question. I've couched these in terms of *moving beyond* orthodox practice. This accepts the validity of the existing frame in certain contexts and conditions but recognizes and embraces a more all-encompassing perspective. One, that is, which *takes complexity seriously*. Each statement indicates the broad shifts in perspective and practice implied by this more reality-congruent view of organizational dynamics. A view which more closely reflects people's everyday lived experience of organizing, leading, managing and participating more generally.

As regards organizational practice, this suggests moving . . .

1. *Beyond well-meaning recipes to the* wiggly reality

Managers and other practitioners would begin by paying attention to their own lived experience. In doing so, they would understand that what can sometimes be useful and anxiety-reducing ways of thinking about the world are nevertheless distortions of what is actually going on. For example, rather than seeing organization as a tangible entity – a "whole" that can be worked upon, changed and managed at will – they would recognize this as an *active process* of organiz-*ing*. A process which is re-emerging continuously from their own and everyone else's participation in it. Coupled with this, the well-meaning but flawed recipes and rhetoric that have grown up around assumptions of certainty, predictability and control would be seen as being at odds with this real-world wiggliness. As would many of the formal trappings of organization and the approach to management practice that these imply. Although embodying a sense of everyday predictability, which allows people to go on together day to day, this radically different view of organization is set within a broader dynamic of uncertainty and unpredictability. This arises naturally from the unbounded interconnectedness of people and the widespread interplay of their in-the-moment interactions.

In working with others, people would recognize that all of these interactions are unavoidably partial, power-related and political. This accounts both for the amazing capacity of people to achieve great things together and, at the same time, for the ever-present possibility of these relationships being played out in ways that are dysfunctional and destructive – whether intentionally or otherwise. You can't have the potential for one to emerge without the risk of the other occurring, too. Former US President Barack Obama put this neatly at the 2019 annual summit of his Foundation, set up to promote 'good citizenship' and the power of people to change things for the better:[3]

> This idea of purity and you're never compromised and you're politically woke,[4] and all that stuff – you should get over that quickly. The world is messy. There are ambiguities. People who do really good stuff have flaws.

Acting with conscious awareness and understanding of these unavoidably wiggly dynamics of organization (*i.e. of everyday human interaction!*) would open-up the possibility of a much more expansive and personally meaningful contribution from those who were willing and able to participate more fully. It would also reduce the likelihood of their being seduced by the fantasies and false promises of the widely peddled, "And they all lived happily ever after" futures. Instead, they would come to recognize and embrace the "beautiful, ugly truth" of organizational life as they actually experience it.[5]

2. *Beyond either-or polarities to* embracing paradox

Clarity and decisiveness are highly rated attributes of conventional management thinking and practice. When faced with competing demands, making clear choices and acting swiftly and decisively to realize these are seen as the essence of leadership. This position tends to be reflected in the comments made whenever management is spoken about in everyday conversation or commented upon in the media. It is the world of either-or.

Whilst this is appropriate in relation to relatively straightforward, techno-rational choices between two mutually exclusive options, it would be recognized that the process of everyday human interaction is fundamentally different from this. It is paradoxical. That is to say, mutually contradictory conditions are simultaneously present and unresolvable. As such, adopting an either-or approach is not credible. Instead, as Stacey argues, "paradoxes require both/and choices at the same time; either/or choices are not possible, nor is a sequential switching between them".[6] Johnson similarly suggests that these need to be seen as tensions to be managed, not problems to be solved.[7] And these tensions need to be managed dynamically, rather than in a once-and-for-all way.

3. *Beyond evidence-based practice to* practice-based evidence

The established notion of evidence presupposes the ability of suitably qualified people to make a direct, unequivocal, and hence repeatable link between cause and effect. However, the process of organization is socially complex. It is not rational in a scientific sense. As such, the dynamics of organization are not amenable to the research and testing protocols needed to provide rigorous evidence of the merit or otherwise of a particular practice. Nor is it possible to carry out 'experiments' in particular settings and expect the repeatability and/or scalability of these to be unproblematic in other contexts. These same dynamics make the relationships between cause and effect untraceable. This means that it is impossible to establish the links between observed outcomes and specific actions in all but a limited set of conditions. Or to justify claims that what is perceived to be successful practice in one context can be reliably generalized to others. Instead, it places a premium on the unique historical background, specific context, current contingencies, and in-the-moment interactional dynamics that are 'in play' at any particular time.

It would be recognized, therefore, that deciding the validity and efficacy of a particular practice is a matter of practical judgement. With the test being one of reason-*ability* rather than scientific rationality. This is a subjective and interpretive task that requires a pragmatic, exploratory and reflexively critical approach to organizational practice. It means managers working with others to make context-specific sense of what's going on; act forwards into the future that is being co-created from their own and everyone else's participation in it; and deal appropriately and imaginatively with the emerging consequences. Expertise in relevant fields might properly be drawn upon to stimulate thinking and provoke new insights, but this would always be circumscribed by the sciences of uncertainty, not certainty. As such, ways forward that emerged from the process would be seen as tentative and provisional. It would be accepted that the success (or otherwise) of particular interventions only becomes evident as outcomes emerge. And that, even then, what constitutes success or failure is a matter of interpretation, not an objective fact. In short, evidence would be seen to be practice-based.

4. *Beyond hollow abstractions to* human agency

One of the current preoccupations within organizational management is the so-called "digital transformation" of processes and practices, which aims to use rapidly advancing technologies to exploit the perceived potential of Big Data, artificial intelligence, robotics and so on. As a result, a world is being constructed, by design, in which the idiosyncrasies and implied inferiority of human agency are replaced by decisions and actions governed by remote and abstract algorithms. In the main, this tends to be uncritically accepted as a welcome advance in practice. In the process, the real-world dynamics of human interaction are ignored, in favour of a utopian view in which there is universal wellbeing, co-operation and harmony, facilitated by technology. This naivety undermines serious consideration of emerging technologies – both in terms of the genuine potential that these might have for improving the human condition, as well as the risks involved in their rapid and unquestioned deployment.

Most significantly here, these changes are being carried out within the confines of what is otherwise an orthodox view of the dynamics of organization and management practice, and the ways that these are mirrored within society more generally. This locks-in the flawed assumptions on which these views of what is good are based. It also imperceptibly reinforces the biases and prejudices that are embodied in the everyday practices of those involved in the development, programming and deployment of the new technologies. This risks further distancing the prescribed ways forward from the very essence of human being and human doing. And from the ethics of its practice.

Instead, imbued with such characteristics as subtlety, nuance, intuition, the capacity for constructive ambiguity, practical judgement, pragmatism and so on, primacy would have been given to human agency, with all of its quirks and foibles. This would not have been subordinated to the supposed sophistication and process efficiencies of ever-advancing science and technology, based on the hollow abstractions of opaque and mind-*less* algorithms and robotics. Technology would be seen as the servant of human being, not its master.

5. *Beyond structured diagnosis to* spontaneous dialogue

Consistent with the above, the currently dominant view of the manager's role is rooted in an understanding of organizational dynamics which assumes that strategic and operational challenges are best dealt with through some form of expert diagnosis, whether the manager's own or that offered by specialist practitioners. Such approaches are based on the notion of objective analysis of 'the facts', in which thinking and doing are thought of as separate and sequential acts. Many are formulaic. They reflect the view that there is a generalizable set of characteristics and/or 'best practice' prescriptions that can be applied universally.

However, recognition of the wiggliness of organizational life would see this as problematic. It would be understood that knowledge and action in a social process are co-created in the moment of people's 'local' interactions (i.e. in small-group and one-to-one settings). These take place both formally and informally, in structured meetings and spontaneously, and occur everywhere from the boardroom to the backroom. These myriad conversations always reflect individual and collective differences of views and values, as well as the personal idiosyncrasies of those involved. They are also historically situated within the vast array of interactions which have gone before – both near and far. And the conscious playing out of these is always infused with participants' in-the-moment intuitive and improvised responses. This means that the patterning of the process and its meaning emerge spontaneously, as thinking and acting are intimately interwoven in a continuous act of sense-making-cum-action-taking exchanges. As a consequence, since structured diagnosis ordinarily draws upon managers' and others' after-the-event rationalizations of their experience, this cannot capture the wiggly reality of what happened in practice.

From this perspective, then, it would be recognized that organization is fundamentally a dialogic process. And that, for managers, *the conversations are the work*. Formal, structured diagnosis of issues relating to the various 'technologies' that might be helping and/or hindering what is going on would still have an important part to play in the broader meaning-making process. But organization is enacted by people in conversation. Understanding and engaging insightfully with these complex and uncertain dynamics can't be reduced to an arms-length task. Or rely on systematic, step-wise procedures and other analytical tools and techniques to make sense of the complex social process through which organization is being continuously re-enacted and outcomes are emerging.

6. Beyond consensus, commonality and conformity to difference, diversity and dissent

If large-scale social organization is to continue to function, and a degree of order and coherence is to be achieved, this necessarily requires people to adhere to certain rules, regulations and behavioural norms. As a result, it has become a central tenet of management orthodoxy that effective performance requires consensus to be sustained around sought-after outcomes; a common approach to be established, to enable these to be consistently delivered; and provisions to be put in place to ensure that people conform to the roles, systems and norms, etc. that have been designed to achieve the desired ends. From this perspective, any deviation from the specified path, or disagreement with it, is considered to be dysfunctional; demanding firm management action.

In contrast, the adoption of a wiggly-world perspective would carry with it an understanding that difference, diversity and dissent are every-present – *and crucially important* – aspects of everyday human interaction. Although these can also be the source of potentially destructive behaviour, it is through difference, diversity and dissent that the seeds of progressive change are sown and that beneficial shifts are achieved in policy and practice. This occurs as themes that run counter to the established narrative emerge from the shadows and are taken up as formal propositions. Responding creatively and constructively to difference, diversity and dissent is therefore central to the task of muddling through with purpose, courage and skill. In essence, this is about:

- seeking to integrate difference, without losing the benefits that difference brings;
- encouraging diversity in all of its expressions, to foster a melting-pot of diverse experiences, perspectives and ideas;
- respecting the expression of dissent, as an important and valued aspect of critically examining what is credible and broadening the scope of what is considered to be sensible; and
- pursuing all of this within a broader narrative of collaborative self-management (below).

7. *Beyond centrally imposed 'solutions' to* collaborative self-management

As a result of the 'do it better and get it right' view of organizational management, there is constant pressure on senior managers to develop and impose organization-wide 'solutions' from the centre that promise order, predictability and control. However, given that actual outcomes emerge through the widespread interplay of myriad local interactions, this task is not within the gift of managers to deliver. In recognizing these dynamics, the emphasis would shift towards more flexible, responsive and improvisational ways of working. Ways that are not constrained by an excess of common structures and centralized edicts, but which recognize the situation-specific requirements, unique perspectives and diverse contributions of those involved.

This more congruent response would encourage and enable the collaborative self-management of people's individual and collective contributions. Its aim would be to facilitate the open and dynamic networking of knowledge, ideas, and resources, to deal with emerging needs *as the real world happened*. This would involve efforts to match individual and collective capabilities to the evolving portfolio of requirements. And doing so dynamically, within more fluid organizational forms.

8. *Beyond managing change to* mobilizing coalitions

According to received wisdom, organizational change happens when managers say that it should. It is considered to be an intellectually sophisticated undertaking, which typically requires the expert application of a formal, structured and commonly applied methodology; the use of 'if you do this, you'll get that' logic; and arm's-length oversight from high-level sponsors and steering groups.

In taking complexity seriously, this episodic and 'done to' view of change would be seen as a fiction. Instead, it would be recognized that change is happening continuously, in the unstructured messiness of people's everyday, local interactions. It is through this ongoing process, which is imperceptibly patterned by the in-the-moment iteration of past sense-making, that people are influenced to think, feel and act in particular ways. In doing so, they tend to coalesce informally around particular themes, in order to initiate, support, or frustrate specific changes. It would therefore be understood that bringing about deliberate changes in policy and practice is a political process. Mobilizing active coalitions of support around organizationally beneficial themes that resonate strongly with a sufficiently powerful constituency of people to cause them to 'sign up'. Rather than this being an arms-length task, involving the mechanistic 'rolling out' of common messages and methodologies, it would be seen as a 'contact sport'. Shifting people's understanding and response by 'pushing at half-open doors'.

9. *Beyond evaluating people to* enabling performance

The established approach to assessing performance is rooted in the supposed ability of managers (and, in other instances, members of public bodies and regulators) to evaluate the actions of other people from a rational, objective and independent standpoint. However well-intentioned such 'assessors' might be, though, they are not dealing with objective facts but rather their own and others' perceptions, interpretations and evaluations of what's going on. In all circumstances, their judgements and actions are subject to a number of factors that belie the notions of independence and objectivity.

To begin with, people are *inter*dependent. Everyone is both enabled and constrained in their thinking and doing by what everyone else is doing and not doing. As such, the performance of any individual is significantly affected by their relationships and interactions with specific and generalized others (one of whom is their manager). Secondly, managers are not 'sitting in the stand', watching from afar how people are performing. They are 'on the pitch, playing'. As such they are continuously affecting what happens, for better or worse, whether knowingly or unknowingly. Thirdly, everything that happens is path- and context-dependent. Successes and failures emerge from the complex interplay of myriad factors, only some of which are attributable directly to the specific individual(s) under review. Others are affected by the actions and omissions of many other people, both currently and historically. Fourthly, since assessments, reviews, inquiries and so on occur after the event, they always take place from a position in which the outcomes of people's practice – and how these have been construed by significant others – are known. And, as noted by Duncan Watts,[8] everything is obvious once you know the answer. Finally, the evaluation process is subject to the same complex social dynamics as those that affect all other conversations. That is to say, it is always infused with the psycho-social, political and cultural aspects of everyday human interaction. Those doing the assessment are themselves immersed in this same complex social process, in which they invariably have 'skin in the game'. As a result, the judgements that emerge are unavoidably partial and subjective.

Recognizing these *natural* dynamics, and the fact that those formally in charge are not in control of what emerges from the widespread interplay of people's myriad interactions, the focus would have shifted to one aimed at joint sensemaking of emerging events and *enabling* people to perform. The aim of those involved would be to achieve beneficial *movement in people's practice* (including their own!), rather than judging people against predetermined performance targets and procedural constraints. Importantly, too, scorekeepers and commentators would no longer be seen as being more important than the players!

10. Beyond paperwork, checklists and SMART-ness *to* purpose, courage and skill

In pursuit of order, predictability and control, mainstream management requires people to operate in line with formally codified policies, systems and procedures. This same line of thinking underpins many regulatory regimes, where regulators impose rigid process disciplines on those covered by the relevant regulations. Managers and other practitioners then need to demonstrate compliance with the mandated procedures – irrespective of the quality of practice and performance outcomes that they might be achieving through other means. General Practitioner David Zigmond, whose well-regarded London practice fell foul of this inflexible, tick-box method of inspection, calls the approach REMIC: Remote Management, Inspection and Compliance.[9]

Central to this is the presumption that effective organization and management practice demands clearly understood and readily measurable deliverables; formal, linear processes, systems, and procedures; extensive documentation; and so on. The call to specify the outcomes required in terms of SMART objectives (where the SMART acronym stands for some variant of Specific, Measurable, Achievable, Relevant, and Time-based) is rarely far away. Overall, the approach tends to be process-heavy and practice-light. The unfailing belief in scientific rationality, predictability, and control further reinforces the illusion that practitioners can ensure that things will turn out as planned – provided that they do things in line with the formally approved 'recipe for success'. They can't.

Instead, recognition of the socially complex nature of organization would reject this mechanistic approach in all but the most technical of situations. That is, limiting its use to those circumstances in which the techno-rational aspects of organization can be dealt with without any need for in-the-moment sensemaking or other forms of nuanced interaction. In all other instances, expert practice would be recognized as being:

- less about programmed instruction and more about personal interaction;
- less about abstract prescriptions and more about active participation;

- less about procedural conformity and more about pattern-shifting creativity; and, encompassing all of the above,
- less about paperwork, checklists and SMART-ness, and more about purpose, courage, and skill.

In relation to the way in which we view the practice of leadership, this suggests moving . . .

11. Beyond elite practice to emergent property

Typically, leadership is spoken about primarily in role-related terms. As the responsibility of those in the most senior positions. Over the past couple of decades, it has also been positioned as something separate from, and superior to, the supposedly mundane task of management. This latter position is perhaps best reflected in the view expressed by Warren Bennis that leaders master the context whereas managers surrender to it.[10] This perspective is both misleading and unhelpful. As regards the role-related tasks of leading and managing, the alternative position set out by Kevin Flinn[11] and mirrored in the view that I have set out here, is much more in tune with the complex reality of what is actually going on. Here, these are recognized as inseparable and complementary aspects of every manager's role – from CEO to the front line.

Crucially, though, *those in formal management roles are not party to most of the conversations that go on day-to-day.* Yet these conversations powerfully influence the ways in which people co-create the meaning of what they and others are doing. As well as mobilizing individual and collective action around one construction of reality rather than another. This means that the actions of managing and leading that we ordinarily attribute to managers are relatively commonplace – occurring routinely in situations in which there is no one present who has formal authority. Many of the perspectives, principles, and practices that affect what people actually do in practice emerge from, and are sustained by, these informal, shadow-side conversations. What, in conventional terms, might be thought of merely as inconsequential small talk, imbues such practices with a sort of 'shadow legitimacy'. Within this, some participants' opinions hold particular sway in the ongoing process through which the future is being perpetually co-created in the currency of people's present interactions.

In the context of this more experience-based view of organization, leadership would be seen as an *emergent property of people in relationship*, not an elite practice confined to those at the top. It would be recognized as being enacted by many people in the normal course of their day-to-day interactions, rather than as a rational, scientific endeavour, practised by a few gifted and formally appointed individuals. Crucially, this is not fundamentally about senior managers deciding, as a design choice, to delegate or distribute formal management authority more widely. Or about adopting one of the more overtly self-managing approaches to organization.[12] It is a natural dynamic, in which individuals mobilize the collective action of others around a particular interpretation of what's going on and/or to bring about sought-after shifts in practice. So, specific acts of leadership can emerge at any time and involve anybody. Punctuation marks in the ongoing conversation of organization.

12. Beyond standing out to standing in

The currently accepted view of formal leadership practice is that this is provided by people with outstanding ability – individuals who stand out from the crowd in terms of their intellectual capacity, charisma, vision, courage, risk appetite, or other personal characteristics that are being advanced at the time. It is also supposedly exercised by standing apart from the minutiae of the action, to see and address the "big picture" from a position of objectivity. It is this narrative, coupled with the notion of leadership as an elite practice, that underpins established patterns of managerial recognition and reward.

However, from a wiggly-world perspective, it is simply not possible for anyone to set themselves apart from what's going on, and to act as an objective observer and controller of other people's actions. A central element of every manager's role would therefore be seen as one of 'standing in' – that is, deliberately being there, in the midst of the action. Paying attention to *what is actually going on* in the detail and patterning of people's day-to-day interactions. Seeing, feeling and sensing pertinent conditions directly, personally and immediately, as opposed to judging on the basis of hearsay or impersonal, arms-length measurement. It implies managers working to establish a visceral connection with what is happening and seeking to shift the patterning and content of interactions through their everyday conversations. They would be doing all of this, of course, from the standpoint of *involved participant* rather than that of external, objective observer.

13. *Beyond certainty to* curiosity

It would be recognized that managers, like everyone else, act into a continuously emerging and unknowable future, in which they don't have all of the answers. Sometimes they don't have any. The search for, and expectancy of, certainty and predictability would therefore have been supplanted by the valuing and practice of curiosity. This signals a shift towards leading through questions, inquiry and critical thinking rather than a presumption that the manager's role is to provide all of the answers. That is, stimulating and drawing upon the curiosity and insights of others, as a contribution to a more reality-congruent form of management practice. It also means exposing and exploring those shadow themes that are organizing people's participation; engaging constructively with the implications arising from the irresolvable paradoxes of organization; and having the ability to articulate these natural dynamics of organization in ways that resonate with relevant others.

In the context of the social world, this is about moving from a search for scientifically verifiable absolutes to the notion of proto-truths.[13] As mentioned earlier, these are contingent and provisional truths that work for now but are always open to review and revision in the light of experience. Above all, it points to the capacity of managers to embrace uncertainty and ambiguity, and to become comfortable in a position of 'not knowing'. Importantly, too, it also means normalizing this practice in the ways in which others are able (and enabled) to deal with the unavoidable wiggliness of organization.

14. *Beyond controlling to* contributing

In face of this inherent uncertainty and complexity, managers (as well as those who judge and comment on their performance) would no longer perpetuate the myth that they were in control of organizational outcomes. They would accept that no individual or group – whatever their formal authority – can predict or control what emerges in practice. Managers are, of course, formally in charge, and as powerful participants in the ongoing interactional process, they contribute to those dynamics and outcomes in important and influential ways – whether intentionally or otherwise. But they are not *in control* of them. Their position would therefore be recognized as one of contributor to, rather than controller of, people's practice and organizational performance.

Within this, helping people (including themselves) to deal with the anxiety of not knowing, would be recognized as an important, complexity-aware and emotionally intelligent contribution for managers to make. As Yiannis Gabriel points out, the myth of management control is a politically and culturally expedient way of helping to reduce anxiety – "fulfilling in fantasy wishes that cannot be fulfilled in actuality".[14] As such, having a sense of being 'in control' can, in some circumstances, satisfy an important psychological need for managers and others alike. Provided, that is, that this idealization is held lightly and its limitations recognized.

The call for people to "control the controllables", which is a popular mantra in elite sporting circles, captures the essence of this and offers a pragmatic response to any suggestion that people's inability to determine what happens overall means that they should just shrug their shoulders and hope for the best. However, recognition of the complex reality does mean that the central theme of a manager's contribution would shift from controlling people's practice and performance to one of enabling them to perform with their own sense of purpose, courage and skill.

15. *Beyond prescribing to* provoking

Conventional management wisdom is rooted in the idealization of outstanding, position-based Leadership (with a capital 'L'), coupled with the vast array of prescriptions that claim to deliver the sought-after conditions of order, predictability and control. From this perspective, those who are formally in charge appear well placed to achieve success. However, recognition of the complex social dynamics of organization would have exposed the mismatch between this 'textbook' position and the practical realities of people's everyday lived experience.

As a result, the tendency for managers to prescribe the ways in which others should proceed would be much less in evidence. Instead, they would set out to provoke individual and collective (self-) reflection, encourage different perspectives, and enable new ways of working to emerge. Frank

Barrett, talks about this notion of provocation as one of creating dissonance by questioning assumptions, exploring tangential ideas, and creating metaphors that stimulate new thinking.[15] Edward de Bono would talk of this in terms of stimulating *movement*, as a departure from the default position of offering 'right-wrong' judgement. From this perspective, actions would be viewed as experimental, contingent and provisional, with knowledge being seen as "applied, pragmatic, and ongoing rather than stable, objective, and predictive".[16]

On a similar theme, sociologists and anthropologists use the complementary notions of "making the familiar strange" (adopting a different way of seeing what has become taken for granted) and "making the strange familiar" (normalizing what, at first sight, might appear odd, impractical or irrelevant). Here again, the aim is to escape from the clichéd patterns of understanding and action, by provoking beneficial shifts in perspective and practice. Indeed, these notions are encapsulated in the central theme of this book. This is aimed at making the well-worn clichés of organization and management appear strange, in the light of people's experienced reality; whilst making the apparently strange dynamics of complexity, uncertainty and paradox reasonable, familiar and natural for people to deal with.

16. *Beyond individual dynamism to* interactional dynamics

The notion that successful organizational performance can be attributed to the personal dynamism of certain, all-powerful individuals would no longer be seen as credible. The emphasis on such attributes as drive, vision, energy, inspiration and so on would have been replaced by a focus on managers' understanding of – and practical engagement with – the complex social dynamics of organization and the muddling-through nature of real-world management practice. It would be understood that a manager's impact depends upon the extent to which they are able to influence these dynamics in organizationally beneficial and ethically sound ways, *through the quality of their in-the-moment participation*. These same considerations apply to those intimately involved in self-managing groups, where authority-based influence is applied more remotely.

This realization would also have called into question the ways in which those in formal management positions (and, especially those 'at the top') are recruited, remunerated, and developed. In particular, the current preoccupation with the traits, styles, competencies, and so on of such individuals (i.e. on the so-called 'best practice' attributes of individual actors) would be seen as of secondary importance. This would have been replaced with something more in tune with the challenge of leading and managing in a world in which people are co-creating the future through their ongoing interactions.

Overall . . .

17. Beyond muddled thinking to muddling through

I began by referring to the "well-meaning recipes" that provide the bedrock of the mainstream discourse on organization and management practice. In most cases at least, these are not pursued with malicious intent. According to the dominant discourse, if you're not in control, you're not leading. So most of those who continue to deploy them are no doubt making a well-meaning attempt to impose order on the (organizational) world and control what happens for the collective good. Well-meaning but wrong. Wrong, because this fails to take account of, and provide a meaningful response to, the unavoidable wiggliness of *what people – including themselves – are actually doing and experiencing day to day.* Continuing to repeat this muddled thinking, and the actions that flow from it, tends to strengthen it still further. Somewhat ironically, this occurs precisely because of the self-organizing, patterning-forming and pattern-using dynamics of organization, which the established discourse seeks to deny!

Rather than persisting with this fiction, there would therefore be an acceptance of, and conscious engagement with, the underlying dynamics of organization. Muddling through would then be recognized as the most meaningful description of what managers and others *actually find themselves doing in practice.* And that muddling through *with purpose, courage and skill* is the *best* that they and anyone else can do, as they act forwards into a future that they and everyone else are perpetually creating together.

18. Beyond colluding to confronting

In support of the above shifts, there would be an increasing tendency for people to challenge the basic myths that sustain current management orthodoxy. A central illusion, that an organization's fortunes can be assured if people take action in line with the latest 'recipe for success', would be less in evidence than at present. The tendency instead would be for managers and others to confront rather than collude with principles, policies and practices that run counter to their lived experience. And this would also extend to the surfacing and exploration of other shadow-side themes and behaviours that were organizing people's everyday conversations and interactions – *including the contribution that they themselves were making to the patterning of thought and action that was emerging.*

19. Beyond . . . to . . .

A radical shift or more of the same?

The above statements reflect radically different assumptions about how organization works from those that currently inform mainstream prescriptions of management and leadership practice. These nevertheless reflect a view of organization that accords much more closely with managers' everyday lived experience. As noted above, it is in the give-and-take of people's day-to-day interactions that the capacity exists for new patterns of understanding and action to emerge and change to arise. And so, if a sufficiently powerful coalition of support were to grow up informally around themes such as those set out above, these might emerge from the shadows and enter the mainstream. If not, the tendency will remain for current narratives, and the flawed assumptions on which these are based, to continue to shape people's understanding of organizational dynamics, management practice and leadership performance – reinforcing these still further and limiting the scope for meaningful improvement.

Hopefully, the former outcome will prevail.

Notes

1 Allenby, B. and Sarewitz, D. (2013) *The Techno-Human Condition.* MIT Press.

2 From the Preface of *The Book on the Taboo against Knowing Who You Are* by Watts, A. Originally published by Jonathan Cape Ltd. (1969).

3 See, for example, https://www.bbc.co.uk/news/world-us-canada-50239261.

4 Paying attention to what's actually going on in society, with its potential for discrimination and injustice (as well as acts of inclusion, fairness and humanity, of course) is at the core of acting skilfully in the midst of the complex social dynamics in which we are all participating. Seeking to circumscribe this emergent activity with a set of rights and wrongs relating to the everyday use of language and behaviour – and calling people out for their perceived transgressions in this regard – is, as Obama suggests, misguided and unhelpful. This is, in a sense, another way in which people seek to 'catch the real-world wiggliness in a net' of imposed rules and regulations, rather than recognizing and dealing with the messy and ambiguous reality, as this is emerging. At the same time, the pressure that this puts on others to conform, often policed through social media, makes this particularly dysfunctional, with its polarizing, "I am right; you are wrong" rhetoric.

5 "The beautiful, ugly truth" is how the leader writer in the *New Scientist* of 28 June 2014 headlined the argument that it is "better to see the cosmos as it is, rather than as we'd like it to be".

6 Stacey, R.D. (2000:13) *Strategic Management and Organisational Dynamics 3Ed.* FT Prentice Hall.

7 Johnson, B. (2014) *Polarity Management 2Ed.* HRD Press.

8 I referred to this in more detail Chapter 5: Watts, D. (2012) *Everything is Obvious Once You Know the Answer.* Atlantic Books.

9 See, for example, Zigmond, D. (2019) *The Perils of Industrialised Healthcare.* A discussion paper from the Centre for Welfare Reform.

10 Bennis, W. (1989: 44) *On Becoming a Leader.* Addison-Wesley.

11 See commentary in Chapter 1 on leadership and management, based on Flinn, K. (2018: 49) *Leadership Development.* Routledge.

12 Sociocracy and holacracy are two examples of approaches to organization that have been lauded over recent years as practical ways of reducing hierarchy and achieving greater self-management. As a design approach, sociocracy dates back to the mid-twentieth century, although its roots go back further still. Holacracy originates from the mid-2000s. It is important to recognize that these forms of organization design and management practice are subject to the same complex social dynamics of human interaction that apply in all organizational contexts.

13 De Bono, E. (1977) *The Happiness Purpose*. Penguin.
14 Gabriel, Y. (1999: 284) *Organizations in Depth*. Sage.
15 Barrett, F.J. (2012) *Yes to the Mess*. HBR Press.
16 Barrett, F.J. ibid: 139.

POSTSCRIPT

PERPETUALLY CREATING THE FUTURE TOGETHER

Over recent years, many articles have been written about the need to "defeat", "overcome", or otherwise "eliminate" organizational complexity. By this, the writers invariably mean the overly complicated structures, systems and procedures that tend to grow up over time, as managers strive to satisfy the expectations of order, predictability and control. Drawing on the imagery of philosopher Alan Watts, I have referred to this general organizing tendency as one of seeking to "catch the real-world wiggliness in a net".

Simplifying unnecessarily complicated ways of working is to be welcomed, of course. But this surface-level, as-designed view of organization says nothing about the underlying dynamics of what's going on. That is, the complex social process of everyday human interaction through which organization is continuously (re-)enacted and outcomes emerge in practice.

Immersed in the 'game of life'

Taking this further, these same dynamics are also at play in our living of life more generally. That is to say, beyond the natural world, *everything* that happens in our life emerges from the worldwide interplay of our own and everyone else's ongoing interactions. Some of these are intentional. Others are habitual. Some are planned. Others occur spontaneously or by chance. Some are bound up in the full trappings of formality, whereas others reflect informal networks of relationships. Some are acted out in person. Others exist solely in our imaginations. This relational process will sometimes be co-operative. At other times the exchanges will be competitive and conflictual. Rarely will the differences be clear-cut. Even though we are conscious of a lot of what is going on, large chunks of our lives remain outside our conscious awareness.

In this way, we seek to go on together, as interdependent beings immersed in the 'game' that we call life. We each act, moment-to-moment, into this continuously emerging future. A future that carries with it a sense of everyday predictability whilst, at the same time, being ultimately unknowable. In doing so, we participate in the co-creation of that very future as it is emerging – in all of its richness and beauty; ugliness and poverty; hope and despair. The values, ethics and morality of our actions are also interwoven with, and emerge from, our everyday interactions with others, near and far. People who are similarly engaged in finding their way through the highs and lows of their own lives, whether with a sense of compassion and respect for others or fuelled by evil intent.

C'est la vie

Despite this ongoing state of not knowing, we can say with certainty that we've managed to make it this far. At least, for me, at the time of writing and, if you're reading this, for you too! Our ongoing interactions with other people – fondly remembered and long forgotten – are both the product and process of the lives we are living. Within this, whatever missed opportunities, mistakes made, and unfulfilled expectations we might each be able to point to, there will no doubt be aspects of our present lives that we would not want to wish away under any circumstances. Importantly, those things that we value most about today have not just come to pass *in spite of* the less-than-perfect episodes from our past, but also *as a consequence of them*; however painful these might have been at the time. This is not about forgetting those who have been a meaningful and cherished part of our lives, but who are no longer with us. Or showing a lack of compassion and concern for the struggles and misfortunes of others. It simply recognizes that today's reality is historically situated and path dependent. These various happenings, arising from the flowing together of our own and others' hopes and aspirations, fears and concerns, choices and omissions, good deeds and bad, have brought us to where we are today. Both those things that we are keen to speak about and others that we might be less willing to acknowledge.

Wherever and whenever people are involved, these complex social dynamics are *always* in play. Things are never merely simple or complicated. They are always complex. This complexity is not something that we can "overcome", "defeat", or otherwise design-out to reach some sort of idyllic state, even if we wanted to. As the Swedish poet, psychologist and translator, Tomas Tranströmer said perceptively, "You'll never be complete, and that's as it should be".[1] So, if our conscience is clear as regards the way in which we've set out to 'play the game', we should not regret what we have or haven't done. Or what did or didn't happen in the past. Instead, we should take comfort in the fact that it is out of this complex social process that all of today's 'good bits' – those that we would not want to wish away under any circumstances – have come to pass.

That, as they say, is life! It is a life in which our myriad actions, inactions and interactions, together with those of everyone else in the world, are perpetually creating the future together. A life in which we have no option but to muddle through the twists and turns that emerge along the way. But one in which we can – if we so choose – seek to do so with *purpose, courage and skill.*

Notes

1 This quotation ("Du blir aldrig färdig, och det är som det skall", in its original Swedish) is taken from Tranströmer's poem, *Romanska Bågar.* It was brought to my attention by a friend, Fredrik Bååthe (2015: 67), who had used it to conclude his PhD thesis. He describes it as, "energizing and soothing all at the same time". Which is the essence of taking complexity and uncertainty seriously!

BIBLIOGRAPHY

Aaronovitch, D. (2020, 1 January) We can never be sure we'd be the good guys. *The Times*.

Allaire, Y. and Firsirotu, M.E. (1984) Theories of Organizational Culture in *Organization Studies* 5(3): 193–226.

Allenby, B. and Sarawitz, D. (2013) *The Techno-Human Condition*. MIT Press.

Ansoff, I. (1976) *From Strategic Planning to Strategic Management*. Wiley.

Argyris, C. (1999) *On Organizational Learning*, 2nd ed. Blackwell Business.

Bååthe, F. (2015) *Physicians' Engagement – Qualitative Studies Exploring Physicians' Experiences of Engaging in Improving Clinical Services and Processes*. Institute of Health and Care Sciences, Sahlgrenska Academy at the University of Gothenburg. Available at: https://gupea.ub.gu.se/bitstream/2077/40438/8/gupea_2077_40438_8.pdf

Barrett, F.J. (2012) *Yes to the Mess*. HBR Press.

Bennis, W. (1989) *On Becoming a Leader*. Addison-Wesley.

Birkinshaw, J. and Heywood, S. (2010, 1 May) Putting Organizational Complexity in its Place. McKinsey & Company [Online] Available at: http://www.mckinsey.com/insights/organization/putting_organizational_complexity_in_its_place

Board, D. and Warwick, R. (2012) *The Social Development of Leadership and Knowledge*. Centre for Progressive Leadership.

Bourdieu, P. (1992) *The Logic of Practice.* Polity Press.

Bridges, W. and Bridges, S. (2017) *Managing Transitions.* Nicholas Brealey.

Burden, P. and Warwick, R. (2015) *Leading Mindfully.* Self-published.

Caldini, R. (2007) *Influence.* Harper Business.

Chater, N. (2018) *The Mind is Flat.* Allen Lane.

Chynoweth, C. (2014, 7 September) Management by muddling through. *The Sunday Times.*

Clarke, J. *et al* (2015) *Making Policy Move.* Policy Press.

Cleaver, F. (2012) *Development Through Bricolage.* Routledge.

Collins, D. (1998) *Organizational Change – Sociological Perspectives.* Routledge.

Culbert, S. (1996) *Mind-set Management.* Oxford University Press.

Cunliffe, A.L. (2009) *A Very Short, Fairly Interesting and Reasonably Cheap Book about Management.* Sage.

Daloz, L.A. (1986) *Effective Teaching and Mentoring.* Jossey-Bass.

Dannatt, R. (2011) *Leading from the Front.* Corgi.

De Bono, E. (1969) *The Mechanism of Mind.* Simon & Schuster.

De Bono, E. (1977) *The Happiness Purpose.* Penguin.

De Bono, E. (1979) *Future Positive.* Penguin.

De Bono, E. (1982) *Lateral Thinking for Management.* Penguin.

De Bono, E. (2016) *Lateral Thinking – A Textbook of Creativity.* Penguin.

Drucker, P. (1974) *Management: Tasks, Responsibilities, Practices.* Heinemann.

Drucker, P. (1986) *Technology, Management and Society.* Routledge.

Drucker, P.F. (2007) *The Practice of Management.* Routledge.

Dunford, R. and Palmer, I. (1998) Discourse, Organizations and Paradox. In Grant, D. *et al* (Eds) *Discourse and Organization.* SAGE Publications.

Egan, G. (1993) *Adding Value.* Jossey-Bass.

Ekman, G. (2001) *Constructing Leadership in Small Talk* in Sjöstrand, S-E, *et al Invisible Leadership.* Thomson Learning.

Elias, N. (1939) *The Civilizing Process.* Blackwell.

Ewing, D. (1968) *The Practice of Planning.* Harper and Row.

Furnham, A. (2015) Write a Business Bestseller. *Professional Manager* (Autumn).

Fletcher, J. and Olwyler, K. (1997) *Paradoxical Thinking.* Berrett-Koehler.

Flinn, K. (2018) *Leadership Development.* Routledge.

Flood, R.L. (1999) *Rethinking the Fifth Discipline.* Routledge.

Flyvbjerg, B. *et al*, Eds. (2012) *Real Social Science: Applied Phronesis.* Cambridge University Press.

Fortun, M. and Bernstein, H.J. (1998) *Muddling Through.* Counterpoint.

Gabriel, Y. (1999) *Organizations in Depth.* Sage Publications Ltd.

Gabriel, Y. (2002) Essai: On Paragrammatic Uses of Organizational Theory – A Provocation. *Organization Studies,* 23(1), 133–151.

Griffin, D. (2001) *The Emergence of Leadership.* Routledge.

Griffin, D. (2010) *Speaking of Managers and Leaders being Ruthless: The Deepening Crisis of Everyday Ethics in Business* in Complexity and Management blog: https://complexityandmanagement.com/2010/04/15/speaking-of-managers-and-leaders-being-ruthless-the-ongoing-crisis-of-everyday-ethics-in-business-2/

Grint, K. (2007) Learning to Lead: Can Aristotle Help Us Find the Road to Wisdom? Sage, *Leadership,* Vol. 3, No. 2, May.

Grint, K. (2008) *Wicked Problems and Clumsy Solutions: the Role of Leadership* Clinical Leader, 1(2), December, BAMM Publications.

Harford, T. (2016) *Messy.* Abacus.

Heifetz, R.A. and Laurie, D.L. (2001) The Work of Leadership. *Harvard Business Review.*

Hernes, T. (2014) *A Process Theory of Organization.* Oxford University Press.

Hickling, A. (1974) *Managing Decisions: The Strategic Choice Approach.* Mantec Publications.

Higgins, J. and Reitz, M.(2019) *Speak Up.* FT Publishing International.

Hirschhorn, L. and Gilmore, T. (1992) *The New Boundaries of the "Boundaryless" Organization.* HBR (May–June 1992).

Hoeyer, K. and Jensen, A.M.B. (2011) Organ Donation and the Ethics of Muddling Through, *Crit Care,*15, p. 109. https://doi.org/10.1186/cc9379

Holman, P. *et al* (2007) *The Change Handbook 2Ed.* Berrett-Koehler.

Horst Rittel, H. and Webber, M. (1973) *Dilemmas in a General Theory of Planning* (Policy Sciences 4).

Janis, I. (1971) *Groupthink Among Policy Makers.* In Sanford, N. and Comstock, C. (Eds.) *Sanctions for Evil.* Jossey-Bass.

Jenkins, R. (2008) *Social Identity (Key Ideas) 3Ed.* Routledge.

Johnson, B. (2014) *Polarity Management 2Ed.* HRD Press.

Kaplan, R.S and Norton, D.P. (1996) *The Balanced Scorecard.* HBR Press.

Kay, J. (2010) *Obliquity.* Profile Books.

Kuper, S. (2014) *'Muddling Through' is the New Politics.* FT Magazine.

Lawler, S. (2008) *Identity: Sociological Perspectives 1Ed.* Polity Press.

Lester, R.K. and Piore, M.J. (2006) *Innovation: The Missing Dimension*. Harvard University Press.

Li, O. (2009) *Keats and Negative Capability*. Continuum International Publishing Group.

Lindblom, C. (1959) The Science of "Muddling Through". *Public Administration Review*, 19(2), pp. 79–88.

Lindblom, C.F. (1979) Still Muddling, Not Yet Through. *Public Administration Review*, Nov–Dec, pp. 517–526.

Lowe, R. (2005) Structured Methods and Striking Moments: Using Question Sequences in 'Living' Ways. *Family Process*, 44(1), pp. 65–75.

Malraux, A. (1976) *Picasso's Mask*. Macdonald and Jane's.

McAndrew, F.T. (2008) The Science of Gossip. *Scientific American Mind*, October.

McKergow, M. and Bailey, H. (2014) *Host*. Solutions Books.

Mead, G.H. (1934) *Mind, Self and Society*. The University of Chicago Press.

Mechanic, D. (1997) Muddling Through Elegantly: Finding the Proper Balance in Rationing. *Health Affairs*, 16(5), pp. 83–92.

Miles, R.E. (1965) *Human Relations or Human Resources*. HBR, July.

Mowles, C. (2011) *Rethinking Management*. Gower.

Nevis, E.C. (1987) *Organizational Consulting*. Gestalt Press.

New Scientist (2014, 25 June) The beautiful, ugly truth. Available at https://www.newscientist.com/article/mg22229751-700-better-to-see-the-beautiful-ugly-truth-of-the-cosmos/

Obeng, E. (1995) *Putting Strategy to Work*. FT Management.

Odiorne, G. (1974) *Management and the Activity Trap*. Heinemann.

Rittel, H. and Webber, M. (1973) Dilemmas in a General Theory of Planning. *Policy Sciences*, 4, pp. 155–169.

Rodenburg, P. (2009) *Presence*. Penguin.

Rodgers, C. (2007) *Informal Coalitions*. Palgrave.

Rolfe, G. (1998) Beyond Expertise: Reflective and Reflexive Nursing Practice. In Johns, C. and Freshwater, D. (Eds.) *Transforming Nursing through Reflective Practice*. Blackwell.

Rosenzweig, P. (2007) *The Halo Effect: How Managers Let Themselves Be Deceived*. The Free Press.

Sachs, J. (2018) *Unsafe Thinking*. Random House Business.

Scott, J.C. (1998) *Seeing Like a State*. Yale University Press.

Shaw, P. (2002) *Changing Conversations in Organizations*. Routledge.

Smith, G. (2018) *The AI Delusion*. Oxford University Press.

Snowden, D. (2015, 9 September) Cognitive Edge blog. Available at https://www.cognitive-edge.com/on-the-value-of-order/

Stacey, R.D. (1996) *Strategic Management and Organisational Dynamics 2Ed.* Pitman Publishing.

Stacey, R.D. (2000) *Strategic Management and Organisational Dynamics 3Ed.* FT Prentice Hall.

Stacey, R.D. (2007) *Strategic Management and Organisational Dynamics 5Ed.* Financial Times/Prentice Hall.

Stacey, R.D. (2009) *Complexity and Organizational Reality*. Routledge.

Stacey, R.D. (2011) *Strategic Management and Organisational Dynamics 6Ed.* FT Prentice Hall.

Stacey, R.D. (2012) *Tools and Techniques of Leadership and Management*. Routledge.

Stacey, R.D. and Mowles, C. (2016) *Strategic Management and Organisational Dynamics 7Ed.* Pearson.

Stacey R.D., Shaw, P. and Griffin, D. (2000) *Complexity and Management: Fad or Radical Challenge to Systems Thinking?* Routledge.

Stokes, P. (2011) *Critical Concepts in Management and Organization Studies*. Palgrave.

Streatfield, P. (2001) *The Paradox of Control in Organizations*. Routledge.

Syed, M. (2020, 29 March) Coronavirus: An Unimaginable Challenge for Our Leaders, but What Great Lessons they Will be Learning. *The Sunday Times*.

Taylor, D. (Ed.) (2010) *Michel Foucault – Key Concepts*. Routledge.

Taylor, J.R. and van Every, E.J. (2000) *The Emergent Organization*. Lawrence Erlbaum Associates.

Traeger, J. and Warwick, R. (2018) *Organisation Development*. Libri Publishing.

Ullrich, R.A. (1976) Organizational Design, Employee Motivation and the Support of Strategic Motivation. In Ansoff, H.I. *et al* (Eds). *From Strategic Planning to Strategic Management*. John Wiley and Sons.

US Marine Corps (1997) *Warfighting*. Marine Corps Doctrinal Publication 1.

Vaill, P.B. (1989) *Managing as a Performing Art*. Jossey-Bass.

Vaill, P.B. (1996) *Learning as a Way of Being*. Jossey-Bass.

Wallace, B. and Ridgeway, C. (1996) *Leadership for Strategic Change*. CiPD.

Warwick, R. and Board, D. (2013) *The Social Development of Leadership and Knowledge*. Palgrave Macmillan.

Watts, A. (2009) *The Book on the Taboo against Knowing Who You Are*. Souvenir Press.

Watts, D. (2012) *Everything is Obvious – Once You Know the Answer*. Atlantic Books.

Weick, K.E. (2001) *Making Sense of the Organization*. Blackwell Business.

Zigmond, D. (2019) *The Perils of Industrialised Healthcare*. A discussion paper from the Centre for Welfare Reform.

INDEX

For Product Safety Concerns and Information please contact our EU representative GPSR@taylorandfrancis.com
Taylor & Francis Verlag GmbH, Kaufingerstraße 24, 80331 München, Germany

www.ingramcontent.com/pod-product-compliance
Lightning Source LLC
LaVergne TN
LVHW010651300926
849161LV00005B/1099
9780367744656